MARYLAND EASTERN SHORE NEWSPAPER ABSTRACTS

Volume 1

1790-1805

F. Edward Wright

HERITAGE BOOKS
2007

HERITAGE BOOKS

AN IMPRINT OF HERITAGE BOOKS, INC.

Books, CDs, and more—Worldwide

For our listing of thousands of titles see our website
at
www.HeritageBooks.com

Published 2007 by
HERITAGE BOOKS, INC.
Publishing Division
65 East Main Street
Westminster, Maryland 21157-5026

International Standard Book Number: 978-1-58549-043-1

INTRODUCTION

Newspapers are one of the most important sources of genealogical and biographical information, but because they have not been indexed the information they contain is difficult to retrieve. The columns may contain vital records such as marriages and deaths, but almost impossible to find. This information is especially critical in those areas where the court house has burned down. Fortunately, in recent years a growing number of genealogists have turned their attention to abstracting and publishing genealogical data from early newspapers.

In this 152 page volume the compiler has presented vital records, legal cases, property sales and rentals, as well as lists of letters in post offices, from Eastern Shore newspapers for the years 1790-1805. Although the items are heavily concentrated in the Easton area, legal advertisements dealing with probate and chancery matters refer to families from all over the Eastern Shore of Maryland.

Not only vital and legal notices are included: advertisements for lost relatives from Europe, runaway wives, fugitive slaves, absconding apprentices, newly arrived merchants and craftsmen seeking customers all appear in the pages of the early gazettes. In addition to the above items, one may find here accounts of such natural phenomena as a swarm of Hessian flies so numerous they covered one man's entire farm in 1793. In 1799 local inhabitants contributed to a fund to pay for a fire engine. Such items while not adding to the bare bones of a pedigree, do certainly give the research something of the flavor of the times in which his ancestors were living and working.

In order to include as much material as possible, Commander Wright has arranged the items chronologically by newspaper, with items from each issue in a separate numbered paragraph. The index is keyed to the paragraph numbers rather than the page numbers, enabling one to find the desired name with a minimum of effort.

To the growing number of basic research tools for Maryland, this book is a most welcome addition, one which will certainly shed new light on many families from the Eastern Shore.

Robert Barnes
Perry Hall, Maryland

Author's Notes

The first Eastern Shore newspaper was established in Easton on May 11, 1790; it was the Maryland Herald and Eastern Shore Intelligencer published by James Cowan. Later in 1793 Chestertown introduced the Apollo or Chestertown Spy replaced the same year by the Chestertown Gazette. A second Easton newspaper came on the scene in 1799 under the title, Republican Star; it was published by Thomas Perrin Smith.

This is the first volume of a planned series of abstracts and extracts of the earliest newspapers of the Eastern Shore. Abstracts have been taken from issues held by the Talbot County Free Library, Maryland Historical Society and Library of Congress. For the period covered by this volume (1790 - 1805) only a few issues are held by the Enoch Pratt Library, an otherwise excellent repository of Maryland newspapers; these issues were duplicative of copies found at one of the other three libraries.

Preceding each paragraph in this book is a sequence of letters, indicating the name of the newspaper and the location of the issue as shown below.

ESHM - Maryland Herald and Eastern Shore Intelligencer/Maryland Historical Society

ESHT - Maryland Herald and Eastern Shore Intelligencer/Talbot County Free Library

ESHC - Maryland Herald and Eastern Shore Intelligencer/Library of Congress

APM - Apollo or Chestertown Spy/Maryland Historical Society

CGM - Chestertown Gazette/Maryland Historical Society

RSM - Republican Star/Maryland Historical Society

RST - Republican Star/Talbot County Free Library

Duplicative or similar items have been avoided when possible. Constant attention has been given to reduce wording while still retaining all genealogical data. A few items have been repeated verbatim (enlosed in quotation marks) when considered in the best interest of retaining the feel of the time, place and style of the period or the situation. If you would like a verbatim transcription (zeroxed when allowed, otherwise a typed copy) send $3.00 for the first article, adding $2.00 for each additional item, to: Family Line, 13405 Collingwood Terrace, Silver Spring Maryland 20904.

Abbreviations used:

a. - acres	inst - instant (current month)
adj - adjoining	QA - Queen Anne's
admin - administrator or administratrix	Rev - Reverend
dau - daughter	Talb - Talbot
dec - deceased	ult - ultimo (last month)
Dorch - Dorchester	Worc - Worcester
exec - executor or executrix	yrs - years

Comments and questions are encouraged.

F. Edward Wright

1. ESHM May 11 1790/Died suddenly 4th inst at his seat in this town Matthew Tilghman in the 73d year of his age, affectionate husband and tender parent/ David Kerr, Easton, admin of Jacob Gibson/Wanted apprentice to carpenter and joiner business - James Vansandt, Easton/Benjamin Stevens; atty for John Gregorie assignee of Quaile Charles Christian requests payment of debts.

2. ESHM May 18 1790/Rev Doctor Connor elected Rector of St Peter's Parish, formerly rector of St Paul's and St Martin's churches in Pennsylvania/Married Saturday 1st inst Hon. Joshua Seney to Miss Fanny Nicholson dau of Commodore Nicholson of New York/A canoe discovered in one of my coves - J. Beale Bordley/ John Needles surveyor & conveyancer,Easton.

3. ESHM Jun 1 1790/Francis Sellers,,Tuckahoe Bridge, admin of Charles Edward Irvine late of Caroline Co, dec/Richard Grason offers reward for negro man Jack who ran away from one of Col. Edward Lloyd's farms on Wye River.

4. ESHM Aug 10 1790/John Hooper, Transquakin River, near the Bridge, Dorch Co offers reward for negro boy Hannibal age about 20/B. M. Ward, Trap, advertises a l ctery to raise 300 dollars for erection of a school/Tanner & currier wanted - John MacMahan, Trap/Jonathan Ozment offers reward f or negroes (unnamed)/Joseph Price offers reward for negro man George Rex/Apprentice wanted for carpenter's & joiner's business - James Croney, Easton/For rent plantation on Chicknacomico River, Dorch Co, where John Hodson formerly lived - John Eccleston, near New Market/James Price Jr offers services in drawing up accounts of guardianships/Richard Harrington reports a stray mare taken up by himion the plantation of Charles Croockshank occupied by Richard Harrington/ Thomas Lockerman offers reward for negro man Edmund age about 23/ James Shaw offers reward for negro slaves: George age about 30 who was hired to a Levin Lecompte of this county; Patience his wife age about 25 and about 6 months gone with child/Thomas Delahay Talb Co, offers reward f or negro man Harry.

5. ESHM Aug 17 1790/Joseph Neall, Easton, offers reward for stray horse/ Jeremiah Garland, Wye River, Talb Co , offers reward for negro man Jacob age about 30, born in Virginia.

6. ESHM Aug 24 1790/Plantation for rent - James Tilghman Jr, Talb Co/William Skinner, Easton, has removed his shop to Washington St opp to Court House & continues to carry on Silversmith business.

7. ESHM Aug 31 1790/Partnership of Baldwin & Richardson requests payment of debts/House for rent - Peter Denny

8. ESHM Sep 14 1790/Robert G ddsborough of Cambridge, a young citizen "in crossing from Kent-Island to Annapolis where for some time he has prosecuted the study of law, the boat was overset ...and sunk... the corpse was found a few days after, ... and interred in the Episcopal burying-ground of Annapolis ...By the same unfortunate accident Mr. Easton, house builder, was drowned."/ W. V. Murray, Cambridge, candidate for congress.

9. ESHM Sep 21 1790/David Sisk, Caroline Co, near Hunting Creek Church, offers reward for apprentice Andrew Merrick, shoemaker, 5 ft, sandy complexion, broad flat face, a very visible halt in his walk, has a brother in QA Co/A school now open at Church-Hill under the direction of James McCoy & James Haughey/Joseph Harrison 3d, exec of Daniel Lambdin of Talb Co dec/G. Duvall admin of Thomas Rutland requests payment of debts from those who had dealings at Thomas Rutland's stores in Oxford & Kingston. Thomas Tibbels to collect in Oxford neighborhood and John Dickinson in Kingston.

10. ESH Aug 3 1790/"We are informed that on the 25th ult. Mr. Solomon Clayton with his child of two years old, and Mr. Charles Blake, with his two sons,, one about 7, the other 15 or 16 years old, and a negro boy, being out on the river Wye, in a sailing boat, were unfortunately overset by a whirlwind. The two

-1-

gentlemen being skilful swimmers each took his child and swam - but alas! - before they had reached the shore, the waves beat so violently over them that the children were suffocated...The elder son of Mr. Blake saved himself by clinging to the boat - but the negro boy was drowned."

11. ESHM Oct 5 1790/Messrs John Scott, Thomas B. Hands and Jeremiah Nicols of Chestertown to receive applications for the position of principal of Washington College/Chestertown Races - Jon Hodgson & Thomas Worell/Joseph & W. Haskins opening their dry goods store at the sign of the Golden Plough nearly opposite William Weaver's Tavern

12. ESHM Oct 12 1790/Quayle C. Christian, "a languishing prisoner in the public gaol of Easton" to petition under the insolvency act

13. ESHM Oct 19 1790/Chancery sale of real estate of John Mitchell of Sussex Co Del, dec, lying in Somerset and Worc counties, Esme Bayly, Gillis Polk, William McBryde, trustees

14. ESHM Nov 16 1790/Chancery court requests creditors of Joseph Williams of Kent Co to present their claims/Chancery sale at the house occupied by Henry Parker in Worc Co, commonly called the Trap, real est of David Evans, late of Worc Co: pt of Mitchell's Dear Park, pt of Long Acre, pt of Friendship - John Done, trustee/Sale of sloop, Mayflower, lying at Kingstown - apply to James King near Kingstown or Richard Johns/Lot owned by Lodge No. 6 for sale - Edward Cox, Thomas Harris, John Harwood/W. Hayward admin of Adam Gray, QA Co dec

15. ESHM Nov 23 1790/Henry Hall, mouth of Mesongo Creek in Acquamack Co Va, offers reward (15 pounds of Virginia currency) for negro man, Leven/Chancery sale of plantation where Benton Harris of Worc Co lived arid all the lands devised to John Rousby Whittington and in the case of his death, without heirs, and the death of his the said Harris's widow, to be sold, as appears in the will of said Benton Harris - Samuel Smith, trustee.

16. ESHM Nov 30 1790/Robert Browne, near Chestertown, informs the public that Isaac Easton (an approved teacher from Newark) had engaged to teach Latin & Greek.

17. ESHM Dec 14 1790/Married Thursday 2d inst by Rev Ferguson, George Robins Hayward of Talb Co to Miss Peggy Smyth of Kent Co/Chancery sale of real property of John Reasin late of Kent Co, lying in Stillpond - Arraminta Reasin, Thomas Angier, trustees/John Meconekin of QA Co offers reward for mulatto man, Jem Calwell age about 25, born in Talb Co bay-side, his mother, if living, is in Annapolis or Balt; she formerly belonged to James McMurdy/Robert Ewing, Kingstown, exec Patrick Ewing late of Dorch Co/S. Cornor Jr, gaoler, offers reward for John Routten, native of VA, about 5 ft 7 inch, pleasant countenance, fair complexion, light hair, blue eyes, has a sister in Hampton Va

18. ESHM Dec 21 1790/Whereas Elizabeth my wife has eloped from my bed & Board ...Richard Ray/Edward Eubanks, Easton, secretary of Lodge No. 6/Edward Cox, Easton, requests payment of debts, is desirous of laying in a sufficient stock of fur.

19. ESHM Dec 28 1790/Wednesday last the schooner Sea Flower, of Wye River, Joshua Gossage, master, was sunk near Turkey Point by ice. - She was on her way to Elk, with about seven or eight hundred bushels of wheat/Martha Yarnell admin of Uriah Yarnall, late of Talb Co, dec. Debts may be paid to Samuel Edmundson in Easton/Houses in Easton, formerly the property of George Miller for rent. Robert Lloyd Nicols

20. ESHM Jan 4 1791/Married Thursday evening last by Rev Dr. Connor John Singleton to Miss Anna Goldsborough both of this co/Died 20th ult Anne wife

of Howell Powell after a tedious illness, age about 37 yrs and on the
following Friday remains were interred at Friends' burying ground of this
place - a tender mother and affectionate wife.

21. ESHM Jan 11 1791/Letters remaining at the post office, Easton: William
Atkinson, Somerset; John Austin, Worc; Mr. Bechan, near Cambridge; Robert
Bazur, Talb; Richard Barnaby, Talb; Henry Barger, Somerset; Samuel Baldwin,
Talb; John Brown, Caroline; John Bruff ,St. Michaels; Dr. Bourk; Thomas Bush,
Easton; John Bush, Talb; Benjamin Shaw, Talb; John Corrie, Tuckahoe; Eliza
Corce, Talb; James Corrie, Tuckahoe; John Collins at Washington Academy; Sarah
Colston, Somerset; Dr. Francis Chency, Somerset; Bennet Chew, QA; Arthur
Carter, QA; Mr. Cochran, Cross-creek; John Dove, Princess Anne; John Dorden,
Talb; Joseph Dearden, Talb; William Dawson sen, Caroline; Michael Flanedy,
Taylors Island; Dr. Fullwill, Northhampton; Mr. Ferrer at Colonel Wilkinson's;
John Gibson, Talb; Woolman Gibson near Easton; Eliza Gibson near Wye Mill;
Mr. Goldsborough; Thomas Goldsborough ,Talb; Hon. Robert Goldsborough; Charles
Goldsborough, Jr; John Gunby , Snow Hill; Levin Gale, Somerset; Hon. George
Gale, Talb; Robert Holmes at Morgan Creek; Francis Hall, QA; Edward Harris,
QA; Samuel Handy, Worc; John Hutchinson, Talb; Miss Delilah Hamilton, Nanjemoy;
Thomas Hughlet & son, Choptank; Thomas Irving A. B.; Richard Johns , Easton;
Sarah Kinneman near Easton; Nathaniel Kennard, Wye Mill; Peter Kirwan , Dorch;
Elizabeth Lamb, Easton; John McIver, St. Michaels; James McAlpin, Accomack;
William Vans Murray; Robert Martin near Oxford; John Pope Mitchel, Worc; James
R. Morris, Worc; William McBryde, Somerset; George Miller, Easton; William
McKellum, Talb; John McClean, Accomack; Robert Noble, Tuckahoe; Henry Nash,
Talb; Robert Postlewait , Caroline; John Purris (Parris?), Somerset; Isaac
Purnell, Worc; Dr. Zabdiel Potter, Caroline; William Richmond, Wye Mill; Andrew
Rabsom , Easton; John Stewart at R. Goldsborough's; John Stewart, Somerset;
Francis Sellers, Tuckahoe; William Thomas, Talb; John Thomas, Talb; James
Tilghman .Talb; Edward Turner, Talb; Charles Vandern, Easton; Benjamin M.
Ward , Talb; Francis Wayman, Easton; Denwood Wilson, Somerset; Margaret Wheland,
Vienna. - John Erskine/Schooner, Lydia continues to run as a packet - Edward
Bromwell, William Trippe, Easton.

22. ESHM Jan 18 1791/Died Saturday last, Talb Co, after a lingering illness
Mrs. Henrietta Burkhead, relict of the late Christopher Burkhead, aged 44.

23. ESHM Jan 25 1791/Edward Vidler, builder, brick or stone, now resides in
Easton/To let, blacksmith shops - Thomas Hughlett and son, Choptank-bridge/
Sarah Davis, Benjamin Davis request payment of debts to estate of Abel Davis/
Henry Pratt, QA Co, offers reward for negro man, Will Potts who may have a pass
signed by Isaac Dickson of Talb Co/Apprentice wanted to the tanning &
currying business - William Ruth, Fast Landing, Kent Co/The shop of John &
Elijah Eliason in East Nottingham was broke open.

24. ESHM Feb 22 1791/On Tuesday night last the house of John Catrop about 3
and 1/2 miles from this place was entirely consumed by fire/William Mansell,
Chestertown, offers small-pox inoculations.

25. ESHM Mar 1 1791/John Erskine assigneee of William Gray late of QA Co,
bankrupt. Persons indebted are requested to pay John Erskine or Samuel D.
Betton.

26. ESHM Mar 15 1791/John Boon forwarns that Francis Hopkins did in a
fraudulent manner obtain a note for 12 pounds/Jeremiah Carter, near Cabin
Creek, Dorch Co, offers reward for negro man, Adam, age about 25/

27. ESHM Mar 15 1791/Died around half past 5 in the 61st year of his age
William Hayward, eminent practioner of law/William Perry to sell young negro
woman

-3-

28. ESHM Mar 29 1791/lot for sale in Easton in Millers Alley - George Miller/
George Robins Hayward admin of William Hayward/Woolman Gibson, Head of Wye,
Talb Co .offers services of his horse,Soldier.

29. ESHM Apr 5 1791/William Blake, within 1 mile of the Three Bridges,
reports stray colt/tract for sale adj lands of Richard B. Carmichael - Robert
Browne, QA Co/John Jenkinson offers the services of his horse, Matchless.

30. ESHM Apr 12 1791/Alexander McCallum offers services of his horse, A
Spanish Jack/Sale of lands on which subscriber now lives, also 1/3 pt of
Woolsey Manor adj same - Randolph Johnson/Anne Bewley, Talb Co, admin of
Joseph Bewley late of Talb Co dec.

31. ESHM Apr 19 1791/Sale of about 1000 a. lying on banks of Marshyhope Creek
Kent Co - Thomas White.

32. ESHM Apr 26 1791/Chancery sale of the estate of James Ayler, an infant,
of tract, Ayler's Fortune in Caroline Co to satisfy unto Henrietta M.
Chamberlaine exec of James Lloyd Chamberlaine - John Lee, trustee/Nicholas
Hopkins now has a schooner to run as a packet from Choptank & Tuckahoe Bridges
to Balt. Thomas Elliott at Tuckahoe Bridge will receive subscriptions/Sarah
Goldsborough, Talb Co, admin of Nicholas Goldsborough.

33. ESHM May 3 1791/John L. Bozman offers reward for negro man, Joe, who ran
away from Mr. Bozman's plantation where Tristram Martin now lives in Talb Co/
Elizabeth Armstrong, Hawkins Downes, admin of Francis Armstrong dec, to sell
which Francis Armstrong occupied near Kingston/William Benson & Edward Vidler,
Easton, have contracted to build courthouse in Caroline Co/Lots for sale on
Washington St, Easton - Samuel Baldwin, Easton/Christopher & Robert Johnston
have opened assortment of dry & wet goods at house lately occupied by Mr.
Benson .Oxford, also seeking apprentices for their factory - apply to
Alexander Gun, Oxford/Farm for sale by John Harwood, Talb Co, who intends to
leave the state this year/Samuel Yarnall, Easton, seeks apprentice to shoe-
making business/Cornelius West, Easton, wants to contract for plank.

34. ESHM May 17 1791/Joshua Kennard admin of William Price & John Price(exec
of William Price) both late of QA Co.

35. ESHM May 24 1791/Stephen Darden offers reward for negro man, Nat, age
about 33 yrs.

36. ESHM Jun 7 1791/Chancery sale of real estate in Worc Co which descended
from William Watson to his only son Benjamin Watson, a minor, the tract,
Golden Quarter - Peter Chaille Jr, trustee/William West running schooner,
Henrietta, a packet from Easton to Balt/John Finley now res Cambridge,
requests payment of debts/Chancery sale of real estate of Jonathan Riggen
late of Worc Co, dec: Safeguard, pt of tract George's Purchase - John Cathel,
trustee, Worc Co.

37. ESHM Jun 28 1791/Sale of plantation where subscriber lives in QA Co upon
Long Marsh - Vachel Keene/Sale of plantation in Dorch Co opp Cabin Creek Mills
on Choptank River - Christopher Birkhead/Sale of 2 bags of coffee from on
board schooner, Industry, Joseph Elliott, master - Nathaniel Ramsay, marshal.

38. ESHM Jul 5 1791/Robert Nicols, Ennalls Martin, Perry Benson, exec of
Thomas Chamberlaine, late of Talb Co.

39. ESHM Jul 19 1791/Robert Goldsborough seeks overseer/Moses Sherwood admin
of Edward Mann Sherwood, late of Talb Co, dec/James Holland admin of William
Holland, late of Talb Co, dec/John Erskine exec of Christopher Love, QA Co.

40. ESHM Jul 26 1791/On Friday fe'night a murder on the body of Sarah Rathell
in Tuckahoe around 8 miles from Easton. On Sunday following her mangled

corpse was found in a thicket a small distance from her house. David Rathell her husband was apprehended on suspicion of murder and committed to gaol for trial. The deceased was far advanced in her pregnancy./Died Friday 15 inst after a short illness Mrs. Mary Bush about 27 yrs old, wife of Captain John Bush, Talb Co, wife and mother/Chancery sale of plantation in Worc Co consisting of tracts: Simpleton and Brother's Contrivance, for debts of Henry Dennis - Littleton Dennis, Worc Co, trustee/Sale of farm on Corsica Creek, QA Co where Thomas Carradine now dwells.

41. ESHM Aug 9 1791/Benjamin Collison, Dorch Co, to petition to record a deed acknowledging the sale to him by William Jones late of Dorch Co of a tract, Goodridges Choice, lying on Cabin Creek.

42. ESHM Aug 16 1791/Francis Sellers, Tuckahoe Bridge offers reward for negro woman, Amy, age about 28.

43. ESHM Aug 23 1791/Married 9 inst James Hollyday to Miss Susan Tilghman both of QA Co/Died Monday 15 inst near this town James Barnwell and on the following day his remains were interred in the family burying ground/Died Thursday last about 7 o'clock in the evening at Peach Blossom after a long and tedious illness Mrs. Henrietta Maria Chamberlaine, interred on Saturday in the family burying ground; Rev Bowie delivered the sermon/Whereas I gave a bond to John Morgin of this co and he assigned it to Francis Hopkins then of this co but has since moved to Duck-Creek/A new land stage from Chestertown to Easton - Richard Newman/John Thomas Jr, tax collector for Talb Co.

44. ESHM Sep 6 1791/Died Sunday fe'night after a tedious illness Mrs. Sarah Webb wife of Peter Webb of this co and after a short illness Mrs. Elizabeth Stevens died aged about 51 yrs, wife of John Stevens of this county/John Martin Needles has commenced a hatting business in the shop previously occ by late Daniel Carnon, in Washington St.

45. ESHM Oct 12 1791/Sarah Dashiel, QA Co, to petition under the insolvency act.

46. ESHM May 1 1792/Died yesterday morning after a short and painful illness James Ewing, Easton, taylor/Waxwork exhibition at Capt Richard Coward's, Easton/William Berridge, register, St Peter's Church/John Erskine, Easton, exec of Christopher Love, late of this place, merchant/Sale at Cambridge of lots of vestry of Great Choptank Parish adj house where Mrs. Caile lives/Bank bills lost - Messrs Samuel & Peter Sharp/Vessel for sale built by Thomas Haddaway. Apply to Mathias Bordley, Wye River/Greenbury Goldsborough admin of Richard Dickinson lat of Talb Co, dec/Henrietta Kemp exec of Alice Kemp late of Talb Co/Sale of 7 slaves at Mrs. Millington's Tavern, Tuckahoe Bridge, formerly the property of William Colston. Attendance given by Dekar Thompson/John Bond, taylor, carries on his business at the house lately occ by John Huron ,Easton/Peter Gordon, Cambridge, admin of Archibald Patison, late of Dorch Co, dec.

47. ESHM May 15 1792/Samuel Swan, taylor, carries on his business opp Mr. Weaver's Tavern, Washington St/John McGrann insolvent debtor/Richard Benson, taylor, keeps his shop in Washington St opp Mr. Bruff's gold & silvershith shop, Easton/Colin Ferguson, treasurer, Washington College, Chestertown/Isabella Heron, Easton, exec of John Heron late of Talb Co dec.

48. ESHM May 29 1792/Samuel Conaway, Long Marsh near the Nine Bridges, Caroline Co, offers reward for hired servant Edward Jackson, 5 ft 7 inch, well set, dark hair, native of Talb Co who left his wife & 2 small children behind him as a burden to his master. He was also a prisoner of Caroline Co sheriff at the time he absconded/Chancery sale of real estate of Henry Ayres son and heir of Henry Ayres dec, consisting of 36 a. in Worc Co - Ezekiel Wise, trustee/Dancing school of Mr. Curley from France. Apply to Mr.

Kalkbrener, Easton

49. ESHM Jun 12 1792/James Douglass, in Vienna, offers reward for horse
supposedly taken away by a certain Henry Bruffit who was raised in the neighborhood of Black-Water, a weaver by trade, and who was in this town (Vienna)
about that time, and wanted to purchase said horse/James Earle Clerk of the
Court/Notice by Peter Edmondson, sheriff Caroline Co to creditors of Samuel
Short, insolvent debtor/Hezekiah Cooper, insolvent debtor, in the custody of
the sheriff of Kent Co/James Sullivane forewarns persons from taking assignment on his bond held by William S. Bond, assigned by John Hooper/Joseph
George, near Wye Mill, QA Co, offers reward for stolen horses/400 a. for sale
on the heads of Miles & Wye Rivers - Benjamin Benny/John Brice, taylor, next
door below Mr. Cornor's tavern

50. ESHM Jun 26 1792/Married at Vienna Dorch Co Mr. ___ Bond of that town,
merchant, to Miss Polly Hayward of Dorch Co/Died at Philadelphia Capt Matthew
Bennet age 51/Died at Philadelphia Bryan O'Hara age 64/English & Grammar
School to be opened at Easton under the direction of Mr. Chandler of the
University of Cambridge/Rachel Thomas, Talb Co, admin of William Thomas, dec

51. ESHM Jul 10 1792/Jacob Seth exec of Thomas Pennington, late of Caroline
Co/John Petty and Co have imported per the William, Capt Bolton, from London
an assortment of goods at their store(late in the occupation of Samuel Logan)

52. ESHM Jul 24 1792/Married at George-town, 5th inst, in the Roman Catholic
Church, Adam King, merchant, to the amiable and accomplished Miss Grace Doyle,
dau of Alexander Doyle, merchant/List of remaining letters at the P. O. Easton:
John Burn in care of Mr. Corner, tavern keeper Easton; Dr. Solomon Birckhead,
Cambridge; Edward Creighe, on Broad Creek, in Sussex Co, care of Messrs Samuel
& Robert Smily, Salisbury; Robert Coran, Dover; Samuel Cheesman, merchant,
Snow Hill; William Clark at Dr. Wilson's, Talb; Mrs. Ann Clark, Talb; Mr. John
Dawson, Talb Court-House; Alexander Douglass, Vienna; Capt. Gors. Dave,
trading to Annemassex, Somerset Co; James Dimond, Princess Anne, Somerset Co,
care of Mr. Neil, merchant; Robert Dennis at Vienna, Nanticoke River; Henry
Elbert, coach-maker in aston; James Earle, Easton; William Ennalls,
Cambridge; Peregrine Fitzhugh, Kent Island; Miss Henrietta Grace, Broad Creek,
Sussex Co; Charles Gardiner, Miles River Neck; John Gunby, Collector, Snow
Hill; John Henry, Easton; Levi Hollingsworth Jr, to be lodged at Easton; James
Hay, Cambridge, North America; William Lynch care of Mr. Philinley, QA Co;
Hugh Lendsay Jr, merchant, Cambridge; John Muir, Collector, Vienna; Miss
Harriet Martin, Talb Co; George Mitchell in Easton; John Pope Mitchell, Worc
Co; William McCallum, Talb; Hon. William Perry, Talb Co; Captain Abner Parrot,
Talb Co; Miss Amelia Palmer, Cambridge; John Smoot, merchant, Vienna; Colonel
John Stewart, Somerset Co; Smith Snead, Northhampton Co, Va; John Stringer,
Northhampton Co, Va; Walter Scott care of James Bryan, tavern-keeper,
Cambridge; John Sutton care of William McBryde, Salisbury, Somerset Co;
Samuel & Robert Smyley, merchants, Salisbury; Stevens Summers, Annemessex,
Somerset Co; Aaron Sterling, Little Annemassex, in Maryland; Captain Thomas
Tennant, Easton; Edward Tucker care of Ollister McBryde, Salisbury; C. T.
Wederstrand, Hermitage, QA Co; Henry Waggaman, Atty at Law, near Cambridge;
Heber Whittingham, Somerset Co; Mr. Shandy Yard, Somerset/Farm for sale at
Miles River Ferry, now in the occupation of Robert Pickering. Apply to Col.
Banning or H. Banning - Benjamin Chew, Talb Co/Houses in Federalsburgh for
rent, lately occupied by John Harrison - Thomas Nicols, Federalsburgh, Dorch
Co/Wanted to buy or rent - farm house with 150 a. Apply to Rev Dr. Connor or
Capt John Erskine.

53. ESHM Aug 1792/Edward Harris, QA Co, submits a letter regarding an article by Joseph Nicholson, atty at law, QA Co/Thomas Jenkins, Talb Co, offers reward for negro man, Job, age 25

54. ESHM Aug 21 1792/Jeremiah Banning to petition regarding an error in the survey of Grundy's Addition which became part of Conjunction, lying on Plain Dealing Creek/For sale - about 20 tons of timothy and clover hay lying on the farm formerly the dwelling of James Dickinson, within 5 miles of Easton - John Singleton/William Lowrey intends to leave Easton in a few weeks - Chambers & Lowrey to dissolve partnership/Risdon Bozman to petition under the insolvency act/John Martin Needles, Easton, intending to leave the state in a few weeks, requests persons to settle their accounts with him.

55. ESHM Sep 4 1792/Thomas Hall, Airey, gives statement he made at QA Co Court regarding the petition of two Edward Harris's negroes for their freedom "...informed Mr. Joseph Nicholson...in favor of the petition..."/John Gibson Talb Co, offers reward for mulatto fellow, Jim Serten, age about 20, has lived with William Sherwood in Caroline Co/Peter Rea, Cambridge, exec of James Smith, tanner

56. ESHM Sep 8 1792/Kent Co - died Sunday 2d inst Miss Milcha Groome, age 19; on Tuesday the 4th her remains were interred at St Johns Church, afflicted with a long and painful illness/Richard Key Heath requests letter from John L. Wilmer and Dr. William Matthews to Mr. E. Key be published in which they accuse Key & Heath of murder/Joel Willes, Kent Co, to petition under the insolvency act/William Hughlett has at his store at Greensborough 900 pounds of dry goods; intends to close his mercantile business as soon as possible and retire to the farming business/Robert Clothier, trustee, Kent Co, requests creditors of Thomas Hynson, late of Kent Co, to present their claims/Peter Edmondson, Caroline Co, to petition to confirm his title to a tract in Talb Co called The Addition by virtue of a contract by James Dickinson atty for late Anthony Richardson, a British subject to the father-in-law of the late Andrew Mein/Richard Grason, Wye River, offers reward for negro Jack, age 37, property of Colonel Edward Lloyd/George Robertson, Somerset Co, to petition under the insolvency act/Jesse Fooks, Worc Co, to petition to remedy error in deed of a tract called Indian Lot in Wecomico Manor bought from Richard Mills of Worc Co/A petition for public road leading from William Akers's Landing/ A farm for rent on Kent Island - Daniel Lamdin, Bay-Side, Talb Co/Edward Cox has reopened a shop (hats) in Easton & will open a shop in Cambridge/John McLaran announces that a taylor & habitmaker has opened shop in Easton in the house of Samuel Baldwin, formerly occupied by James Ewing, taylor/James Polk, surveyor of Somerset Co/Stephen Christopher to petition under the insolvency act/Isaac Bassett, dentist

57. ESHM Oct 2 1792/Friday 14th ult died after a short illness in 63d year Peter Stevens of Talb Co/John Petty has rec'd at his store in Easton a large assortment of merchandize/Jonathan Hodgson & Thomas Worrell, Chester-Town announce Chester-Town races/To let a plantation on Long Marsh, QA Co, adj lands of Vachel Keene formerly occupied by Henry Henrix - Thomas Boon at Greensborough alias Choptank Bridge

58. ESHM Oct 16 1792/Elijah Christopher confined to Snow Hill gaol for sundry debts to petition under the insolvency act/Parish of St Peter's, Talb Co, is without an incumbent, the Rev James Conner having voluntarily relinquished his agreement for the remainder of the year/Joseph Haslett, QA Co, to petition under the insolvency act/Mill-Store for sale - Matthias Bordley, Wye River/ List of letters remaining at the P. O. Easton: Dr. Moses Allen near Easton; Samuel Baldwin, Easton; Nathaniel Bell, Nanticoke River; Captain Richard Barnady, Oxford; Capt Edward Bromwell near Easton; John Bustard care of Captain John Blair, merchant, Cambridge; John Blair, merchant, Cambridge; John Bennett, merchant, Easton; Joseph Bruff, Easton; Tristram Bowdle, Easton;

Samuel Dickerson, Talb; Downes & Barrow, merchants, Tuckahoe Bridge; Mons.
De Graves, teacher of dancing; Thomas Dance, Easton, care of James Earle;
Henry Elbert, coachmaker, Easton; Joseph Foster, Talb Co; John Gooding,
merchant, Hunting Creek; William Hemsley, Wye; Edward Jones, Federalsburgh;
Alexander King, gardiner to the Honourable Matthew Tilghman, Bay Side, Talb;
Capt James Lloyd, Talb; Miss Lydia Lewis care of Alexander McCallum; Hugh
Lindsay, Easton; Alexander McCallum near Easton; Benjamin Massey now at
Easton; Donald MacLeod, Cambridge; Thomas O. Martin, Easton; Edward Noel care
of Edward Cox, Easton; The Hon. William Perry, Talb Co; William Perry Jr;
James Powell, Talb; James Price, Easton; Joseph Purden, saddler, Choptank
Bridge; Robert Polk living with Mr. Needles at Easton; John Pitt, Transquken,
care of Captain Trippe; Benjamin Parrott, Easton; Mr. McPiersoll, merchant,
Easton; Jesse Richardson, merchant, Easton; Patt(?) Reynolds, merchant,
Easton; William Sawyer, merchant, Easton; Alexander Stevens care of John
Smoot, merchant, Easton; William Stevens, merchant at the Trap; Henry Stock,
Cambridge; Samuel Swan at the sign of the George and Dragon, French Town in
Baltimore; John Stewart at the Honourable Robert Goldsborough, Talb; North
America; The Hon. James Tilghman, now at Easton; John Turner, Talb Court House
care of Henry Elbert; James Troth, Easton; Mr. Weaver, tavern keeper, Easton;
Dr. James Wilson, Head of Wye; William Wiley care of Capt James Ewing,
merchant, Princess Ann, Somerset Co; Capt Nathaniel Wright, merchant, near
Talb/John Blake offers reward for apprentice lad, Peregrine Sprous, age 20/
Plantation for sale near Head of Wye adj Mr. Gibson's Mill - Jere. Nicols,
Chester-Town/Solomon Barwick to petition for confirmation of his right to a
tract, Co-Partnership, in Caroline Co, sold by John Goslin of Dorch Co to
William Thomas of Dorch Co in 1762 afterward on same day assigned to Alias
Barwick, mother to subscriber, Solomon Barwick, by said William Thomas. And
for as much as John Goslin moved to North Carolina before he conveyed to Alias
Barwick.

59. ESHM Nov 6 1792/Sale of tract lying in Tuckahoe Neck within 2 miles of
Denton on main road from Tuckahoe Bridge to Denton - Robert Wright, Thomas
Wright, Solomon Wright/John Wynn Harrison to apply at Talb Court to bound
tracts: Dover Marsh, Dover, and Lower Dover

60. ESHM Nov 13 1792/B. M. Ward, Trap, Talb Co, master of an English School/
Marshall & Dawson, painters in Easton/John Carter, Caroline Co, about 15 miles
below Choptank Bridge, offers reward for stolen mare/Samuel Sharp admin of
James Horney/Chancery decree to creditors of William Garey, late of Talb Co,
Jeremiah Garland, trustee

61. ESHM Nov 20 1792/Rebecca Aldern forbids hunting or cutting timber on
her plantation in Talb Co/William Tripp, Easton, rec'd barrel marked W. G.
among his goods shipped from Philadelphia/Sale of property of Traverse
Garland late of Talb at his late dwelling house - Matthew Greentree, exec/
James Bowdle, gold & silversmith, has removed from next to Owen Kennard's
store into a house adj Samuel Baldwin's store/Tanyard for sale with 1/2 mile
of Easton; apply to Thomas Wickersham near Akers's Ferry or to Samuel Stevens/
Thomas Ozment offers reward for negro Jack age 37, who ran away from Col.
Lloyd's farms in Wye and also negro David age 36

62. ESHM Dec 4 1792/A few elegant fancy feathers, plumes, and wreaths just
rec'd - Watts & Fowle, Trap/James Delihay Jr, admin of Thomas Delihay, late
of Talb Co, dec/Chancery sale of tracts in Kent Co 3 miles from Chester-Town.
To see the property persons will be attended by Nathaniel Comegys res upper
part of county, William Burnaston of Chester-Town, or Thomas Nicholson, tenant
in possession - Nathaniel Comegys, John Scott, trustees, Kent Co/Ann Welch,
John Green admin of William Welch, late of QA Co, dec, to meeting of creditors
at Charles Stewart's store-house in QA Co at Hall's Cross Roads/Fisker Rakes,
QA Co, near Tuckahoe Bridge, offers reward for negro man, Davy or Dave, age 23,

-8-

63. ESHM Dec 18 1792/House for let at New Market - Cyrus Mitchell, New Market/700 a of land for sale at head of Chickmecomico River - James Sulivane/ Jacob Gibson, Miles River, seeks teacher for small children/Chancery sale of real estate in Worc Co which descended from George Stewart to his son James Stewart - Zadok Sturgis, trustee/Direction of Classical & English School in Easton undertaken by Rev Owen F. Magrath grad of Univ of Dublin & min of P.E. Congregation of this parish/Benjamin Stevens clerk of Talb Court/Sale of 400 acres adj Cross Roads within 1/4 mile of Cambridge and a lot in Cambridge between the lots of William M. Robertson & William V. Murray - Charles Goldsborough Jr

64. ESHM Jan 15 1793/Married 23 Dec Dr. Moses Allen of Talb Co to Mrs. Margaret Maxwell of Kent Co/Married Sunday 30 ult Dr. Tristram Thomas of Talb Co to Miss Susan Geddis of Wilmington/Married Friday 11th inst Mark Benton to Miss Polly Trippe both of this co/Richard Martin, Blackwater, Dorch Co, offers reward for negro man, Sam, age about 27/John Fonerden, Easton, seeks two apprentices to blacksmith business/Letters remaining in P. O. Easton: William Acres, near Easton; Jacob Aldridge in Kingstown; John Bennett, merchant , Easton; William S. Bond, merchant, Easton; James Blades near Easton; Nathan Bailey, Caroline; John Ballard(?) care of Mr. Blair, Cambridge; Captain Edward Bromwell near Easton; Bennett Chew, Wye River; Solomon Corner; Mrs. Coats, Easton; Nancy Clark, Easton; Messrs Dennis & Higson, merchants, Cratchers' Ferry; Samuel Edmondson, Easton; Henry Elbert, coach-maker, Easton; John Freman, Easton; Captain James Frazier or James Byus; Archibald Foster, taylor, Huntington Creek; Edmond Farrell at William Salier's; Matthew Greentree, Talb; Howes Goldsborough; John Gibson Jr, Head of Wye; Mary Gybs; William Hemsly; John Higbee living at Pollard Edmondson's near Easton; William Harrison at Dr. Wale's Mill at Big Elk, near Little Elk; Adam Jobe(?) Jr, Easton; Thomas Kallender near Cambridge care of John E. Gist; Owen Kennard; Charles Lester care of Henry Elbert, Easton; William Bond Martin, Cambridge; William Meluy, Easton; Samuel Nicols, Easton; Tristram Needles, Easton; Hon. William Perry; James Price, Easton; Captain Abner Parrot, Talb; Mr. Richardson treasurer Eastern Shore; Mary Ringgold, Easton; Benjamin Stevens, Easton; William Sawyer, Easton; Robert Sulivane, care of Mr. Bond Easton; Captain William Trippe; Richard Trippe near Easton; Dekar Thompson, Caroline; John Thomas, Collector of the revenue Easton; Mrs. Vidler, Easton; Rev Charles Wheelan, Easton; James Wilson, merchant, Head of Wye/Sarah Vicker near Turner's Mill, Talb Co, reports a mare straying onto her plantation/Dwelling house in Easton for rent, late the property of Joseph Bruff dec. Apply to Capt William Trippe in Easton - Mark Benton

65. ESHM Jan 29 1793/Hester McCallum, Peter Webb, exec of Alexander McCallum, late of Talb Co/Chancery sale of lands in Kent Co, part of the estate of the late John Gleaves, lying within 3 miles of Chester-Town - Nathaniel Comegys, John Scott, Kent Co, trustees/Chancery sale by Robert Clothier, trustee, of realestate of Thomas Hynson dec in the cause of William Rogers & others against James Thomas Hynson heir of Thomas Hynson/Pollard Edmondson forbids hunting on his lands in the Neck where he lives

66. ESHM Feb 12 1793/Tract of 500 a. within 3 miles of Cambridge; apply to Dr. William Maynadier near Easton or Henry Maynadier, Annapolis/David Kerr offers reward for negro lad, Shadrach age about 15 who ran away from Peter Denny's near Easton/Thomas O'Bryon, sheriff QA Co, has committed to QA jail negro man, Moses but since Mingo, and says he belongs to Joseph Denny, Talb Co; he had in his possession a spoon marked W. W./Josiah Mitchell, William Purnell, commissioners, Worc Co/Josiah Riley, insolvent debtor/ Joseph Haslett insolvent debtor/ Edward Smith, insolvent debtor/Sale of house in Cambridge improved by John Finley, late of Cambridge, now res Philadelphia; the house is now in the tenure of Messrs Gordon & Brown - Peter Ferguson, Cambridge & Robert Henderson who hold power of atty/Owen Kennard, Easton, offers reward

for negro man, Isaac age 23 formerly property of William Thomas late of Kent
Co, near George-Town Cross Roads, dec, & has for several years been employed
in that neighborhood, principally by a Mr. Maxwell and lastly by Messrs. John
& James Carmack, as a waggoner/Chancery case - James Steele of Dorch Co has
filed a petition setting forth that John Kennedy of Somerset Co and Priscilla
his wife and Lebulon Wingate and Ann his wife and Sarah Tayler conveyed unto
him land situated in Dorch Co: pt of Leinster, pt of Tayler's Neglect and
Addition to Leinster; John Kennedy having since removed out of this state/
District Court of U. S. - Whereas Charles Kirby master of schooner Lively did
not make entry of goods, valued at ten hundred dollars, nor make a report
thereof to district of Snow Hill, whereas Daniel Johnson, Inspector of the
Customs for the District of Snow-Hill seized the vessel

67. ESHM Feb 26 1793/Benjamin Blackiston, Kent Co Del, living on the road
from Head of Chester to Duck Creek, offers reward for stolen horse/John
Harwood,secretary of Lodge/Report from Captain Ebenezer Handy in St
Bartholomew's on board the schooner Lively Lass/Edward Smith insolvent debtor

68. ESHM Mar 12 1793/Richard Johns, Sheriff, Easton, offers reward for negro
man, Henry Simpson, age about 60 who broke out of gaol/James Eareckson Jr
insolvent debtor of QA Co/Chancery sale of tract purchased by Richard Gould
of Samuel Bruze lying in Caroline Co near Rev Samuel Keene's, 300-400 a.; also
to be sold at John Rolph's in Chester-Town two lots which lie near Washington
College, Martha Gould, trustee/Sale of farm of 600 a. in Talb Co; also a tract
in Caroline Co of 200 a. situated in Tuckahoe Neck now in the occupation of
Mrs. Downes - Solomon Birckhead, Cambridge/John Roberts, guardian for the heir
of John Cooper late of Caroline Co, dec/Married February last Thomas Wright
of QA Co to Miss Susan Keene of Dorch Co/Married 21st ult Abraham Eves to Miss
Elizabeth Spencer of New-Castle/Gideon Clark insolvent debtor

69. ESHM Mar 26 1793/Sale of waggon and gears and horse - Thomas J. Seth,
Mount Mills, QA Co/Meeting of Grand Lodge - Charles Gardiner, sec/Elijah
Christopher involvent debtor, lately in the custody of sheriff of Worc Co/
Married Sunday last William Lowrey, merchant, to Miss Betsy Stevens, both of
Talb Co/Chancery sale of real estate of Henry Ayres dec by Ezekiel Wise

70. ESHM Apr 9 1793/Letters remaining at P. O. Easton: Matthew Doyle, Trap;
John Duncain care of William Stevens, Trap; Capt Robert Ewing, merchant,
Kingston; Henry Elbert; Archibald Foster; Charles Gardiner; John Gibson, late
commissary of wills at Queen Anne's; William Hughlett, Easton; James Harris;
James Hutchins, Kent Island; Richard Jones at Richard Tilghman's; William
Meluy, Easton; Mrs. Hetty McCallum; Tristram Needles, Easton; Robert Pickering,
Miles River; Jesse Richardson, Easton; James Rheu(?), Easton; William Sawyer,
Easton; Walter Scott care of Mr. Weaver; Capt Severn Teackle; William
Tilghman; Dr. James Wilson care of ...; James Wilson living with ...; William
Warrin, Talb/Frederick Kreamer, Easton, seeks two journeymen plasterers/
Catharine Goldsborough, John Singleton, exec of Thomas Goldsborough, atty at
law of Talb Co, dec/Sale at the dwelling house of Nicholas Loveday of his
personal property - John Turner(for creditors)/Talb Co sheriff offers reward
for mulatto man, Levin Maddin, who broke out of gaol at Easton

71. ESHM Apr 30 1793/George Robertson insolvent debtor lately in the custody
of sheriff of Somerset Co/Richard Goodman, QA Co, near Kent Narrows, offers
reward for a negro man, Phill, age about 25/Edward Cox to establish a shop in
Cambridge and continue in Easton; requests debts be paid to James Nabb/John
McLaran, taylor & habit maker has quantity on hand of Peter's Beer, Porter in
Bottles & other sundry articles/Letter from Thomas Cooper regarding declar-
ation of Capt. Charles Sherwood involving sale of wheat which was shipped to
Baltimore/Death of Miss Milcha Groome of Kent/Buffaloes on display at Mrs.
Bruff's Alley/C. T. Wederstrandt, near Kent Island, offers reward for mulatto
girl, Mabb, age about 16; her mother lives in Wye Neck/Lucretia Haddaway admin

of Okley Haddaway, late of Talb Co/Arthur Rigby, Talb Co, admin of Moses Rigby, late of Talb Co, dec/William McBryde & Co, Salisbury, announce the Macgilvrce is now loading in Wicomico river & will sail to Port Glasgow around 10 May/ Sale of two tracts in QA Co and Talb Co - Charles Daffin/Sale of 1500 a. on water from Kent Narrows to Jackson's Creek - John Sayer Blake

72. ESHM May 7 1793/Capt Richard Coward of Easton about to leave the county with the intention of going to sea - John Singleton, trustee; the boarding house will still be continued by Mrs. Coward/William S. Bond has been joined by Captain William Buchanan in business; they have just rec'd a part of their supply & a complete assortment of groceries/Lots for sale in Cambridge - Thomas Hicks

73. ESHM Jun 4 1793/Sale of house in Cambridge occupied by Mrs. Elizabeth Caile - Robert Harrison near Cambridge/Charles Goldsborough, Horn's Point, near Cambridge, offers reward for negro fellow, Ned Wheatly, age about 26/ Chancery case - Samuel & Robert Smyly versus heirs of James Houston (if there be any) dec, regarding a lot owned by Houston in Salisbury, pt of Mill Security/Peter Cooper, Talb Co, forewarns he will not pay debts of his wife Anna Cooper/Farm for rent at mouth of Hunting Creek, Caroline Co whereon Capt. Teakle now lives - Charles Goldsborough, Cambridge/John Lecompte, Lecompte's Bay, Dorch Co, offers reward for negro man, Levin, age about 21/Edward Bromwell Sr in Oxford, offers reward for mulatto man, Perry age about 25

74. ESHM Jul 2 1793/James Robardet to open Dancing School in Easton/157 1/2 a. adj Vienna, Dorch Co; Apply to Mr. Bond living in Vienna - William Campbell, Gabriel Duvall/Samuel Sharp, Easton, admin of James Horney, dec/ Jere. Banning, collector for the district of Oxford/Sale or lease of 7 years of part of Charles Pickering's land - Greenbury Goldsborough/Chancery sale of real estate of Edward Smith, insolvent debtor - Alexander Douglass, trustee/ Stephen Fleharty, late inspector tobacco) at Richardson's Warehouse on great Choptank River/Sale of house in Cambridge where he now lives - Samuel Birckhead/Sale of 508 1/4 a. land on Corsica Creek, QA Co - James Earle, Chester-Town/James Booker, Easton, forewarns persons from trespassing on his orchards situated near Cow Landing/Joshua David admin of James Davis, late of QA Co/Tenements adj Plain Dealing for rent: Head of the Creek Plantation and The Oak - Robert Lloyd Nicols/John Erskine request payment of debts/John Singleton, Howes Goldsborough, William Goldsborough, trustees of Foster Goldsbough, late of Caroline Co, dec, to sell his tract, Hog Island; Rachel Goldsborough exec of Foster Goldsborough/Wanted - journeyman carpenters - James Vansandt at Col. Nichols's

75. ESHM Jul 23 1793/John Dickinson, Caroline Co, offers reward for negro man Caesar, age about 21/Chancery sale of tract Pitt's Range at Hole in the Wall, late the property of Edward M. Sherwood - Robert Sherwood, trustee/Chancery sale of part of the real estate of William Garey, late of Talb Co, dec, adj plantation whereon he lately dwelt - Jeremiah Garland, trustee/House for rent where Thomas J. Bullit now lives - Benjamin Stevens, Easton/Plantation for rent in Tuckahoe Neck (Caroline Co) now occupied by Samuel & Ambrose Kinnament - Apply to Sarah Troup or Charles Troup, Easton/Letters P. O. Easton, Jul 8th: Ester Banks at Mr. Muray's Cambridge; John Blake, Easton; Charles Baker to be left at Talb Court House; John Bennet, merchant, near Easton; Isaac Cox, merchant, Talb Court House; John Carter, brick maker, Talb; John Dickinson the 4th; Solomon Dickinson, Easton; James Dawson, Talb Co; Dr. John Elbert near Wye Mill; Horatio Edmundson; William Frazier, Caroline; Philip Frees, Easton; Woolman Gibson near Easton; John Goldsborough Jr, atty at law; Robert Goldsborough student of medicine; John Harrison, Talb; Thomas Harrison, merchant, Broad Creek; Capt John Hughes, Easton; William Hemsley, QA; Giles Hicks, Tuckahoe Bridge; John Herster (or Hertter?), Easton; William Knox, blacksmith, Talb; Mr. Meluy, saddler, New Market; Charles McClaran; Hon.

-11-

William Perry; John Powell; Jesse Richardson; Pat. Reynolds; William Richmond, Queenstown; James Saunders, Dorch Co; William Sawyer; Dr. Sullivain Jr, Newmarket; Thomas Sherwood, Miles River; Cyrus Sharpe of Somerset Co, now at Easton; James Seth, merchant, Easton; Charles Vanderen, Newmarket; Colonel Weaver, Inn Keeper at Talb Court House; Lazarus Winsor, Devil's Island; Rev Charles Whealan near Easton; Henry Waggaman, atty at law, Cambridge

76. ESHM Aug 27 1793/Died Tuesday 20 inst John Nesmith a native of North Britain, in Easton, age 67; he engaged in the civil commotions of his country in 1745 and "having been upon the unfortunate side of the question, he was in consequence obliged to emigrate, and sought this country as an assylum. - For many years previous to the American Revolution he conveyed the mail from this place to Philadelphia ..."as a member of Lodge No. 6, members attended his remains to the grave/Peter Edmondson, sheriff of Caroline Co, has committed to gaol a negro man, who calls himself, Sam Clarke, sold & taken from this co last fall to Georgia from whence he says he ran away/William Benson, Caroline Co, to petition to establish a levy for the purpose of completing the court house/Chancery sale at the house of Elijah Christopher in Worc Co - Benjamin Dennis, trustee/William Rose, Easton, forewarns persons from trespassing on his plantation/Two farms for sale in Caroline Co, known as Old Town and the Quarter Plantation, part of the estate of Thomas Goldsborough - John Singleton/ John Ozman reports a stray mare/Blacksmith shop for rent between Greensborough and Frederica - William Hughlett; also a farm for sale 1 1/2 miles from Rev Samuel Keene's/Letters remaining at P. O. Chester Mill on 1 Jul 1793: John Nicolls, William Colman; Robert Brazier; Edward Harris; James Starr; Miss Susan Livingston; Benjamin Young, QA Co - James Kent, Post Master

77. ESHM Sep 3 1793/John Goldsborough Jr, Easton, candidate for representative in General Assembly/Charles Troup, David Kerr, exec of John Nesmith late of Talb Co/Talb Co sheriff offers reward for Robert Carnon, by trade a saddler & harnes maker, of a dark complexion, around 5 ft 7-8 inch; he had on a brown coat, black vest, and breeches and a round hat; he broke out of gaol of Easton

78. ESHM Sep 10 1793/Several letters involving statements by John Roberts, Col. Edward Lloyd, Dr. Bowie on Lloyd's treatment of his slaves/Peter Edmondson sherriff of Caroline Co offers reward for negro slave, Nuba, property of Peter Rich of Caroline Co, age around 25/James Lloyd, chariman of committee, Kent Co, in resolution to President George Washington/Col. John Eccleston, chairman of meeting of landholders & other citizens of Dorch Co in support of President G. Washington/H.Sherwood of Huntington, candidate for Assembly/Petition to lay off the town of Salisbury and ascertain the boundary between Somerset and Worc counties - Ebenezer Handy, William Chaille, Salisbury/Trustees of the poor, Talb Co: John Singleton, Robert Lloyd Nicols, Samuel Chamberlaine, Henry Nicols, Henry Banning;James Dwiggins, QA Co, overseer of Mr. William Richmond's farm, reports stray mare/Chancery sale by Robert Sherwood of real estate of Edward Mann Sherwood

79. ESHM Oct 1 1793/Benjamin Kirby, Bay-side, wants to purchase negro woman/ John W. Harrison, near Easton, offers reward for mulatto man, Will Busby, age about 21/Randolph Johnson, Dorch Co, to petition under the insolvency act/ George Bell to petition to condemn a stream of water near Tuckahoe Creek in Caroline Co owned by heirs of Richard Lockerman and to erect a mill/Susanna Rakes wid of Fisher Rakes, QA Co, near Tuckahoe Bridge, offers reward for negro man Davy, age about 24, last reported to the kitchen or negro quarters of Peter Edmondson, sheriff of Caroline Co, by the name of Jacob Inlows/ Whereas my Rebecca having eloped from my bed and board ...George Hall

80. ESHM Oct 8 1793/Died Mon 30 Sep last Mrs. Margaret Maynadier of Talb Co after a long and painful illness..."gone from a disconsolate husband and young and numerous offspring ..."/Moses Sherwood admin of Edward Mann Sherwood late

of Talb Co, dec/Sale at Mr. Weaver's tavern in Easton, lands of Mrs. Hollyday lying in Talb Co, about 800 a.- Samuel Chamberlaine, Nicholas Hammond, Easton, agents/Peter Webb exec of Alexander McCallum, late of Talb Co, dec/William Keene Dorch Co to petition under the insolvency act/David Kerr, E aston, candidate for representative

81. ESHM Oct 15 1793/Married Thursday evening last by Rev Collin Ferguson, Joseph H. Nicholson to Miss Rebecca B. Lloyd dau of Col. Edward Lloyd of Talb Co/Thomas Hill, Unicorn Mills, near Head of Chester, QA Co, offers reward for stolen horse/Leather manufactory co-partnership of Atkinson & son will dissolve at close of the year and the tanyard within 1/2 miles of Easton will be carried on by Israel Corse & William J. Atkinson/Letters remaining at P. O. Easton: Medford Andrews, merchant, near Cambridge; Capt Edward Bromwell Jr, near Easton; Manuel Blodget, Easton; John Blake, Easton; Joseph Brown, merchant, Eastern Branch Ferry; James Batman, Easton; Charles Baker near Easton; Christopher Driver, Caroline; Mr. Elbert, carriage maker, Easton; James Edmondson, merchant, Caroline; Archibald Foster care of John Gooding, Hunting Creek; George Frost, Easton; William Gray care of William Reade, Easton Town, America; William Hughes, Dorch Co; John Herster, Easton; Amos Heald, bricklayer, Easton; Joshua Hitch now at Eston; William Hicks , Oxford care of Samuel Baldwin; P. Kelly, Cambridge; William G. Killune near Easton; Charles Locount near Cambridge; Thomas M. Cutchen, pedler care of William Weaver; Andrew Mitchell, Doctor in Caroline Co; Capt Thomas Neighbors; Capt Abner Parrott, Talb; Jonathan Pinkney at Mr. Baker's, New Market; John Powell, Talb; Patt Reynolds, Easton; Mr. Rutter; Jesse Richardson; James Rheu; William Rowe to be left at Mr. Dawson's, Cambridge; Peter Rich, Caroline; Sheriff of Talb Co; Benjamin Sylvester, Caroline; William Scott, miller, Head Kings' Creek; Jacob Smith, Kings Town; Capt Hugh Sherwood, Oxford; Francis Sellers, Tuckahoe; John Stevens near Talbot Courthouse; Joseph Stone, St. Michaels; Messrs Sulivane & Ennalls, New Market; William Thomas, Talb; Edward Vidler, Easton, America; Charles Wheeler, Dorch, care of Edward Cox, Easton; Henry Waggaman, Cambridge; Joseph Welsh care of Rev Beveridge, Cambridge/William Keene, Dorch Co, to petition under insolvency act/Joseph Dodson, Dorch Co, near Middletown, offers reward for apprentice, John Carroll, about 20 yrs old, 6 ft, brown hair

82. ESHM Nov 5 1793/Tracts for sale: Lane's Addition, Kinnomonts' Outlet in Caroline Co, Dawson's Neck, New Port & New Port Addition in QA Co; apply to James Kent, merchant, QA Co or Reubin Gilder, Balt/Isaac Sharp, near Hall's Cross Roads, QA Co, offers reward for strayed mare/Tavern for rent, lately occupied by Thomas Mansfield in Queens-Town - John Williams, Queens-Town

83. ESHM Dec 10 1793/Farm for sale near Easton pursuant to the will of William McCallum, lateof Talb Co: his dwelling plantation: pt of Mount Hope, pt of Proprietary, pt of Manor; apply to Solomon Neall or John Needles, exec/ James Hindman, Bennett's Point, Wye River, intending to leave the country in May next, to sell farm known as Bennett's Point on the mouth of Wye River/ John Stevens, Candidate for sheriff/Philemon Auld, Bay-Side, Talb Co, offers reward for negro man, Isaac, age about 28/Andrew Boyer, limner, Easton/James Tilghman, William Tilghman, exec of James Tilghman, late of Chester-Town/Mary Martin of Talb Co offers reward for negro man, Daniel, age about 25, who ran away from Andrew Callender/Sale at the dwelling house of the late William Lavall(?) of Talb Co, near KingsTown, horses, cows, household furniture, farming utensils - William Sawyer

84. ESHM Dec 24 1793/Died 6th inst Charles Gardiner of Talb Co/Robert Kersey watch & clock maker has opened shop opp Court House

85. ESHM Jan 7 1794/Married Sunday evening last by Rev Dr. Bowie Richard Trippe to Miss Hariot Edmondson dau of Pollard Edmondson/Died Tuesday 31 Dec of a pleurisy at Hunting Creek, Dorset Co, William McBride, merchant at

Salisbury/Chancery sale in Kent Co, late the property of William Hanson, dec, land which the dec purchased of Robert Little, 480 a. - Simon Wilmer of Ed., trustee, Kent Co/J. E. Gist, Cambridge admin of Patrick Kelly, late of Cambridge, dec/Thomas S. Denny candidate for sheriff/Charles Blair of Caroline Co seeks wet nurse

86. ESHM Jan 21 1794/Tanyard for rent in Cambridge - Peter Rea, Cambridge/ Christopher Cox, QA Co, exec of James Bordley, late of QA Co/Letters remaining at the P. O. Easton Jan 14 1794: William Aljoe care of Capt John Erskine; Jacob Bromwell; James Butcher, Church Hill; John Blair, merchant, Cambridge; John Blake, Easton; Samuel Chew of John, Lyon's Creek; William Clayland, Easton; Mr. ___Clift near Easton; Richard Carmichael, Wye River; Mrs. Dawson, Easton; Joseph Darden, Island Creek; Pollard Edmondson; William Fountain near Easton; Capt W. Frazier near Easton; Wolman Gibson near Easton; Jeremiah Garland; Lucas Gibbes, Easton; Robert Hewet care of Peter Ferguson, merchant, Cambridge; Robert Harrison at Appleby, near Cambridge; William Hay, merchant, St. Michaels; Joseph Harrold, merchant, Easton; John Hughes, Easton; David Hull care of Samuel Edmondson; Michael Hart, merchant, Easton; Martha Jordain, Talb; Mrs. Sally Kellum; Nicholas Kellum; Patrick Kelly, Cambridge; Rev James Kemp; William Lavins care of Capt John Erskine; Thomas Lockerman, Cambridge; Thomas Mews care of Samuel Baldwin; Elijah Massey; Benjamin Massey; Thomas McKeel; Daniel McDonnell, Cambridge; Henry Martin near Easton; Mrs. Mary McMullen; Howel Powel; John Pitts, Dorset Co; Abraham Palmer, Talb; John Reed care of Peter Ferguson, Cambridge; James Robardet; Patrick Reynolds; James Ramsey, merchant, Belvidere; William Smith, merchant, Easton; William Sawyer; Benjamin Sylvester, Caroline; Samuel Sharp; Robert Smith, Talb; Rev Mr. Teasdale at Wally Kill near Newtown, Sussex Co; William Thomas, Talb; Charles Vanderen, merchant, New Market; John Duncan Wright care of William Stevens, Talb

87. ESHM Jan 28 1794/Died Saturday night last Captain Severn Teikle of this town/James Price exec of Jeremiah Garland, late of Talb Co/Daniel P. Cox candidate for sheriff Talb Co/John Bracco, Miles River Neck, Talb Co, offers reward for negro man Oliver, age about 22/Samuel Sharp, Easton, admin of James King/Samuel Foudray wants apprentices to the hatting business/James Shaw register for land office, Eastern Shore, Easton

88. ESHM Feb 4 1794/Whereas my Mary Dobson has eloped from my bed and board ...William Dobson, Talb Co/Clover seed for sale - William Dawson/Impey Dawson Jr admin of Stephen Dawson

89. ESHM Mar 4 1794/Married Sunday 23 ult by Rev James Kemp, Peter Webb to Miss Sally Trippe, both of this co/Paddy Whack, horse of Doctor Robert Lemmon is available for service/Wanted by Doctor Lemmon in Salisbury a few workmen at the shore & bootmaking business/John Townsend, Caroline Co, to petition under the insolvency act/Daniel Fiddeman, Bay-side, Talb Co, offers reward for negro lad, Juba, age about 18/Thomas Worrell, secretary, announces Chester-Town races/Chancery sale of real estate of Cuthbert Heron, Anna Heron, and Harriot Heron, orphans and heirs of Cuthbert Heron, late of Dorch Co, dec, a house in Vienna - James Shaw, trustee/Waggon & gears for sale - John Dougherty/Joseph Douglass admin of John Smoot late of Dorset Co/B. M. Ward, Easton, admin of Captain Edward Delahay, late of Talb Co, dec/John Calahan of New Castle Co, Del, forwarns that he will not honor assignement passed to James Slaughter of Caroline Co, being "Fraudulently obtained."/Chancery sale of real estate of Levin Kirkman, Robert Kirkman, Peggy Kirkman and Nancy Kirkman, orphans and heirs of Levin Kirkman, late of Dorch Co: Blackwalnut Landing, 245 a, within 4 to 5 miles of Vienna - James Shaw, trustee/Thomas Burnett, Island Creek Neck, Talb Co, seeks to hire a teacher/William G. Killum forewarns persons from hunting on his plantation in the neighborhood of Easton/ House for sale adj Easton - James Tilghman/Dorcas Barrow offers reward for

horse which strayed from plantation of Thomas Barrow at Miles River Ferry, Talb Co; for reward deliver horse to her plantation in Caroline Co near Tuakahoe Bridge/Margaret Gardiner, Samuel Barrow, Nathan Gregg Bryson, Miles River Neck, exec of Charles Gardiner

90. ESHM Apr 15 1794/Tanyard for sale lately occupied by William Corbit Jr and Co at Beaver Dam causeway, QA Co - William Corbit admin of William Corbit Jr, George Vt. Mann and William Thomas surviving partner of William Corbitt Jr/ James Smith insolvent debtor/John Brown exec of William Brown late of Kent Co Del/Jacob Alborn, hair dresser, bleeder and tooth drawer, carries on business where Mr. Wickersham formerly lived; has for sale a small assortment of perfumery/James Slaughter responds to "slander" by John Calahan/Married Thursday last by Rev James Kemp Dr. John Eccleston to Miss Mary Sulivane dau of James Sulivane of Dorch Co/William Paca, Balt Town offers reward for negro Dick who crossed the Bay to Kent Island/W. Buchanan, Easton, admin of William Stevens Jr, late of Talb Co, dec/George Bell, Caroline Co - whereas my wife eloped from my bed and board .../Richard Johns, sherif of Talb Co offers reward for negro woman Peg Cornish age about 25, 5 ft 4-5 inch, convicted of stealing, has mulatto child about 18 months old named Frisby; her mother is Beck Cornish in Easton/Tanyard in Cambridge for rent - Peter Ray, Cambridge/ John Brown, Nixon Sherwood, admin of Francis Sherwood, late of Caroline Co, dec/William Burke insolvent debtor/John Walters Jr insolvent debtor/Isaac Boon exec of Joseph Boon, late of Caroline Co/William Whiteley, Charles Jones, admin of Robert Dixon, late of Kent Co, Del/Farm for sale in QA Co adj Chester Mill; apply to Richard Tilghamn - Ed. Tilghman, Philadelphia/Talb Co sheriff has committed to gaol negro Sam, age about 30, who says he belongs to James Coultrain of Georgia, purchased by a Mr. Ervine of Joshua Clark of Caroline Co

91. ESHM Apr 22 1794/John McLaran, taylor, to keep a grocery & fruit store in Cambridge

92. ESHM May 13 1794/John McCoy & James Ratliff, taylors near Captain Wright's store, White Haven/Plantation for sale in the bottom of Dirty Neck, Talb Co, known as Long Point or Elston's Point, about 196 a. - William Shield/ Letters remaining at P. O. Easton, Apr 25 1794: Francis Baker, Talb; John Bennet, Easton; John Blake: Messrs Benjamin & Thomas Boyd, New Market; Richard Chamberlain, Talb Court House; Daniel P. Cox; Edward Coursey on Wye; Messrs Crozier & Elliott near Tuckahoe; James Diamond, Great Choptank; Cornelius C. Elmerdorph, North East Town; James Earle Jr; Thomas Elliot Jr, Tuckahoe; Messrs Thomas & Richard Emory, Queens-Town; Horatio Edmondson; Capt Joseph Foster, Easton; Archibald Foster, taylor, Hunting Creek; Woolman Gibson Jr; Mrs. Gibson; Robert S. Gamble, Caroline Co; Mrs. Prudence Harrison, Talb Co; William Harper, Nine Bridges; Richard Hickman; Richard Haners, St. Michaels; John Hance Hambleton, Dorch Co; Michael Hart, merchant, Easton; George Knok, Wye Mill; Benjamin Kemp, Talb Co; Messrs. Solomon Martin & William Mackey, Talb Co; Edward Roberts; Patrick Reynolds, Easton; William Sawyer; Dr. James Sulivane, New Market; Daniel Sparkes, miller, Dorch Co; Francis Smyth, Easton; Miss Martha Smith, Easton; Thomas Stevens, Talb; Henry Travers, Dorset Co; Levin Travers, Dorch Co; Thomas Tillotson, Tuckahoe Bridge; Col. T. Woolford; Joshua Willis Jr; Dr. James Wilson, Head of Wye/Samuel Thomas master of the schooner Betsy, Easton to Balt packet/James Ewing admin of James Meredith late of Caroline, dec/Samuel Sherwood, boot & shoemaker, Easton

93. ESHM May 20 1794/Alexander Kinney, Easton, has just rec'd a neat assortment of goods/John Walters Jr insolvent debtor, lately in the custody of the sheriff of QA Co/Chancery sale at Denton of the property of Robert Casson, dec - Thomas W. Loockerman, trustee/Chancery sale at Denton of a tract in Caroline called Golden Grove of about 725 a. which descended to James Dixon, heir of Robert Dixon, late of Delaware State, dec, to satisfy claims of Richard Darnall and Bennett Darnall - P. Edmondson, trustee/Partnership of John Watts & Jacob Fowle, Talb Co dissolved

94. ESHM May 27 1794/"... to certify ... what I can gather respecting what has been reported on Mr. Samuel Cox concerning my saddlebags, clothes and money, that I gave in the possession of Josiah Sterling at Northwest-fork Bridge, as he the said Mr. Cox was accused with the fact, I have since got great reason to believe that he is clear, and that his character I hope may not be considered any the worse, for I believe that he is quite innocent of the charge. John Peay. Witness, Samuel Swan"

95. ESHM Jun 3 1794/The schooner, Tartar, Captain Pamphilion, to run a packet from Easton to Balt every Wednesday; commands may be left at the store of John Erskine/Henry Bowdle, cabinet & chair maker, has opened a shop in Washington St adj Mr. Wilmot's (clockmaker) a little below Mr. Mullikin's Tavern

96. ESHM Jun 10 1794/Mill for sale called Potts's Mill - James Tilghman Jr, Easton/Houses for sale at the Walnut Trees in Caroline Co - William Gibson, Denton

97. ESHM Jun 17 1794/Benjamin Wilmot, secretary, announces meeting of Lodge No. 6/John Carey, near Queen's Town, QA Co, offers reward for stolen mare/His dwelling place for sale in QA Co, 4 miles from Centreville near road leading to Chester Town - W. Bruff/House for rent where James Shaw lives - Sarah Troup/ A list of appointments in the militia of this state (only the officers of the Eastern Shore of Maryland are listed here) - Brigadier Generals - Caecil & Harford, Josiah C. Hall; Kent & QA, James Lloyd; Dorch, Caroline & Talb, John Eccleston; Somerset & Worc, Alexander Roxburgh; Somerset-Lieut Cols: John Stewart; John Gale; Majors: Levin Gale & Samuel Wilson; Littleton Dennis & Esme Bayly; Worc-Lieut Cols: Levin Handy; Isaac Houston; Majors: John Holland & Thomas Martin; Edward Henry, James Handy & William Chaille; Caroline-Lieut Cols: William Whitely; Majors: Thomas Mason & Joseph Richardson; QA-Lieut Cols: Samuel T. Wright; James Bruff; Majors: Edward Coursy & Richard Emory; Joseph Forman & Edward Downes; Dorch-Lieut Cols: James Steele; ___; Majors: Moses Lecompte & ___; ___ & ___; Talbot-Lieut Cols: John Hughes; Perry Benson; Majors: Daniel P. Cox; Robert Lloyd Nicols; Hugh Sherwood; & William Goldsborough; Caecil-Lieut Cols: Edward Oldham; Henry Hollingsworth; Majors: Thomas P. Forman; Ezekiel Ford; John Hartshorne & Samuel Maffitt; Kent-Lieut Cols: Benjamin Chalmers; Philip Reed; Majors: John Bordley; John Bowers; Isaac Freeman; & Robert Wright/Married Sunday evening last by Rev Bowie, James Earle Jr to Miss Nancy Tilghman dau of Col. Peregrine Tilghman of Talb Co

98. ESHM Jun 24 1794/John Hardcastle, Caroline Co, offers reward for negro woman Pegg, age about 26; it is expected that "she has been conveyed away by a noted villain by the name of Alexander Wilson; he is a blacksmith by trade ...committed for a felony in Caroline Co about 2 yrs ago; he broke jail and has left the place; he took up with the aforesaid woman about 3 yrs ago; he has declared to some of the family that he would have her away with him; he is a native of Ireland and is about 40 yrs of age and is a well set fellow.."

99. ESH Jul 1 1794/Sale at Thomas Stewart's, Cambridge, a tract of about 500 a. in Transquaking; apply to Thomas Hicks, Cambridge or Levin Porter on the premises/Robert Griffith, Dorch Co, offers reward for 2 negro men: Harry age about 24 and Stephen age about 24/Whereas my wife Mary has absconded from my bed and board without any lawful cause ... John Shearman

100. ESH Jul 8 1794/Peter Rich inspector gives notice that the justices of Caroline Co have discontinued Bridge Town Ware House at Choptank Bridge. "I request all those who have any tobacco in said warehouse to take it away ..."/Chancery sale of part of two tracts lying in Kent Co Md on Langford's Bay: Kimbolton & Smith's Venture, about 443 a. - Ben: Chambers, trustee

101. ESH Jul 15 1794/Letters remaining at P. O. Easton July 15 1794: David Austin, Easton; Henry Banning, Talb; Capt John Bush, Talb; Messrs. Benjamin & Thomas Boyd, New Market; Charles Brown, house carpenter, Talb;

Daniel Bannerman care of Peter Ferguison, Cambridge; Au Citoyen Nadal Tillew
a Bay Side Church, Talb Co; Edward Coursey, Wye River; Mrs. Henrietta Craig,
Easton; Miss Mary Caldwell at Mrs. Russell's, North East, Md; James Cheston,
Easton; Matthew Driver, Caroline Co; James Earle Jr; John Fisher near
Tuakahoe Bridge; Capt Joseph Foster, Easton; Samuel Foudray, Easton; James
Fisher care of Messrs. Ennalls & Sullivan, New Market; Levin Gale at James
Dickinson's, Talb; Greenbury Goldsborough, Easton; Mrs. Catharine Goldsborough,
Talb Co; Amos Haild near Easton; Thomas Harrison, merchant, Broad Creek;
Robert Hewat care of Peter Ferguison, Cambridge; Miss Elizabeth Jordan in
Talb Co; Hugh Lindsay near Easton; Jeremiah O'Brian care of· John Blair,
Cambridge; Samuel Randel, New Market; Jesse Richardson, Easton; Patrick
Reynolds, Easton; Absalon Swaney, Easton; Miss Nancy Smith, Easton; Charles
Stewart, Merchant, Hall's Cross Roads, QA Co; Capt William Trippe, Easton;
Dr. Thomas, Easton; William Thomas, Easton; Mrs. Elizabeth Topping, Easton;
Charles Wheeler, Dorch Co, near Charles Lecompte care of Edward Cox, Easton;
James Wilson, Easton; Dr. James Willon or Mr. John Thomas, Head of Wye/
Chancery sale of two tracts formerly the property of Joseph Brater, dec: pt
of Craton's & Showel's Addition, Crooked Lot - 270 a. situated on the head of
St Martin's River, Worc Co - William Purnell, trustee, Worc Co/John Nabb Talb
Co to petition under the insolvency act

102. ESHM Jul 23 1794/James Sykes, John Laws, Edward Miller, Dover Del app
to examinine specimens of Peruvian bark, sold as a medicine/To form a society
of architects & house carpenters of the Eastern Shore at Easton - James
Benson, Cornelius West, James Vansandt/Slave, Molly's Jack now is custody of
Talb Co sheriff/James Gunn, soon to depart for Georgia, offers reward for
negro man, John Scott, age about 24/To let a stand in New Market for a tavern
with a billiard table, now in the tenure of Charles Stuart/Matthew Bendle,
Dorset Co, near White's Warehouse, 5 miles from Cambridge, offers reward for
a man who stole a horse; the thief is William Thomas, a stout, strong man,
about 6 ft high; the horse has since been recovered, and the thief taken up
by William Coursey & John Ewing of Caroline Co, since which the thief has
made his escape.

103. ESHM Jul 29 1794/Slave Harry now in custody of Talb Co sheriff/Chancery
sale of pt of tract, Neglect near Church Hill, 200 a., which hath descended
to Richard Earle Clayton, William Jackson Clayton and Julianna Clayton from
Solomon Clayton, dec, of QA Co, for the use of James Hindman & William Hemsley
- Peter Edmondson, trustee/Chancery case - Thomas Jones versus heirs of
Matthew Bright. Thomas Jones applies for a decree for recording a deed from
said Matthew Bright, executed 3 Mar 1767, for conveying unto Robert Wilson a
tract in Dorch Co called Grove which has since been conveyed by said Wilson
unto the complainant & his heirs. The bill states that the said Bright, since
the execution of the said deed, hath died without leaving any known heirs/Farm
for sale 4 miles from Chester Town - Charles Baker, New Market, Dorch

104. ESHM Aug 5 1794/Grist mill for sale in Caroline Co 2 miles from Choptank
Bridge on road that leads to Dover; also a good stand for a retailer's store
& blacksmith shop - William Jackson/A petition to straighten road from the
south end of the lane between Benjamin Sylvester and John Tolson, to intersect
the public road leading from Choptank Bridge to Tuckahoe Bridge, near Robert
Postlewaith's new building/Joseph Bruff informs officers of the militia that
he offers newest and most approved patterns for sword mounting/William Jackson
claims that Benjamin Sylvester fraudulently recorded in Annapolis a resurvey
of a tract called Dublin/Negro man Phil, age about 40, in custody at Talb Co
gaol who was sold by John W. Harrison of Talb Co to Mr. Irvine of North
Carolina who sold him; from thence he says he made his escape/Sale according
to the will of William Sawyer, late of Easton, dec, of the dwelling plantation
of William McCallum, around 200 a. lying in Talb Co within 1 mile of Dover

-17-

Ferry - Mary Sawyer, William Meluy, John Needles, Talb Co

105. ESHM Aug 12 1794/Sale of farm within a mile of Dover Del - Robert Clark of Dover Del/Tract for sale in Somerset Co: Friends Assistance, around 280 a. - Isaac Henry, John Henry/William Keene insolvent debtor

106. ESHM Aug 19 1794/William Hindman candidate for U. S. Conrgress/Recruiting notice to join army of the United States; Lieutenant Geddes at Mr. Hodgson's or Mr. Joseph Williams, Commissary, Chestertown/John Tarr offers reward for negro man, Paris, age 29 ,who ran away from Mr. Sherwood's plantation on Miles River

107. ESHM Aug 26 1794/The Light Infantry, of the first Battalion, of the 4th Regiment, are hereby notified that they are to assemble at their usual parade, with arms and accoutrements, on Saturday next at three o'clock, P.M. agreeable to law. By order of the Captain, Samuel Sharp, clerk, Easton/William Keene of Caroline Co, Tuckahoe Neck, informs friends and acquaintances that he is not the same William Keene who is petitioning for relief under the insolvency act/ Margaret Cornish, Talb Co, to petition under the insolvency act/A petition to lay off anew the town of Salisbury and to establish a road which leads from William Winder's mill toward Broad Creek/Thomas Anderson, Hunting Creek, Dorch Co, offers reward for slaves: negro woman, Nell and her children: boy, Brian, age about 16, girl, Sal, age 12 or 13; girl, Ann, age 4; girl, Fan age about 2; her husband is John Brian, age about 42, who was emancipated by Philip McKey of Talb Co/James Matthews, 4 miles from Easton, offers reward for stolen horse; it is suggested that a mulatto man named Stephen Richards has carried him off; Stephen Richards is well set, about 5 ft high, has a bushy head, has a bright complexion.

108. ESHM Sep 9 1794/Notice is given by Schoolfield Parker that he "being imposed on by a certain Sarah Noble, (which married, now Sarah Parker) that I mean to petition ...for a divorce.."/Gustavus Scott, Baltimore, offers reward for negro fellow, Juba, age about 25, who escaped to Talb Co; he is a native of Dorch Co; of late he res in Talb Co/Announcing prices agreed upon by a meeting of tanner & curriers in Easton - William Rose, Israel Corse & William Atkinson, James Dawson, Christopher Nice, James Richardson/Sale at the house of Walter Jenkins, late of Talb Co, dec, carriage, household furniture, horses, cattle, farming utensils, a boat built for pleasure - Catharine Jenkins/Thomas Ozment, Hammond's Farms, Wye River, offers reward for negro men who absconded from Col. Edward Lloyd's plantation: Jacob, age about 28 and Sam age about 20, and Toney/Nat. Kennard, Wye Mill, Talb Co, offers reward for saddle mare/Charles McMachan to leave Easton with the drafted troops as a volunteer

109. ESHM Sep 16 1794/Kings Creek, Daniel P. Cox "Being called on by the Commander in Chief of this state to march out against the insurgents in the back counties of Pennsylvania, flatters himself that the Free Voeters of Talbot County, and his friends in general will exert themselves in his favor in the ensuring election for their Sheriff, as it is very improbable that he can be present at that time, and their favours will be gratefully acknowledged by their friend and humble servant."/To petition to condemn land of Thomas Dale, Worc Co, used as appertnent to the mills of Joseph Adkins, Hannah Adkins, David Adkins, Ayres Parker, Worc Co/Samuel Foudray former partner of William Wood to petition under insolvency act/Addition to the roll of officers - Doctor Daniel Sullivane of New Market, Dorset, Surgeon; Doctor John Murray of Cambridge, Dorset, Volunteer Aid to General Smith/Cambridge 11th Sept. 1794: The embarkation of the Dorset Volunteers took place yesterday afternoon about five o'clock under Captain Newton and Lieutenants Trippe and Wright, by orders from Brigadier General Eccleston. One hundred men, officers included, embarked on this solemn occasion amidst the huzzas... This morning they set sail at sunrise with a fair wind to Baltimore, from whence with the other

militia of this state proceed to the scene of action.../Farm for sale in
Caroline Co of 300 a. adj Mrs. Ennall's land, known as Poplar Neck - John
Clayland

110. ESHM Sep 23 1794/John L. Bozman candidate for house of Delagates/Mules
for sale - George Talcott, Chester Town/Thomas Baynard offers reward for
apprentice lad, Henry Hill, age about 20, brought up to the farming business/
John Jenkinson reports a stray steer/Edward Bourke, Hog Island, Caroline Co,
reports a stray mare/Edward Cox, Easton, to petition to import into this state
a negro man, Ned, a slave that was bound by my father to certain Edward
Collins of Kent Co, in the Delaware State, until he arrives to the age of 25
years, which time expires November next." Edward Cox says "As I am about to
leave Maryland to join the troops against the insurgents ... to authorize Mr.
John Thomas, Junr to settle my accounts .." books and papers to be delivered
to Samuel Sharpe if Cox prevented from returning to Easton by death or
accident./Tract for sale near Denton, 180 a. and tract within 2 miles of
Whitleysburgh, Kent Co, Del, about 260 a.; apply to William Hughlett at Spring
Mills or to Thomas Berry at Whitleysburgh/Houses and blacksmith shop to let
near New Market, now occupied by William Knox; apply to Pollard Edmondson/
Benjamin Sylvester, Caroline Co, responds to earlier charges by William
Jackson with statement submitted by George Martin, surveyor of Caroline Co in
which he refers to tracts: Mill Security adj tracts, Bloomsbury, Irish
Discovery, and Garratt's Look Out; Martin states that Benjamin Sylvester said
he had reason to believe part of 35 a. of vacant land had been surveyed by
Richard Tilghman Earle and Caleb Ricketts/Plantation for sale where he now
lives on Miles River, 150 a. - Samuel Tenant/Partnership of William Buchanan
& William S. Bond, Easton, dissolved

111. ESHM Sep 30 1794/Died at Chesterfield, QA Co, in the night of 20th inst
after a long and tedious illness, Doctor John Bracco in 31st year of his age
...He left a fond & youthfull wife with a tender infant, to bewail his loss/
John Goldsborough Jr, Easton, declines to be a candidate for office/John
Erskine, Easton, candidate for representative in Assembly/Sale of Horses,
cattle, sheep and household furniture at Dover Ferry by Charles Nabb/Cornelius
West to petition for losses in building courthouse for the county of Talbot/
Lots for sale owned by John Haynes, Easton, on Harrison St

112. ESHM Oct 7 1794/John Ward of Caroline Co to petition under the
insolvency act/Married Saturday 26 Sep by Rev Kemp, William Murray Roberson
of Cambridge to Miss Henrietta Maria Murray of the same place/Chancery sale
at Centreville plantation known as Hayfield, being a part of Long Marsh which
formerly belonged to Griffin Fauntleroy, dec, and which was devised by him to
his daus: Anne Bushrod Fauntleroy and Elizabeth Fauntleroy - to be sold
subject to a life-estate of his widow Sarah Fauntleroy - Dekar Thompson,
trustee/The schooner, Betsey, Easton packet, still continues to run - Samuel
Thomas/To petition for road from corner of Phil. Macky's Road

113. Oct 14 1794/John Bracco's plantation in QA Co for let, within 1 1/2
mile of Col. Hopper's dwelling & now in the possession of Solomon Sinnit's
widow where the subscriber (John Bracco) formerly lived; apply to the
subscriber, John Bracco, near Miles River Ferry/Chancery decree ordered that
on the application of Thomas Leverton, trustee of Jeremaih Coleston, of
Caroline Co, to set day for settlement of claims by creditors of Jeremiah
Coleston/Ann Weaver admin of William Weaver late of Talb Co, dec/Sale at the
house of subscriber of horses, cattle, sheep and hogs and farming utensils -
Christopher Bruff

114. ESHM Oct 21 1794/Deserted at Frederick from the Eastern Shore Militia
-Daniel Macquay, James Pickering, John Burgess, John Jobb, Robert Newnam,
William Merchant, James Rally, Nathan Hunter, Cornelius Durgin, Robert Wales,
William Dean, Daniel Brookes, Samuel Thornton, John Willoughby, Robert Cops,

Abraham Purnel. For any one of the above deserters being delivered to this Regiment, Six Cents will be given, and one cent per man for the whole in a body - by Perry Benson, Lt. Col. Comdt. September 30 1794/A 2-story brick house for sale nearly opp Francis Seller's near Tuckahoe Bridge - William Smith/Died Frieday 10th inst Richard Martin of Dorch Co aged 42/John Erskine, Solomon Corner, admin of Andrew Brown, carpenter, dec/House for rent where James Roper lives and storehouse lately occupied by Robert Gillis; apply to John Erskine

115. ESHM Oct 28 1794/Sale at the dwelling house of William Weaver, Talb Co, dec, household furniture, farming utensils, horses, cattle, sheep and hogs - John Thomas Jr admin/Sale of 300 a. on Head of Chiconecomico River and house now in tenure of Charles Stuart in New Market - James Sulivane/Died at Dover Del Mrs. Mary Neill in the 31st year, consort of William Charles Neill, a wife and parent/Sale of personal property of Robert Brown late, dec, at house of John Ward, overseer on the estate of the dec - William Richmond, QA Co/ Bank notes lost by John Singleton last wrapped in a small piece of paper, on which is an account of some sugar bought of William Lowry. On one note is "I believe, wrote Thomas Coward..."

116. ESHM Nov 4 1794/Horatio Edmondson and John Edmondson exec of Pollard Edmondson, late of Talb Co/Mary Thompson admin of John Thompson, late of Talb Co, dec/Letters remaining P. O. Easton: Capt R. Barnaby, Oxford; Robert Benson, Talb; Richard B. Bewley near Easton; William P. Chandler, Easton; Lambert Cayton,living with Samuel Sherwood, Talb; Peter Denny near the Head of Wye; John Deale, Easton; Messrs. Thomas & Richard Emory, Queens-Town; James Earle; Peter Ferguson, merchant, Cambridge; Archibald Foster care of John Gooding, merchant, Hunting Creek; Massy Fountain near Tuckahoe Creek; Hanover Gibon(?) care of Thomas Callender, Fishing Creek; John Gooding, Hunting Creek; Wolman Gibson Jr near Easton; William G. Gibson, Easton; John Grace or Graice, Easton; Messrs. John & George Johnson, merchants, Cambridge; Messrs. Daniel Knock & Co, Eastern Shore of Maryland; Messrs. William Knock & Co, merchants, Eastern Shore of Maryland; Nicholas Killum, Easton; Capt Aaron Mitchel near Easton; Thomas McKeel, Easton; Goodwin Pierce care of Thomas Hicks, Cambridge; Benjamin Parsons, Talb; Mrs. Thomas Snowden; Rebecca Smith, Easton; James Shaw, Easton; John G. Thomas, Talb; Henry Travers, Dorch Co; James Vansandt, Easton; Samuel Willis near Easton care of Dr. James Wilson; Dr. James Wilson, Head of Wye; Thomas Wickersham, Easton; John Willis, merchant, Oxford; William Weaver, Easton; Mrs. Elizabeth Walker near Easton; Miss Priscilla Walker, Easton; Charles Wheeler, Dorch Co; Philemon Willis careof John Willis of Oxford/James Rolph reports a stray horse/Tract for sale, 411 a. in Tully's Neck, QA Co - Joseph Price, Greensborough/Sale at dwelling house that formerly belonged to Mr. Maccallum where his widow now lives, property belonging to Edward Carslake in QA Co - household furniture, horses, cow, beds - Joseph DeFord, admin

117. ESHM Nov 11 1794/John Blake admin of William Martin late of Talb Co, dec/Died Thursday last John Blair, merchant of Cambridge/Died on Friday last in an advanced age, John Bracco at his seat near Miles River/By virtue of an agreement between David Wilson & Worc Co, Henry Steele, Dorch Co, the subscribers will act as trustees for the sale of a tract, Clover Fields lying in Somerset Co on Rewastico Creek formerly owned by Samuel King. Trustees - Levin Winder, Esme Bayly, James Steele/William Ford near Queens Town offers reward for negro man, Emanuel/House for rent at present occupied by Captain Hugh Auld on Dover St a few doors from Washington St - Tristram Needles

118. ESHM Nov 18 1794/Died Friday morning 14th inst Thomas Jordan of Talb Co aged 16 yrs/House for rent owned by Samuel Troth Jr next door to James Wainwright's in Dover St/John Bowie reports stray gelding/House to let & garden at corner of Washington & Dover St where Mrs. Teikle lives -

Peter Denny/Blacksmith shop for rent in Caroline Co on road from Choptank to Tuckahoe Bridge - James Boon/To be sold at his dwelling near Miles River household furniture, farming utensils, horses, cows, sheep - Matthew Greentree/

119. ESHM Nov 25 1794/Alexander Lawson reports that his carriage horse was stolen out of the stable of Charles Brown near Queens Town/Robert Tuite near Wye Mill offers reward for 2 negro men: Jacob age about 22 and Bob age about 21/James Holland admin of William Harrison

120. ESHM Dec 2 1794/B. M. Ward, Easton, admin of Dorothy Richardson, late of Talb Co, dec

121. ESHM Dec 9 1794/William Marsh Catrup forewarns persons from hunting on his plantation on Bolingbrook Creek & Choptank River which he pruchased of Randolph Johnson/Died Sunday evening last John Dickinson the 4th of Talb Co/ Died about 4 o'clock this morning John Stevens one of the ass ociate justices of Talb Co after a sudden illness/Storehouse for rent now occupied by Joseph Haskins; apply to William Hayward/Storehouse, houses, and lots at Oxford for rent - Thomas Coward/Chancery case - John Chrisfield versus Priscilla Falecner, Charlott Falecner, Mary Falecner and Julia Falecner. The complainant applies for a decree to record a deed indented in 1787 by Gilbert Falecner for conveying unto the complainant a piece of ground in Bridgetown in Kent Co, pt of a tract, London Bridge Renewed. Since the execution of the deed the grantee hath died intestate and defendants are his heirs/Chancery case - Samuel Crench exec of William Dooley versus Rebecca Falecner and Philip Cline. Claimant applies to have a deed recorded, indented in 1788 by said Rebecca Falecner and Philip Cline for conveying unto William Dooley a lot adj Chester Town, No. 11 in a survey by John Williamson. The lot was the property of Jacob Falecner dec that defendents sold to said William Dooley under the last will and testament of said Jacob Falecner as his exec and said William Dooley hath departed this life having appointed complainant as his exec/ Chancery sale at Mr. Hyat's tavern in Queens Town of a tract, Broomley Lambeth of about 50 a., part of the estate of James Croney ,dec - William Richmond, trustee/John Hardcastle.Jr, Talb Co, surviving admin of John Hardcastle Sr, late of Talb Co, dec

122. ESHM Dec 16 1794/Chancery sale of a tract in Talb Co called Advantage, formerly the property of William Garey of Talb Co, dec, James Shaw, trustee

123. ESHM Dec 23 1794/Orson Turner exec of John Allen Reed, late of Talb Co, dec/Mrs. Rebecca Jones consort of John Jones died Saturday 27 inst after a long and tedious illness/Forty Dollars Reward for apprehending, delivery at the post, or securing in jail the following deserters: (1) Charles Rhoads, a native of Dorch Co, around 23 yrs of age, 6 ft high, florid complexion, light hair, blue eyes, and a handsome well made fellow. He had on when he deserted a short uniform, blue and buff coat. He inlisted at Chester Mill the 3d, and deserted the 15th of September last. The said Rhoads is well known about Hunting Creek and Tuckahoe Neck, where he has relations and is supposed to be now skulking. (2) Henry Smith - says he is a native of Somerset Co, about 22 yrs of age, 5 ft 9-10 inch high, brown hair, well made, but has an impediment in his speech. He laboured about Chester Mill the last summer - was detached with the militia, inlisted at Chester Town the 12th September, and deserted the 6th October last - He had on a jacket and overalls and took with him a blanket and pair of soldiers shoes, high in the instep and laced before. (3) James Smith, a relation to, and went off with, the above deserter - also said to be a native of Somerset - about the same age of his companion. He is slander and appears to be a temperate man. His clothing is unknown, only that he took with him a blanket and a pair of shoes as above described. (4) Martin Davis - an Englishman, formerly a serjeat in my company, about 27 yrs of age, 5 ft, 7-8 inch high, fair and florid complexion - says he was formerly in the British service (17th light dragoons) that he has been in this country

a considerable time as a clerk in a store, and a schoolmaster in Somerset Co
from whencehe came in company with a youth to Baltimore in the latter part of
July last, inlisted the 2d August, obtained a furlough the 4th October of
Lieutenant Smith for a fortnight - and I am informed is now keeping a school
in the same couty, but denys his having inlisted....J. Bruff. Capt
Artillerists & Engrs. Comdt. Fort at Whetstone Point. Baltimore. Dec 10th
1794/Sale at the dwelling of the late John Dickinson, the 4th,dec, household
furniture, cyder, horses, cows, hogs and farming utensils, John W. Harrison,
exec/Francis Caulk offers reward for negro man, Thomas, age about 27/James
Booker requests persons having claims against the estate of John Bracco, late
of Talb Co, to present to him/James Sulivane admin of Mrs Anne Ennalls, dec

124. ESHM Jan 13 1795/Jesse Fooks versus heirs of William Winder dec regarding a deed indented by William Winder in 1783 conveying unto Richard Mills
36 a., pt of Cox's Choice, Worc Co/Margaret Gardiner, Nathan G. Bryson, exec
Charles Gardiner, late of Talb Co/Mrs Mansell to continue boarding school in
Chester Town/Sale ordered by Orphans Court, Dover Del of a tract where
Bennedict Brice died in Murderkill Hundred, about 1500 a. being the property
of Bennedict Brice; Mary Cook admin/House to let in Easton, lately occupied
by Philip Horney, property of James Troth

125. ESHM Jan 27 1795/Letters remaining at P. O. Easton, Jan 26 1795: Capt
Edward Bromwell or Captain Robinson; Jacob Bromwell; John Brown, Greensborough;
William Bell Sr, Caroline Co; Samuel Baldwin, Easton; Daniel Powell Cox, Talb;
Thomas Cooper, merchant near Easton; Thomas Corse, Middle Town, Dorch Co; John
Dale, Easton; Messrs. Impey Dawson & Co; Capt Robert Dawson at Emerson's
Warehouse; Adam Dill, Caroline Co; Isaiah Dockery, Cambridge; Samuel Edmondson,
Easton; James Earle Jr; David Fountain, Caroline Co; Archibald Foster; William
Graig, Easton; Mrs. Prudence Harrison care of Thomas Harrison, Talb Co;
Michael Hart, Easton; William Humes, Oxford Township; Charles Lecompte,
Cambridge; Capt Aaron Mitchell, Cambridge; William McGuire Tabbs; Capt Edward
Right, White Haven, Dorset Co; James Ralston, Easton; Richard Sherwood, Talb
Co; James Sulivane Jr, Dorset Co; Capt William B. Smith; Henry Thompson care
of Francis Sellers, Tuckahoe; Edward Truitt, St. Michaels; Robert Trail, atty
at law, Easton; John Willis, Oxford; Alexander Warfield, QA Co/House for let
occupied by the late James Shaw, Easton; apply to Mr. Haskins or William S.
Bond atty for Anne Shaw admin of James Shaw/James Tilghman Jr, William
Tilghman, exec of James Tilghman/John Needles atty in fact of Dr. Samuel
Cooper, to sell his land in Talb Co consisting of tracts: Hampton and pt of
a tract in the tenure of James Mills bounded by lands of William Hayward and
Hugh Work - And a plantation, pt of Dudly's Choice and pt of Strawbridge, now
in the tenure of John Kemp, bounded by the land of William Hayward and George
Wilson

126. ESHM Feb 24 1795/Sale at the dwelling house owned by Charles Blair
where Dr. Andrew Mitchell now lives - household furniture/Sale of a lot in
Centre Ville by Henrietta Bracco, Chesterfield/Peter Edmundson, trustee
requests creditors make claims against the estate of Solomon Clayton, late of
QA Co, dec/Jacob Gibson, Talb Co, offers reward for negro man, James Grace,
age about 45, late the property of Robert Newcomb, dec, manumitted by James
Newcom without any authority; deliver to Robert Lesage 5 miles from my
quarters or to me (Jacob Gibson)/Jacob Graybell, marshal, announces sale to
be held at Vienna, Dorch Co, order by Court of Admiralty/Z. Gregory forwarns
persons from cutting wood on his tract, Stopard's More/Sale at dwelling house
of David Nice, Easton, the personal property of the late Christopher Nice,
dec, household furniture, cows, hogs - Elizabeth Nice, David Nice/A lot for
sale on Dover St - John Fonerden/Robert Sherwood, mercantile business at The
Hole in the Wall, Talb Co/John Coats, register of the Land Office for the
Eastern Shore of Maryland/James Bennitt, Robert Dashiell, Samuel Smyly to

petition to sell real estate of Elijah Austin, dec, to satisfy claims of his creditors/Chancer sale of estate of Griffin Fauntleroy, dec, by Dekar Thompson of a tract in QA Co, Hayfield

127. ESHM Mar 10 1795/Died Sunday 1st inst Doctor William Maynadier/Chancery sale of tracts in QA Co, late the dwelling plantation of William Falconar, dec, within 3 miles of Head of Chester: Harris's Hazard, Friendship, Tilghman's Friendship, around 202 1/2 a. - Abraham Falconar, trustee/B. M. Ward admin of Capt Edward Delahay/Apprentice wanted to the tanning & currying business - William Starky Denton/Tract for sale: Cook's Hope within 2 1/2 miles of Easton - William G. Killum/Storehoue for rent at the Trappe lately occupied by William Stevens Jr, dec - Samuel Dickinson/Joseph Turner, living Colonel Edward Lloyd's farm called Hacker's at the head of Wye, reports a stray mare/James Ridgaway exec to house at Hole in the Wall, property of the late Joseph Ridgaway, about 5 a. Also at the plantation lately occupied by said Ridgaway near Samuel Abbott's mill horses, cows, sheep and hogs for sale. Also to lease the plantation which formerly belonged to Lewis Jenkins at the Trappe.

128. ESHM Mar 17 1795/Died Sunday 8 Mar Mrs. Ann Roberts wife of Edward Roberts of Talb Co who left an infant about 3 weeks old/Farm for sale situated on Head of Wye River, QA Co, 700 a.; apply to C. Theodore Wederstrandt, QA Co/Anna Elbert admin of Doctor John Elbert late of Talb Co/ James Nabb requests payment of debts to the estate of Charles Nabb, late of Talb Co

129. ESHM Mar 24 1795/Thomas Anderson, Hunting Creek Dorch Co, offers reward for negro slaves taken by John Bryan and Dick his brother that Philip Mackey set free, the following slaves: negro woman, Nell, Ann age 4-5 , Fan, age 2-3, and two other children. They were at a quarter in Caroline Co near Bromwell Andrew's mill in March 14 to 16th/John Bradshaw to operate ferry-boat from Cambridge to Philemon Mackey's Landing in Talb Co/A lot for sale in Easton - Mary Bruff/A lot for sale in Easton - Thomas Wickersham/Farm for sale near the Trappe on which Richard Hickson lately lived, pt of Wales, Irish Freshes, and Alexander's Chance, about 500 a. - William H. Nicholson

130. ESHM Mar 31 1795/John Jones near Easton forwarns persons from hunting on his farm/John Turner exec of John Chambers

131. ESHM Apr 21 1795/For sale - 1400 a. on waters of Kent Narrows & Jackson's Creek - John Sayer Blake/Letters remaining at P. O. Easton, Apr 18 1795: Mary Bordley, Talb; Francis Baker, Talb; Edward Chatham, Easton; William Carmichael, Cambridge; Joseph Chaplin; Edward Cox; Matthew Driver; Joseph Everitt; James Earle Jr; Samuel Hopkins, Dorset; William Hambleton Jr; Alexander Kinney; William Keney; Benjamin Kemp; Ezekiel Long; Frisby Lloyd; Mary Lacey; Cyrus Mitchel, New Market; Mr. McLaran; Ezekiel Merrick; Joel Munson; Hugh Martin, Queens Town; Thomas McKeel; Capt William Mackey; John Pitts; James Price; Benjamin Riggin; Capt Amasa Robinson; William Richmond; Dekar Thompson; Henry Travers; William Weaver/Sarah Welch exec of Thomas Welch/John McLaran has opened a public house in New Market, also a grocery store/Sale at dwelling plantation of James Seth, late of Talb Co, dec, horses, cows, sheep - Christiana Seth, exec/Inhabitants of Worc Co to petition for road from William Davis blacksmith shop to Cornelius Ennis's (sen.) Landing/ Henry Maynadier exec Dr. William Maynadier, dec, Talb/Anna Elbert admin of Dr. John Elbert, late of Talb Co, dec

132. ESHM May 1795/Died Sun 4th ult at his res Snow Hill, James Round Morris, Clerk of Worc Court/Died Friday morning 1 May at this place Mrs. Rebecca Kearny, age 71, having passed a long life chequered with many misfortunes/Wheat farm for sale, 340 a. on St. Michaels Creek - Henry Maynadier/John T. Birckhead to sell his land in Talb Co adj the plantation of William Richardson Jr, pt of tract Little Bristol, about 480 a. - Apply to

Peter Webb/John Reed, living near Vienna, offers reward for negro man, Eli, age about 33, bought from James West Sr, late of Somerset Co, but now of Worc Co near Snow Hill; a John Smithson in law of said West removed likewise into the neighborhood of Snow Hill, who owns his wife/Margaret & John R. Bromwell exec of Edward Bromwell Jr/Samuel Swan requests payment be made to him of all persons indebted to Henry Nicols (of Balt) for ground rent due in Easton/ Thomas Kemp of St. Michael offers reward for silver table spoon stolen from his house.

133. ESHM May 19 1795/Daniel P. Cox, sheriff Talb Co, offers reward for Isaac Williams, age about 30, who broke gaol, 5 ft 9-10 inch; he has kept school in Caroline and Talbot Counties near Tuckahoe Bridge, where he has a sister now living/E. J. Alborn, hairdresser and surgeon barber, has opened his shop opp the widow Troth's tavern/Mark Benton requests a public meeting with Benjamin Willmott of Easton to answer his charges/James Hicks, Caroline Co, exec of George Bell, late of Caroline Co/The Justices of the Levy Court for Talb Co have ascertained the following to be the Public Roads, and have laid them off in districts as follow: to wit: 1. From Easton to the Three Bridges 2. From the Three Bridges to Wye Mill, and from the fork of the road leading by Dr. Wilson's and John Gibson's to Emerson's Warehouse 3. From Pitt's Bridge to Robert Goldsborough's Quarter, and from Mr. Bowie's to Miles River Ferry 4. From Pott's Mill to Miles River Ferry, leading by Dundee, thence to William Dawson's Gate, from Miles River ferry to Wye Town, thence to Dundee 5. From the Three Bridges to the New Chapel, thence to Tuckahoe Bridge, thence to Wye Mill, leading by the late Dr. Elbert's Dwelling Plantation 6. From the Chapel to King's Creek Bridge, thence to Kinston, thence to the fork of the road leading to Tuckahoe Bridge from Easton 7. From King's Creek Bridge to Dover ferry, thence to Easton, from Peter Denney's to Solomon Neale's from thence to Robert Neale's 8. From Solomon Neale's fence to Abbett's Mill, from the corner of Dr. Maynadier's fence round to where it intersects the road at Ivy Town, from Dr. Maynadier's shop to the end of the road that intersects the road leading from Easton at Chamberlaine's Hill 9. From Easton to the Hole in the Wall, thence to Dr. Maynadier's shop, thence to James Delahay's near Isaac Cox's Mill 10. From the Hole in the Wall to Oxford, from thence to the corner of Bozman's fence, from thence down to the bottom of Island Creek Neck, thence on the other side of the Neck up to the Trappe 11. From the Hole in the Wall to the Trappe, from the fork of the road near Eve Berry's to the Church, from the corner of Eve Berry's fence until it intersects the road near John Stevens's fence, thence to the Breeding Hickory, from the Trappe to Abbott's Mill 12. From Abbott's Mill to the bottom of Banbory thence round the Neck by Samuel Stevens's plantation, thence to Jamaica ferry, from Chancellor's Point to the White Marsh, thence to the Cross Roads by James Parrott's 13. From the White Marsh to the Trappe, from the Little Quaker Meeting House to James Goldsborough's gate, from James Tobin's shop to Mackay's fence, from the fork of the road T T until it intersects the road leading from Abbott's Mill to Chancellor's Point 14. From Easton to John Dawson's shop, thence Jere: Banning's gate 15. From John Dawson's shop to St Michael's Church 16. From St Michael's Church to Nabb's Narrows 17. From the Royal Oak to Oxford ferry - from thence to Rebecca Auldren's plantation 18. From the Bay Side road to George Dawson's plantation, thence to the plantations of Thomas Ball and Robert Dawson./James Ridgaway exec Joseph Ridgaway late of Talb Co/Notice regarding attendance by William Spencer, paymaster of militia "lately called into the service of the United States, that marched into Pennsylvania, who are entitled to the additional pay allowed them by the act of Congress of the 2d of January last."/Thomas Wooters insolvent debtor/Sarah Long has opened a boarding house in Easton/Tract for sale: Barker's Landing, 320 a., in Talb Co - Apply to William Perry, Colonel Nicols or Jere. Nicols, Chester Town

134. ESHM Jun 1795/Woollen manufactory - a generous price will be given for
work by Zebulon Hollingsworth & son, or Francis Partridge, Elkton/Buchanan &
Clayland, about to remove from this shore; those indebted may settle accounts
with William Buchanan/Thomas McKeel, standard keeper of the county, Easton/
A new fulling-mill has been erected on the Head of Robins's Creek, which makes
out of Great Choptank, about 10 miles above Dover Ferry where cloths are
fulled, & dyed all colours - William Potts, living in Caroline Co/Thomas B.
Hands president of the Board of Visitors & Governors , Washington College,
Chestertown/Greenbury Neale has opened a handsome assortment of dry goods in
the house adj Mrs. Taikle's & formerlyoccupied by Robert Gilliss/Philip Rigby
& Thomas Rigby offer reward for two negro men, brothers: Ishmael, age about
24 who sailed part of last summer in one of the Easton packets with Capt
Hugh Auld and Jethro, age about 26 who has a wife at Samuel Chew's quarter
near Chester Town

135. ESHM Jun 16 1795/Plantation for sale 3 miles from Easton, about 70 a.
- John Dougherty/Receiving subscriptions at the house of Mrs. Suter in George
Town for erecting a bridge over Patowmack River - William Deakins Jr, James
M. Lingan, Uriah Forrest , Georgetown/A farm to let where I now live lying in
Caroline Co near Seth's Mill, Tuckahoe Neck - Mable Daffin/Died Thursday 4
inst after a lingering illness of the small pox in the natural way, Mrs.
Margaret Trippe relict of Henry Trippe of Dorch Co in the 72d year; she was the
last surviving child of Doctor William Murray/Tract in Del for sale - J.
Hughes, within 1 mile of Miles River Ferry/John Jones, Lydia Troth, admin of
James Troth, late of Talb Co, dec/William Dimond offers reward for 2 horses
which strayed from the farm which he rents of Edward Tilghman near Chester
Mill/Partnership of Peter Gordon & Samuel Brown, Cambridge, dissolved

136. ESHM Jun 30 1795/James Bell, Tuckahoe Neck, offers reward for apprentice
lad, Morgan Kelly, age about 15/House for sale on Harrison St adj Samuel
Sharpe - William Benny, Easton/Gabriel Duvall admin of Thomas Rutland,
requests person indebted to the Thomas Rutland for dealings at his store kept
by the late James King at Kingstown are requested to make immediate payment
to Thomas Tibbels of Talb Co/William Bruff having established his res in Balt
in the Commission Line/Sale of the subscriber's house in Cambridge at this
time in the occupation of Thomas Hicks, merchant - Robert Harrison, Cambridge/
Perry Benson of Talb Co offers reward for negro lad, Wat, age 18; he ran away
once before & was taken up at Duck Creek

137. ESHM Jul 14 1795/John Keene, Dorch Co, offers reward for negro man,
Levin, age about 25/Charles Shenon, Dorch Co, offers reward for negro man,
Dick, age about 30; he has relations in Somerset or thereabout/Letters remain-
ing at P.O. Easton: Dr. James Boardly, Talb; Capt Perry Benson; John Brown,
Greensborough; Samuel Baldwin, Easton; Thomas Barry near Choptank Bridge;
James Brown, Sussex Co, Del; Jacob S. Bromwell, Talb; James Barns, Bay Side,
Talb; Nathan Gregg Bryson, Easton; Bryson & Roney; John Currie, merchant,
Caroline Co; Carter Cocking care of John Blake, Talb; Capt William Cannon,
Easton; Edward O. Clark, Miles River; Miss Sarah Constable at George
Hayward's; Daniel Powel Cox, sheriff of Talb; Thomas Cooper near Easton;
Thomas Eggan, Talb Co; James Earle, Clerk General Court; Archibald Foster care
of John Gooding, Hunting Creek; John E. Gist, Cambridge; William Elliot
Griffith; Thomas Harrison, Broad Creek, Talb; Rachel Harring near Dover Ferry;
The Rev Mr. Kemp, Dorch Co; James Kindrick, Talb; David Kerr, Easton; William
Lerrotte at Mr. Wederstrandt's, QA Co; Miss Rachel Lowry, Talb; William Lowry
care of John Erskine, Easton; James Lecompt, Caroline Co; Charles Lecompt,
Dorch Co; Thomas Wynn Loockerman, Talb Co Court House; Dr. Robert Moore; James
Mills, Talb; Joel Munson, singing master; John Vorse, Milford; Hugh McColl,
Dorch Co; Henry Nicols, Easton; Samuel Nicols; William Pitt, inspector of
Ennalls's ferry warehouse; Capt Abner Parrott, Talb; William Rose, Talb;

Jesse Richardson, John Reid at Peter Ferguison's, Cambridge; Mitchel Russum, Hunting Creek; Joseph Stone, St. Michaels; Alice Sherwood below Easton; Edward Stevens, Talb; Henry Somerville, merchant, Easton; Captain Maryland Skinner, Hunting Creek; Dr. Sloan care of Mr. McDonald of Cambridge; Dekar Thompson; Henry Travers, Dorch Co; Levin Travers, Dorch Co; Joshua Williams, Dorch Co; John Watts at the Trappe; Isaac Wickersham, Easton/Letters remaining at Princess Anne: Doctor Richard Elliss, Somerset Co; Doctor William Ellis, Somerset Co; Samuel Casey, Somerset Co; Thomas Evans, Somerset Co; James Weir, Somerset Co; Samuel Tull, Somerset Co - Robert Jones, Postmaster/Commissioners for building new gaol at Easton: N. Hammond, S. Sharp, T. J. Bullit, S. Logan, J. Haskins/Chancery sale on the premises, near Vienna, a tract called Laurel Hill, property of the late James Shaw - John Randall, trustee

138. ESHM Jul 28 1795/Wind mill for sale with a new bolting cloth & miller's house - Abner Parrott, Easton/John Harrison, 2 miles from Dover Ferry, Caroline, offers reward for negro man, Sam, age about 21/Alexander Kinney, Easton, intending to remove from this state this fall, has dry goods & groceries at lowest prices/James Moore, Somerset Co, offers reward for negro man, Charles, age about 24

139. ESHM Aug 18 1795/Died after a long and tedious illness, Mrs. Elizabeth Roper, consort of James Roper, aged 38 yrs/Joseph Martin exec, requests payment of debts to estate of John Stevens, late of Talb Co and Benjamin Stevens, late of Talb co/John Dwigans, Caroline Co, forewarns persons from harbouring wife, Elizabeth Dwigans nor will he pay her debts/W. Meluy & Wainer about to close their partnership/Chancery sale of 200 a. on Corsica Creek descended to Richard Earle Clayton, Walter Jackson Clayton and Juliana Clayton from Solomon Clayton, for the use of James Hindman & William Hemsley/John Tootel, sheriff Dorch Co, offers reward for negro James, age about 25, property of Elijah Marshall of Dorch Co, who broke gaol. Also negro Bob, formerly the property of Peter Harrington of Dorch Co, broke gaol/Rebecca Withgott forewarns persons from hauling seins on Choptank River or Cabin Creek that extends along her land

140. ESHM Sep 29 1795/Married Sunday evening 27th by Rev John Bowie, James Wilson of Philadelphia to the amiable Miss Mary Jacobs of Easton/House for sale in Easton where Alexander Wynn lately occupied as a tavern - Mark Benton, Hole in the Wall/Samuel Sherwood offers reward for negro man, Harry, blacksmith, age about 25/Ebenezer Handy, Salisbury, to petition for a road/House for let at the Trappe in which Jacob Fowle at present occupies and subscriber formerly lived. Apply to John Harrison - Robert Moore/Tract for sale in Caroline Co adj plantation of Thomas Hardcastle - Henry Banning, Talb Co/To petition for road from Col Benson's to Miles River Ferry by continuing Col. Benson's road until it intersects the division line between Mrs. Gordan and subscriber, Jacob Lockerman/Joseph Briscoe, a long time confined in jail for debts to petition under the insolvency act/William Hughlett admin of Johannas Glinn, late of Denton, dec/James Hardin offers reward for negro man, Jacob, age about 40/W. Goldsborough near Easton, offers reward for white mulatto lad Harry age 18 or 19/James Bowdle collector of the Revenues/Chancery sale of pt of tract, Hard Labour situated in Dorch Co within 2 miles of Chicknecomico Bridge, about 150 a. late the property of Levi Charles Craft, dec - John Craig, trustee/Inhabitants of Worc Co to petition for public road from Ruak's near John White's Tavern to Locust Landing (near the Bay Side)/James Porter, QA Co, to petition under the insolvency act/House for rent where Edward Rounds now lives at Hunting Creek; also house where John Norwood lives at Chanceller's Point - Charles Baker, Chancellor's Point/James Ringgold, Chester-Town leasing 18000 a. in Va/Lots to be sold in Vienna - John McGuire/"Whereas about the year 1783 or 1784 two tracts of land called Limbrick's Old Field and Addition to Limbrick in Worc Co was sold under the confiscation law of this state as

the property of a certain Ephraim Tilghman, whom it was alledged went to the British in the time of the American war and thereby subjected his property to confiscation. And whereas Col. Peter Chaille of this county at the sale of the said land, was purchaser of the same, being the higest bidder...(intend) to petition to restore to the subscriber possession of the land which he is entitled to under the will of his deceased father, Gidden Tilghman - and which never having been the property of the said Ephriam Tilghman, was not subject to the confiscation laws of this state - Isaiah Tilghman, Worc Co/ John Ward, Caroline Co, to petition for relief under the insolvency act

141. ESHM Oct 13 1795/Lands for sale belonging to Mrs. Anna Maria Hollyday situated in Talb Co - Samuel Chamberlaine, Nicholas Hammond, agents/Chancery case - Robert L. Nicols, David Kerr and Thomas Chamberlaine versus Thomas Cooper, heir of John Cooper, dec - John Roberts, trustee, regarding the sale of Sylvester's Addition, Webb's Chance, Cooper's Vineyard, Baynard's Discovery and 3 a. of Webb's Chance sold to Henry Martendale/Chancery sale by John Roberts, trustee of lands in Talb Co mortgaged by Abner Broadway unto James Lloyd Chamberlaine: Sam's Fields, Straw-bridge, pt of Broadway's Meadows and pt of Ramak/Henry Brnett, Caroline Co, near the Head of Hunting Creek, offers reward for negro man, Ned, age about 22/Rebecca Hambleton exec William Hambleton, late of Talb Co/Samuel Tenant, Talb Co, offers reward for negro lad, Juba, age about 20, property of Miss Anna Fiddeman/H. Dickinson, Dorch Co, offers reward for negro man, Scipio, age about 25/Samuel Sherwood is having a sale at his dwelling of cows, sheep and horses/James Hardin, Talb Co, offers reward for negro, Bob, age about 40

142. ESHM Oct 27 1795/Died at an advanced age on Thursday morning last Thomas Sherwood of Talb Co/Nancy McGinny, near Hole in the Wall, exec of Daniel McGinny offers reward for negro woman, Henny/Andrew Orem acting admin, requests payment of debts to the estate of Nicholas Orem, dec, at Thomas Stewart's Tavern, Cambridge/A packet running between Easton & Balt - William Ashman, Edward Trippe/Thomas McElderry admin requests payment of debts to the estate of Samuel Logan be made to Bennet Wheeler at Mrs. Logan's Easton; busines is carried on as usual at the store of the deceased/Talb Co sherriff offers reward for free negro man, Charles, set free by William L. Murray, dec of Dorch Co, committed to gaol for felony/Letters remaining at P.O. Easton, Oct 6th: Samuel Barrow, Tuckahoe Bridge; John Blair, Cambridge; Thomas Boon, Hunting Creek; Charles Blair, Caroline; Thomas Cooper; John Corrie, Tuckahoe; Thomas Corse, Middletown, Dorset; Levin & Solomon Charles, Choptank; Thomas Chapman, Talb; Mrs. Dewsborough, Miles River; Peter Denny; Thomas S. Denny; James Dueling, Talb; Charles Emory, Greensorough; Mrs. Ann Edgill, Caroline; James Earle, Clerk of the General Court; Jacob Fowle, Trappe; James Goldsborough; Mrs. Prudence Harrison, Talb; Thomas Harrison, Broad Creek; Henry Herring, Talb; Mrs. Hart, Easton; Rachel Harring, Caroline; John Kersey; William Knox, Talb; Hugh Lindsay, Fowling Creek; Captain James Lloyd; Solomon Martin; Capt Aaron Mitchell; Capt William Mackey; Joseph Nicols, Federalsburgh; John Nabb Jr; John Otto, schoolmaster, Easton; Mr. Pitts, Dorset; Isaac Purnell, Caroline; W. Richmond, Queens-Town; Jesse Richardson; George Rosse, Easton; William Semer at Mr. Hayward's; Samuel Sherwood near Easton; John M. Stevens, collector of the revenue, Easton; William Smith, Tuckahoe Bridge; James Somerville, of Holms, Easton; Thomas Starr, Talb; William Skinner, Caroline; Jesse Turner, Caroline; John Watts; George Ward, Dorset; Philemon Willis, Hunting Creek; Thomas Whealer, Dorset/Catharine Watts admin of John Watts

143. ESHM Nov 3 1795/Richard Bewley & Robert Bewley, exec of Ann Bewley, late of Talb Co/Saturday evening last Honourable James Wilson, Judge of the Federal Court for the District of Maryland arrived in town with his lady/Sale at the place where Thomas Hughey now lives, near Pott's Mill(now Mr. Tilghman's Mill) of horses, sheep, hogs, and farming utensils - James Holland

144. ESHM Nov 10 1795/Sale at the farm whereon the late Mrs. Margaret Trippe lived and whereon the subscriber has h ad a quarter for some years past, in Dorch Co, near the mouth of Hunting Creek, cows, steers, oxen, sheep, horses -Charles Blair/Thomas J. Seth seeks to employ a miller/Greenbury Goldsborough admin of Thomas Mewse, limner, late of Talb Co/House for sale in Easton where Christopher Wynn occupied as a tavern; also store house for rent, now occupied by Samuel Yarnel - M ark Benton

145. ESHM Dec 8 1795/To be sold on the plantation of John Needles, lying on the Choptank River above Kingstown, horses, cows, hogs, and sheep - William Edmondson/A small yawl found by John Kersy, Bay Side, Talb Co/J. Birkhead & Brother have opened an assortment of goods/House for rent at the Trappe where Doctor John Tripp now lives - Levin Stevens

146. ESHM Dec 15 1795/Married Thursday evening last by Rev Bowie, Major Hugh Sherwood to the amiable Miss Betsey Tilghman, both of Talb Co/500 a. of land adj Trappe, property of William H. Nicholson, to be sold/Dwelling house for sale by Christiana O'Donnell & James Vansandt, exec of Edward O'Donnell, dec/ John Tootell, sheriff Dorch Co, has committed to his custody, a negro man, Charles who says he is the property of Noah Dawson, Caroline Co; also committed is a negro woman, Abby who says she is the property of John Spencer of North Caroline, who purchased her from John Griffin, Dorch Co/Store room compting room, granaries & cellar for rent - William Jones, Vienna/Matthew Doyle, Trappe, seeks apprentice to blacksmith trade

147. ESHM Jan 5 1796/Richard Ray, Miles River Neck, offers reward for negro man, Peter, age about 26/Letters remain at P.O. Easton: Stanly Byus, Easton; Arthur Bryan ; Samuel Baldwin, Easton; .... Burke, Caroline; James Bowden, Easton; Mrs. Jane Blair, Cambridge; John Corrie, Tuckahoe Bridge; Edward O. Clark; William Clark at Mrs. Watts's, Trappe; Israel Corse near Easton; Thomas Catrop; Miss Sally Constable at Mr. Hayward's; William Corin, Hunting Creek; James Cleland, Eastern Shore, Maryland; Solomon Cooper, Caroline; Thomas Cooper, Talb; John Campbell, Talb; Edward Caddell, Trappe; Captain Robert Dawson near Easton; Mathew Deroachbrune, Talb; Robert Duhamell care of J. Gooding Hunting Creek; Mrs. Harriot Dickinson ,Cambridge; Col. John Eccleston; James Earle, Clk, Gen. Court; Jacob Fowle, Trappe; Peter Fergus, Cambridge; Archibald Foster; Joseph Turner, head of Choptank; Samuel Fodury, Easton; Massey Fountain, Talb; John Genn, Choptank Bridge; John Gooding, Hunting Creek; Mrs. Caroline Goldsborough, Cambridge; Thomas Hicks, Cambridge; Robert Hay, St. Michael's; John Harrison, Talb; Mrs. Prudence Harrison, Talb; John Jenkinson, Talb; Nicholas Killiam, Easton; William Lowry; Charles Lecompt, Cambridge; Capt William Mackey; William Bond Martin; James Newcome; Dr. Perry E. Noel; William Richardson - treasurer; Jesse Richardson; William Richmond, Queens-Town; Philip Rigby; Henry Somerville, Cambridge; William Skinner, Easton; John Singleton; William Stevens ,Talb; Job Smith, Talb; James Shannahan, Hunting Creek; Captain Philemon Sherwood; Samuel Sherwood, Talb; William Trippe, Easton; Henry Tibbels; Dekar Thompson; John Tompkins care of Major Astin(?) near Cambridge; Nathan Thomas near Hock Town; Mrs. Susan ιhomas, Easton; Dr. James Wilson; Joshua Williams, Caroline; Charles Winrow(?) Cambridge; Joseph Withgott, Cambridge; Mrs. Elizabeth Watts at the Trappe/

148. ESHM Jan 12 1796/Married Sunday evening last by Rev Bowie, Edward Eubanks to the amiable Mrs. Anne Sturgess, both of Talb Co//Byus & Willson have opened in the store-house formerly occupied by Samuel Baldwin, Easton -General merchantize

149. ESHM Jan 19 1796/Parson & Hopkins, taylors in Washington St adj Capt Trippe's store, Easton

150. ESHM Jan 26 1796/Jacob Gibson in answering a grand jury regarding a

charge of cheating in the measurment of wheat and using false measures
includes the following statements: 1. that William Mason is mistaken in saying
that he lived with Jacob Gibson in 1792, that I the subscriber lived with said
Gibson in that year and also 1793 - John Tarr; 2. I Sally Blades widow of
James Blades, deceased...that my husband James Blades died May 1790... who was
tenant to Jacob Gibson; 3. Rec'd 26th Sept 1788 of Jacob Gibson the sum of 35
pounds in full, for a months wages on board his sloop - James Lowrey; 4. ...
I heard Samuel Tenant say, that he had measured Jacob Gibson's corn barrel and
said it was large enough - Nathaniel G. Bryson; 5. being in company one night
August last with Jacob Gibson at St. Michaels ...William Winstandley, Sen;
6. William G. Dawson also in company with Jacob Gibson & William Windstandley
at St. Michaels; 7. I followed William Mason and Robert Gossage from
Gossage's house, when Jacob Gibson was going home on the night spoken of in
the above certificates of William Winstandley & William G. Dawson, that I sew
the said Mason & Gossage go in Mr. Hay's vessel (then on the stocks) that I
heard them throwing stones at Mr. Gibson, as I did suppose - William
Windstandley Jr; 8. ...that Henry Connolly (William Mason's brother-in-law)
told me that Mason stole Thomas Wayman's canoe or caused it to be done -
Jesse Blades/Died Friday 22 inst, Samuel Sharp, merchant of this town/Lots for
sale by Charles Goldsborough which he purchased of the exec of James Tilghman

151. ESHM Feb 2 1796/Jacob Gibson continues his side of the regarding Thomas
Coward's insinuation that he (Gibson) cheated in delivery a quantity of wheat,
"In December 1794 Mr. Samuel Sharp engaged T. Coward's vessel to collect a
load of wheat from serveral persons, viz. John Goldsborough, Richard Trippe,
William Dawson, William Winstandley and myself ... consigned to Capt. Peter
Sharp at Baltimore... Jesse Robinson was the skipper when the whole of the
wheat was delivered.   Statement of James Price: "I certify that Archibald
McNeale and Captain Thomas Coward appeared before me to have a dispute between
John McNeale (son of said Archibald) and the said Coward(resolved)"/Robert
Goldsborough forbids persons from hauling seins on his shores/Buchanan &
Clayland, Balt, formerly of Easton, requests debtors to settle accounts with
Richard Earle/Died Friday last Mrs. Elizabeth Price consort of James Price in
the 21st year of her age, wife and parent

152. ESHM Feb 9 1796/Died Tuesday last after a lingering illness, Captain
William Trippe of this town/Far sale, Easton Packet owned by Samuel Thomas/
Ann Shaw admin of James Shaw late of Talb Co, dec/Chancery case - Benjamin
Comegys against William Falconer's heirs

153. ESHM Feb 16 1796/Open letter to Samuel Tenant from Jacob Gibson - "...
you well know I gave Dick Miller a barrel of corn per head for whiping three
ruffians ..." and refers to a "laugh at able story about the smiling daughter
Beckey Porter, yourself and Fiddler Dick..."/Tract for sale - Hanbrook's
Point in Dorch Co within 2 miles of Cambridge owned by Elizabeth Caile,
Easton; apply to owner or Colonel Robert Harrison near Cambridge /James Milliss
Jr offers reward for negro lad, Israel/Chancery sale of tract, Pearle,
formerly the property of Walter Meeds, dec, lying in QA Co on Chester River
- James Scott, trustee

154. ESHM Mar 8 1796/Peter Gordon gives notice to persons indebted to Gordon
& Brown that papers are in the hands of William B. Martin & Josiah Bayly/More
certificates in the continuing dispute of Gibson and Tenant: 1.that Nancy Mason
came to my house where negro Dick had stopped to warm himslef, that she kept
teazing the fellow to go home with her ...Sarah Blades; 2. I know of no
deference nor ill will at present between Mr. Jacob Gibson and his neighbors
in the neck, Col. Benson excepted - Obadiah Garey; 3. Mr. Gibson and myself
has lived very neighborly for many years - W. Dawson; 4. ...we have been
acquainted with Jacob Gibson a good many years, particularly as a neighbour

- Henry Bullen, B. Stanfield; 5. that Mrs. Gibson acknowledged that Mr. Gibson never did strike her with either cow-skin, switch, or whip, or that they ever had a word of defference on the subject of infidelity - W. Dawson; 6. I was present when Mr. Gibson called on John Blades to relate the circumstances of Samuel Tenant's taking his (John Blades) fodder - Frederick Stanfield, William Winstandley; 7. George Bromwell's statement regarding some person had scattered fodder from a fodder house/Sale of property of William Loveday, Talb Co, dec, by John Roberts, trustee/Talb Co sheriff has committed to gaol negro man, Greaves End, age about 30, property of Depal Antencke, living on the island of Havannah, who has escaped and returned to Maryland/Sale at the house of Mrs. Briscoe in Elkton, the tract, Widow's Lot, situated at the Susquehanah Canal

155. ESHM Mar 15 1796/Lot for sale on Miles River - James Barrow

156. ESHM Mar 22 1796/Letters remaining P.O. Easton Jan 1 1796: Charles Blair, Caroline; Jonathan Bonnel; Richard Barnaby; Easter Benson care of Samuel Brown in Cambridge; John Cockey, Oxford; Capt Robert Dawson near Easton; James Edmondson, Caroline; Charles Foreman, coach maker, Easton; Capt William Frazer; Alexander Gun, merchant, Federalsburgh, Dorset Co; John Goldsborough Jr; Mrs. Catharine Goldsborough, Talb; Sidney George; John Harrison, merchant, Broad Creek; Edward N. Hambleton; Philip Jenkins, Talb Court House; John King, Tuckahoe; Michael Kirby near Easton; William McMechan; James Morison, Little Annamessex; Messrs. Thomas Nicols & Co, Federalsburgh, Caroline; Miss Nancy Parramow living with Mary Seney on Miles River; Colonel William Richardson; John Reid care of Peter Fergusson, Cambridge; John Roche, New Market; James Ralston, Easton; William Spencer now at Easton; Absolom Swaney; John Singleton; Robert Seney; Messrs. Sullivan & Ennells, New Market; James Starr, Nine Bridges, Caroline Co; John Swepson; William Spencer; William Trippe; William Tibbels; John Tall, Little Choptank; Mrs. Mary Valant, Deep Neck; John Willis, Oxford; Philemon Willis; Cornelius West/Chancery case - to obtain a decree for vacating a fraudulent instrument of writing, purporting to be the last will and testament of Mary Elbert wherby she devised all her estate of every kind to James McCabe and also a deed by which the said Mary conveys to the said James McCabe two tracts of land in QA Co, called The Reward and Macklin's Addition; it is stated that the said James McCabe hath absconded and left the state/Household furniture for sale - James Price/A plantation for sale laying in Caroline Co, bordering on the Bee Tree Swamp and the Long Marsh containing 500 a. which tract the subscriber bought of Simon Weekes of Kent Co - John Weams, AA Co /Nathan Gregg Bryson offers a certificate in response to Samuel Tenant from James Roney, junior, of Philadelphia, cordwainer(a native of the county of Antrim, Ireland) and John Campbell also of the county Antrim, Ireland. James Roney saith that he has been well acquainted with the said Nathan Gregg Bryson since his the said Bryson's arrival in this city of Philadelphia (which he believes happened about three years since.) and that Bryson hath a good name and reputation in Ireland and America. A certificate from County Altrim: James Bryson and Robert Bryson, both of Cresshill, in the parish of Killead and county of Antrim, farmers, and Mary Bryson wife of the said James Bryson, ... made oath that on or about 1775 Nathaniel Gregg Bryson, son of the aforesaid James and Mary Bryson, (now of Trap, Worcester county, in the state of Maryland, merchant) was bit on the left side of his head by a horse, which occasioned a scar on his left cheek, and likewise a part of his left ear bit off.../G. Jenkins admin of James Consodant, late of Talb Co, dec, requests claims against the estate be made at the house of John Mullikin, Hole in the Wall/ Sale of a farm in Dorch Co of 500 a. now under rent to Capt. Jacob Wright about 2 1/2 miles south westward of Hunting Creek Mill - Richard Tilghman 4th, Chester-Town/Ferry running from his landing to the Western Shore of Maryland - William Webb Haddaway, Bay-Side/Seek to employ school master in area of Dover,

on the Choptank River, Talb Co, John Regester, Robert Neall, Joseph Parson, William Scott, Tristram Martin

157. ESHM Mar 29 1796/Peter Sharp requests payment to estate of Samuel Sharp late of this town

158. ESHM Apr 12 1796/Died at Balt Wednesday 30th ult in 30th yr of his age, Jeremiah Banning Junr, eldest son of Capt Henry Banning of Talb Co/Died Wed last Mrs. Mary Bruff, relict of Major Joseph Bruff of Talb Co/Elizabeth Turner exec of Joseph Turner, Talb Co/Sale of tracts 3 miles from Vienna – Nathaniel Manning/James Vansandt, Easton, seeks apprentices to carpenters and joiners business/Edward Bromwell having erected a blacksmith shop in Oxford, gives notice of smith work done by Joseph Foreman/William Sharp collecting debts owed to the late partnership of John Watts and Jacob Fowle/My wife Hannah Ingram has eloped from my bed and board... -Robert Ingram

159. ESHM Apr 19 1796/Chancery slae of lots in Cambridge of Joseph Dawson, dec, now occupied by James Steele – Burton Whetcroft, trustee/Howes Goldsborough, William Goldsborough, admin of Anne Goldsborough/Sale of lots adj Cambridge-Robert Muir, Cambridge/James Birckhead & brothers have wide assortment of goods at reduced prices/William Parrott, King's Creek, Talb Co, offers reward for negro woman, Cate, age about 20/Levi Hopkins, Somerset Co, offers reward for mulatto fellow, Charles, age about 23/Benjamin Purnell (of W.) to petition to reclaim a water lot at Cornelius Ennis's Landing, Worc Co

160. ESHM Apr 26 1796/Sale of a lot at Hook Town – James Faulkner/Tanyard for rent at Hole in the Wall – John Macmahan, senr, Head of Island Creek

161. ESHM May 3 1796/List of letters remaining in the P. O. Easton: Richard Barnaby, Oxford: James Booker; John Broof, Saint Michaels; John Blake; Polly Barclay; James Comsate (?), Trap; Mrs. Anna Maria Chew; Samuel Calahan, care of R. Chamberlaine; James Clayland; Robert Duhamell, care of John Gooding; William Donean(?); Mathew Driver; James Earle; Capt William Frazier; John Gooding; Samuel Hopkins, Cambridge; Col. John Jones, near Indian river, Del; Daniel McDonnell, Cambridge; William Mackey; George Miller; Messrs Martin and ...; William Needles; Mrs. Susannah Pickering; Samuel Swan; Philemon Sherwood; John Smyth(?); Thomas Smith; Isaac Sidmon; Henry Somerville, Cambridge; Edward Turner; Charles Wheeler, care of Edward Cox

162. ESHM May 10 1796/Tract for sale of 621 a. in Caroline Co – Thomas Loockerman, Hunting Creek, or Jacob Loockerman, Miles River Ferry/Lot for sale on Miles River – Richard Ray, Miles River Neck, Talb Co/Sale of property of Jonathan Clain – John Jenkinson/Daniel Fiddeman offers reward for negro man, Jacob, age about 22

163. ESHM May 17 1796/Arthur Bryan admin of James Holland, exec and admin of John Bowman or William Harrison late of Talb Co dec

164. ESHM May 24 1796/Arthur Bryan, Head of Wye, Talb Co, offers reward for negro woman, Mary Ann, age about 40, in company with mulatto man, Martin Madden/James Dudley, inspector, gives notice that Levy Court of Talb has discontinued use of Kingstown warehouse

165. ESHM May 31 1796/Greenbury Neale has opened dry goods store/Sale of plantation by Robert Harrison, Dorch Co, which formerly belonged to Thomas Stewart, 3 miles of Cambridge; also property that belonged to Thomas Barnett within sight of Cambridge/Sale of tract on Hog Island, 5 miles below Dover Ferry in Caroline Co – Edward Bourke/Vestry of P. E. Church in St. Peter's Parish: Samuel Chamberlaine, John Coats, John Singleton, Easton/Henry Bullen, near Easton, offers reward for negro man, Daniel, who has carried away with him a negro woman, Florah

166. Jun 7 1796/Hugh Work, Rosannah Work, exec of Charles Pickering, dec, to sell his houses & lots in Trappe; the store-houses are occupied by William Sharp & Mr. Nuton/John Erskine, John Thomas, admin of Richard Johns, Talb Co, dec/Sale of store house in Princess Anne - apply to John Landrith of Somerset Co

167. ESHM Jun 14 1796/Grammar School opened in Easton by Rev Joseph Jackson/ Sale of property of John Leatherbury at Princess Anne, the tract Old Berry of 400 a. and 6 negros: Harry, Rose, Jesse, Littleton, Edward and Stephen; and property of James Bennett: tract Last Choice, pt of Mount Sinai, Addition to Little Eden, Fox Island, Jenkins Mistake, Hannah alias Havannah and 4 negros: David, Joe, Ibby and Cassa - all purchased at a sheriff's sale - William Richardson for William Marbury, agent for state of Maryland/House for sale on road leading from Easton to Judge Goldsborugh's - Robert Sharp Harwood/A pale red silk umbrella was left on subscriber's schooner - William Mackey

168. ESHM Jun 21 1796/James Hindman, Bennett's Point, offers reward for information on the persons who set fire to his fields/John Dougherty admin of Thomas Cain, Talb Co, dec; Tristram Bowdle, Easton, seeks apprentice to house carpenters and Joiners business/James Earle Jr, Easton, seeks apprentice to General Court office

169. ESHM Jun 28 1796/James Boon, admin of James Webb, late of Caroline Co, dec, requests persons to present claims against the estate at the house of Benjamin Denny at Denton/John Turner, Near Tuckahoe Bridge, seeks miller to employ/Michael Rogers, Caroline Co, has erected a fulling mill on Head of Robens Creek, Caroline Co, about 1/2 mile from main road leading from Dover Ferry to Denton/James Price exec of Capt William Trippe, late Talb Co/Mills. and tavern for rent at Hunting Creek (now in the possession of Edward Smith) - John Eccleston

170. ESHM Jul 5 1796/Charles Ferrow, Cabinet maker, Chester-Town/Solomon Corner & William Corner request payment of debts/William Akers, Akers Ferry, has taken out a tavern license/Elizabeth Turner, Head of Wye, offers reward for male slave, Phil, age 20, property of Mrs. Esther Hindman/William Vickars, 2d, Inspector, gives notice that the Levy Court of Dorch Co has discontinued use of White's warehouse

171. ESHM Jul 12 1796/Letters remaining at P.O. Easton Jul 9 1796: Charles Blair, Caroline; Jonathan Bonnel; Richard Barnaby; Easter Benson care of Samuel Brown in Cambridge; John Cockey, Oxford; Capt Robert Dawson, near Easton; James Edmondson, Caroline Co; Charles Foreman, Coach maker, Easton; Capt William Frazer; Alexander Gun, merchant, Federalsburgh, Dorset Co; John Goldsborough, Jr; Mrs. Catharine Goldsborough, Tabl Co; Sidney George; John Harrison, merchant, Broad Creek; Edward N. Hambleton; Philip Jenkins, Talb Court House; John King, Tuckahoe; Michael Kirby, near Easton; William McMechan; James Morison, Little Annamessex; Messrs Thomas Nicols & Co, Federalsburgh, Caroline; Miss Nancy Parramow, living with Mary Seney on Miles River; Colonel William Richardson; John Reid care of Peter Fergusson, Cambridge; John Roche, New Market; James Ralston, Easton; William Spencer, now at Easton; Absolom Swaney; John Singleton; Robert Seney; Messrs Sullivan & Ennells, New Market; James Starr, Nine Bridges, Caroline Co; John Swepson; William Spencer; William Trippe; William Tibbels; John Tall, Little Choptank; Mrs. Mary Vallant, Deep Neck; John Willis, Oxford; Philemon Willis; Cornelius West

172. ESHM Jul 19 1796/Sale at the plantation of Nathaniel Manning late of Dorch Co, dec/Sale of cattle, sheep, horses - Thomas Barnett for Mary Manning exec/Henry Tibbels, William Tibbels, admin of Thomas Tibbels, late of Talb Co

173. ESHM Jul 26 1796/Margaret Hughes, living in Dorset Co, near Transquaken

bridge, offers reward for negro man, Daniel, age about 23/For lease a farm in Caroline Co, 8 miles from Easton, by William Frazer/A lot for sale on the main road from Easton to Potts Mill about 1/4 miles from Hook's Town - J. Bowie/ Samuel Thomas announces the availability of the schooner, Eleanor/Jonathan Porter, living in Hopkins, 6 miles from Easton, offers reward for negro man, Grant, age about 25/Thomas Barnett agent for Mary Manning exec of Nathaniel Manning, late of Dorch Co/Samuel Swan wishes to purchase negroes/The partnership of Meluy & Wainer dissolved with business to be continued by L. Wainer/ Chancery sale by James Scott of real estate of Walter Meeds/Brick building and houses for sale, now occupied by Samuel Swan house now occupied by Henry Elbers and lot purchased by subscriber of Henry Nicols - Robert Lloyd Nicols/ Junifer Tayloy, living in Mispillion Hundred, Kent Co, Del, offers reward for negro man, Joe, age about 40/William Vickars, tobacco inspector, Dorch Co/ W. Hindman candidate for congress/Pott's Mill for sale and several small farms - James Tilghman, Easton/For sale - mill and mill seat on one of the branches of Wye River - Woolman Gibson/Solomon Corner & William Corner request payment of debts/300 a. in Caroline Co for sale near Dover Ferry - William Perry of Perry Hall/James Boon admin of James Webb late of Caroline Co

174.   ESHM Aug 2 1796/Plantation in QA Co for sale where Richard Lowman now lives adj land of Edward Downes, 273 a.; also farm for rent adj Denton, formerly property of Michael Lucas where he now lives, about 350 a. - Thomas Boon, Denton/Elizabeth Lloyd, Wye House, exec of Hon. Edward Lloyd/Charles Emory, surveyor, also available to draw up deeds of conveyance/For rent in QA Co, about 1200 a. near the lands of Richard Tilghman of Chester Town; Mr. Larwood who l ves near the premises, will shew the land; lot # 2 in QA Co of about 900 a. near Kent Narrows Ferry; lots 3 & 4 in Caroline Co adj my farm in Tuchahoe Neck at present occupied by James Love & Mrs Garey, the 1st 200 a. cleared and the latter about 120 a.; lot # 5 in Caroline Co of about 800 a. adj the dwelling of Rev Keene; lot # 6 in Kent Co adj land of General Lloyd on Farley Creek of about 500 a.; lot # 7 in Cecil Co in Elk Neck on Elk Neck river of about 600 a. - Arthur Bryan, Head of Wye/Married Sun 24th ult by Rev Keene, Dr. Perry E. Noel of Talb Co to Miss Sally H. Nicholson of QA Co/ Charles Ferrow, cabinet maker, Chester Town

175.   ESHM Aug 9 1796/Tract for sale, formerly belonging to Dr. Solomon Birckhead, 618 a. on Choptank river, Talb Co - William Richardson Jr, desirous of leaving this shore/John Craig, Droch Co, exec of Colonel Joseph Daffin, late of Droch Co

176.   ESHM Aug 16 1796/Thomas Jackson, admin of Archibald Jackson Jr, late of Caroline Co, dec/Subscribers to the Dover & Easton Post (Joseph Huzza) are requested to pay their respectiver subscriptions; Thomas Boon, of Denton, will receive payment from the subscribers in his neighborhood

177.   ESHM Aug 23 1796/James O'Bryan candidate for elector to choose President of the U. S./Dwelling plantation of Nathaniel Manning late of Droch Co, dec, for let - Thomas Barnett, Dorch Co/Christianna O'Donnall, James VAnsandt, Easton, exec of Edward O'Donnall late of Talb Co, to sell his property in Easton/Berrt's Mill & dwelling house, Head of Kings Creek for rent - Ephraim Parvin/Greenbury Goldsborough admin of Thomas Mewse, late of Talb Co, dec, to sell his house on Dover St., Easton/Doctor Noel now settled in Easton as practioiner of medicine, opposite the court house/Edward Needles admin of John Needles & William McCallum, late of Talb Co/Tract for sale in Caroline Co , about 5 miles east of Dover Ferry and l mile from the back of Peter Edmondson's smith's shop, about 400 a. - William Needles/David Nice, Easton, offers reward for strayed cow, boutht from Joseph Deford (Tuckahoe)/Farm for sale in QA Co at Head waters of Wye, about 1000 a. - Edward Harris, QA Co

178. ESHM Aug 30 1796/William Edmundson, Easton, to petition under the in insolvency act/Francis Neall, admin of Joseph Parsons, late of Talb Co, dec/ Hall & Redhead - groceries/James Booker, admin of John Bracco, late of Talb Co/Jacob Fowle to petition under the insolvency act

179. ESHM Sep 6 1796/Rebecca Hobbs, Princess Anne, admin of Josiah Hobbs

180. ESHM Sep 13 1796/Richard Barroll Sr, announces the Chester-Town races/ James Price, exec of Capt William Trippe, late of Talb Co/John Rolle, living in Talb Co, bayside, offers reward for mulatto man, Andrew, age about 28/Rigby Thomas, living in Caroline Co near the road from Hunting Creek to Northwest Fork Bridge, withing 3 miles of bridge, offers reward for stolen horses/John Dames, near Centre-Ville, offers reward for stolen gelding

181. ESHM Sep 20 1796/John Rowles, Airy Hall, Kent Co, admin of Rezin Rowles, to sell farm on Kent Island, QA Co, previously occupied by Rezin Rowles/ William Jones, near Dover Ferry, Talb Co, offers reward for negro woman, Easter, who formerly belonged to Rev Bowie, age about 22/Philemon Murphey, near Centre Ville, offers reward for stolen mare/Farm for sale on which I now reside in Caroline Co, between Dover Ferry and Kingstown - John Dickinson/ Thomas Stewart & William Price announce the Cambridge races/Peter Spencer Corbin & Co to petition to erect mills on main branch of Dividing Creek from the lands of Jonathan Tull of Somerset Co to the lands of William Corbin of Worc Co

182. ESHM Oct 11 1796/David Kerr, Easton, has just received a handsome assortment of fall goods/For sale - horses, cattle, sheep and hogs and household goods - Nehemiah Noble/For sale at the dwelling house hte personal property of Charles Gardiner of Talb Co, dec, by Margaret Gardiner, Samuel Barrow - Miles River Neck, exec/John Erskine, John Thomas Jr, Easton, admin of Richard Johns, to sell his saddle and work horses/House and lot to let, presently occupied by John Goldsborough - Lydia Troth, Easton/Thomas Cuthcart, whereas he proposes to leave the county, offers for sale a farm in Talb Co, about 300 a./Robert Cross, QA Co, offers reward for mulatto woman, Cumfort, age about 25, with 11 month old child/Edward Clayton, Easton, surviving partner of Richardson & Clayton, plans to continue a general assortment of goods/Samuel Baldwin, Easton, surviving partner of firm, Baldwin & Richardson, which partnership was dissolved some years ago, requests payment of debts/ Margaret or John Bromwell exec of Edward Bromwell Jr, dec/Inhabitants of Worc Co to petition for public road through the lands of Col. William Morris, Charles Hammond, James Selby, and Littleton Robins and to condemn 1/2 a. of land of Littleton Robins for a public Landing/Negroes, Jacob, Pat, and Grace to petition for confirmation of manumission/House to let where Sarah Cockayne now lives on Dover St in Easton - James Berry

183. ESHM Oct 18 1796/Robert Wright presidential elector candidate/Building for rent, formerly occupied by Mrs. Mary Bruff in Easton, now occupied by Richard Harwood as a Public House, the house where Samuel Yarnel keeps his store - Mark Benton/Benjamin Denny requests payment of debts/Henry Pratt to petition for the recording of a deed from William Yoe of QA Co to Christopher Cross Roach(?) dated 17 Jan 1794/John Thomas Jr, candidate for sheriff, Talb Co/Edward Cox, candidate for sheriff, Talb Co/Farm for sale on which I now res in Caroline on the Choptank river between Dover Ferry and Kingstown - John Dickinson/For sale - horses, cattle, sheep and household furniture - W. Richardson Jr/Letters remaining at P.O. Easton on Oct 17: Nathaniel Badley, Dorset Co; Capt W. S. Bond; Messrs Bowdle & Needles; Mrs. Lilly Blake at Col. Richardson's; Henry Carter; Polly Clark, care of Robert Stewarts, Cambridge; The Clerk of the General Court; Thomas Ennalls, Dorset Co; Peter Elliot, Cambridge; Samuel Edmondson, Easton; Messrs Farrel & Oldson, Beaver Dam; Jacob Fowle; Mrs. Margaret Gun; Mrs. Mary Grace; Citizen Henry Haskins,

Cambridge; Mrs. Hurst; David Hughes at Q. Charles Christians; John W. Harrison; Miss Milley Lothy, Oxford; Dr. Andrew Mitchell; Henry Nicols; Nathaniel Pearce, near Camden, Kent Co; Howell Powell; Sarah Roberts, Miles River; John Stanford, Cambridge; James Sullivan, New Market; Henry Smoot; James Scott; James Starr, Caroline Co; Mrs. Scollars, care of John Mackey; Dekar Thompson; John D. Thompson; Miss Nancy Tilghman; Samuel Troth; Edward Turner; Samuel W. Thomas; Dr. James Wilson; Thomas Wright, Reed's Creek; Nancy Wright; John Willis; Philemon Willis

184. ESHM Oct 25 1796/Joshua Taggart admin of Jesse Richardson, otherwise called Jesse Taggart, late of Easton, dec, of the firm of Richardson and Clayton (Edward Clayton)/Joseph Neall seeks apprentice to the cabinet business/ Tan-Yard for rent in Cambridge - Peter Ray/William Dimond, lvigin near Centreville, offers reward for strayed mare/Sale at late dwelling plantation of William Banning in Tuckahoe Neck (Caroline Co)/Sale of horses, cattle, sheep and household furniture - Valentine Green/John Nabb, William Barwick, exec of William Barwick

185. ESHM Nov 8 1796/William Charles Neill insolvent debtor, QA Co/Chancery sale of remaining real estate of Griffin Fauntleroy, dec, tracts: Suder's Purchase & Sudler's Fortune, both on Kent Island, QA Co - Dekar Thompson, trustee (also admin of Charles Daffin & Mrs. Mabel Daffin, both late of Caroline Co)/Greenbury Neale has a good assortment of dry goods/Michael Corse admin of Thomas Jones, Kent Co, Md, requests creditors to make claims at the house of Francis Skirven, Chester-Town/Solomon Etting, Balt, offers reward for negro woman, Darkey, lately purchased of Samuel Swan of Easton who purchased her of Capt Richard Besswick on the head of Wye river, Talb Co/Sale of horses, cattle, sheep and hogs - Richard Ray, Miles River Neck, Talb Co/Robert Speden exec of ___ Speden, late Talb Co/Joshua Hobbs, Somerset Co, offers reward for apprentice boy, Littleton Durman, age about 15/Edward Stevens, Island Creek, Talb Co, exec of Thomas Stevens Jr, late of Talb Co/W. Richmond, QA Co, exec of Basil Brown

186. ESHM Dec 6 1796/James Sherwood admin of Philip Horney, late of Talb Co/ Robert Hopkins, Easton, offers reward for strayed cow/Richard Barniby has opened dry goods & wet goods store at Oxford/Sale at late dwelling houseof Dr. William Kemp at head of Wye of household furniture, horses, cattle, sheep and hogs - Samuel Barrow exec of Christiana Seth exec of James Seth, late of Talb Co, dec/Peter Sharp requests payments be made to the estate of Samuel Sharp, or to the late partnership of Samuel & Peter Sharp/John Plummer Jr reports a stray mare which broke in upon William Griffin's plantation in QA Co where subscriber resides/For rent in Salisbury a Tavern House and Concerns wherein William Furniss now lives - Robert Lemmon/Daniel P. Cox, sherriff Talb Co, will attend Solomon Corner's Brick Room, Easton, for purposes of receiving assessment road tax and officers' fees; also Mr. Bailey's Inn in Wye, Mr. Barrett's Inn at Williamsburg, Mr. Mullikin's Inn at Holeinwall for the same purposes/Henry Summerwill requests payment to himself or James Ball of debts due to the partnership of Summerwill and McDannell/Ephraim Parvin exec of Benjamin Parvin late of Talb Co/Henry Elbert, Easton, seeks blacksmith

187. ESHM Dec 13 1796/The physicians who examined William Brinsfield and Philip Cason are requested to re-examine these cases/Kitty and Harriot Hutchings, Kent Island, exec to sell negroes, horses, cattle, sheep, horses, and farming utensils at the late dwelling of James Hutchings dec on Kent Island, QA Co; claims on estates should be made to Richard T. Earle, Centreville/Joseph Jackson seeks assistant of grammar school, Easton

188. ESHM Dec 20 1796/House for rent on Harrison St - Apply to Jonathan N. Benny, living with Benjamin Willmott, Easton/Howes Goldsborough admin of James

Tilghman, late of Talb Co, dec/Arabella Hardcastle, Caroline Co, offers reward for negro man, Jacob, age about 21/Tract for sale near Easton, 200 to 300 a. - Moses Allen

189. ESHM Dec 27 1796/House for rent in Easton on Harrison St, occupied by Benjamin Ward, school master - James Neall, Easton

190. ESHM Apr 11 1797/Philemon H. Able, the Trappe, offers services of his horse, Black & All Black/Letters remaining at P.O. Easton Apr 10th: William Armstrong, merchant, Cambridge; Samuel Baldwin; Edward Burk, Wye Neck; Charles Blair, Caroline; Stanley Byus, Easton; Mary Berry; Edward Cox; William Corner; William Dawson, house carpenter; Capt Robert Dawson; John E. Denny, near Wye Mill; Capt Samuel Elliott, Fishing Bay; Samuel Edmondson; Horatio Edmondson; Thomas Foster, Dorset Co; Archibald Foster, itinerant preacher; William Farrell, Beaver Dams; John Fisher, near Tuckahoe; Mrs. Mary Gordon; Richard Grisham, Wye River; Alexander Bunn, Northwest Fork Bridge; Gilbert Gardner; Robert S. Gamble, near Choptank Bridge; Daniel & James Groome, Langford Bay; RebeccaHenesy, near Tuckahoe Bridge; John Holland; William Harris, merchant, Easton; Cynthia Haslett, Greensborough; William Hardcastle, merchant, Maryland; Philemon Horney; William Harper & son, Nine Bridges; Capt Jesse Harding, Dorset Co; Henry Johnson; Richard Jones, merchant, Easton; Richard Kennard, Greensborough; Mrs. Margaret Knox, Cambridge Cross Roads; Nicholas Kellum; Solomon Lowe; Philemon Leary; Capt Charles Lecompte, near Cambridge; John & John Massitt; Cyrus Mitchell, New Market; Frances Goreman(?) Massey; Solomon Martin; John Maddox; Martin & Spedin; John McWay, Beaver Dam; Richard Newman; Leaton Nogdon; Samuel Nicols; John Othoson, Peach Blossom; John Opp; John Price; John Quinn, coachmaker; Colonel Richardson; Richardson & Clayton; James Steel, Cambridge; William Skinner; Samuel Sherwood; Joshua Taggart; Ross Thomson; William Troth, Dover Ferry; Mrs. Catharine Watts, Trappe; Cornelius West; Joseph & Rubin Withgott; Cabin Creek; Dr. James Wilson; Robert Williams, Head of Wye; John Young, Tuckahoe Bridge/Intending to leave the Eastern Shore of Md, John Harwood offers for sale his farm adj Kings Town on the Great Choptank river, about 200 a. - Apply to subscriber or Capt Robert Ewing at Kings-town/Samuel Dean displays Bison at Cambridge & Easton - 1/8 of a dollar admittance/Fanny Gooding admin of John Gooding late of Dorch Co; Thomas Boon of Caroline had taken the books of the late John Gooding(of the partnership of Boon and Gooding)/Jacob Gibson, Miles river, seeks overseer/James Clayland, Head of Wye of Talb Co, offers reward for negro man Jem Downes/Farm for sale in Caroline Co, 6 miles from Tuckahoe Bridge, adj land of Isaac Purnel - J. Hughes, Easton/Farm for sale late the property of Thomas Cuthcart on Evans Bay, Choptank River in Bolingbroke Hundred, about 280 a. - David Kerr, Easton/Samuel Troth exec of Ephraim Parvin/Rebecca Goldsborough, Richard Goldsborough, admin of Howes Goldsborough, late of Talb Co, dec/ Patrick McIntire has opened wet & dry goods store at Wye Mill/William Hemsley, QA Co, admin of Philemon Tilghman requests creditors to make claims at the tavern of Mrs. Sarah Dashiel, Centreville/Hugh Sherwood of Huntington, Talb Co, offers reward for negro, Paris, age about 25/John Kean, Sexton and William Berridge, Register, of St. Peter's Parish/For sale - 350 a. in QA Co, about 2 miles from Parson Keene's Plantation, formerly owned by Thomas Elliott, dec, who purchased it from Nathan Wright; present propietor lately from Kentucky - John Elliott or Peter Denny/Nixon Sherwood has commenced riding as a post from Dover by way of Denton & Tuckahoe to Easton/Henry Buckley candidate for sheriff, Talb Co/John Jones, near Easton, offers services of his horse, Young Morwick Ball/Nicholas Watts offers the services of his horse Brillian/Sale at the late dwelling house of John Stevens, cows, sheep, a solo carriage, household furniture - Joseph Martin/Edmund Weyman admin of John McQuay, late of Talb Co, dec

191. ESHM Apr 18 1797/Mr. Miniere proposes a dancing school in Easton/Rebecca Jones admin of William Jones, late of Dorch Co/For sale - Greenwood, late the

-36

res of Alexander Lawson on Wye River - W. Richmond/Chancery case - Leah Townsend versus Thomas Robertson & Charlotte his wife and others regarding the estate of Joshua Townsend, late of Wroc Co, dec, father of Charlotte Robertson; Thomas & Charlotte Robertson res Delaware

192. ESHM Apr 25 1797/Peter Sharp, Easton, refuses to pay bond given to Rev Philip Hughes of Susex Co, Del/Solomon Corner requests payment of debts/Andrew Price has opened store (wet and dry goods) in Greensborough, Caroline Co

193. ESHM May 2 1797/James Ringgold has a brickhouse for sale in Chester-Town/ For rent, place where I now live on Choptank River, mouth of Third Haven Creek, about 16 a. - Jeremiah Colston/Joseph Bruff has household furniture for sale in Easton/Thomas Jackson, Caroline Co, admin of Archibald Jackson Jr, late of Caroline Co requests creditors present claims at Benjamin Denny's, Denton/ Plantation of late Benjamin Parvin, Talb Co, for sale; also apple brandy for sale - by Thomas or Mark Parvin/

194. ESHM May 9 1797/Charles Stewart, QA Co, insolvent debtor/Thomas Lea, QA Co, insolvent debtor/John Ringgold, near Church Hill, QA Co, offers reward for negro man, Jack/John Jenkinson requests creditors make claims against estate of Jonathan Clash, dec, late Talb Co/Tract for sale in Caroline Co adj Denton, about 250 a. - John Lucas

195. ESHM May 16 1797/Plantation for sale, lately the p roperty of Andrew MacDonald and now the property of subscriber on the Nanticoke river, 4 miles below Vienna; apply at my res Northwest Fork Bridge, Alexander Gun

196. ESHM May 23 1797/Farm for sale, 450 a., Thomas Hayward, Talb Co/William Lowrey, Trappe has received assortment of goods/John Erskine admin of James Slaughter, dec, to sell personal property at Easton/William S. Bond to settle accounts of Greenbury Neall, late of this place, and to sell his house now in the tenure of Rev Joseph Jackson

197. ESHM May 30 1797/Farm for sale where Dr. William Maynadier dwelt, now in the possession of James Nabb, 300 a.; apply to William Maynadier, Baltimore Town, Joseph Haskins, Easton, or Henry Maynadier, near Annapolis/Samuel Swan reports theft of jewelry/Joseph Hopkins and Thomas Harrison, Bay side, Talb Co, offer rewards for two negros: Tom, age about 25 and Daniel, age about 15

198. ESHM Jun 6 1797/Gully & Cuthcart have received fresh supply of goods/ B. Willmott - repair of watches and clocks/Charles Baker to sell his res in upper part of Chanceller's Point, 196 1/2a./Elkanah Meeds of Giles Meeds, late of Caroline Co, living in Routhsbourgh, QA Co/Joshua Driver, Caroline Co, admin of William Robinson, late of Caroline, dec/Farm for sale on Island Creek Talb Co, now occupied by John Pritchard -William Sharp Island Creek/William Rose admin of John Jacobs whose partnership now dissolves

199. ESHM Jun 13 1797/Friday last, pursuant to his sentence, Robert Parker was executed for the crime of burglary/Wind mill for sale at St. Michaels - Robert Hay/Matthias Alford, Caroline Co, near Dover Ferry, offers reward for stolen horse;there is reason to believe horse was stolen by Philip Mack/ Thomas Wickersham admin of Charles Vickers, late of Talb Co

200. ESHM June 20 1797/James Trippe, Dorch Co, offers reward for two negro fellows: Ned, age about 20 and Ned Philips, belonging to Mrs. Sarah Byus/ Robert Goldsborough, Centre-Ville, offers reward for negro man, Bob, age about 22, formerly owned by John Bracco, Talb Co/Richard Ray, Talb Co, offers reward for strayed horse

201. ESHM June 27 1797/Tract for sale: Gatterly Moor Resurveyed, near Easton, now in the occupation of Henry Elbert - Thomas J. Bullit, Easton/Baley Warrin, Talb Co, gives notice that he & wife Mary have separated/Edward Trippe running a packet from Easton to Balt

202. ESHM Jul 4 1797/Married Sunday evening last by Rev Kemp, James Price of this town to Miss Anne Ennalls of Dorset Co/Married Sunday evening last by Rev Jackson, Joseph Meuse of Cambridge to Miss Sophia Kerr daughter of David Kerr of this town/Letters remaining at P.O. Easton Jul 3: Henry Allen, Hill's(?) Point; John Anderson, Dorset; George Anderson, Cambridge; Robert Bruff, St. Michaels; Thomas Bruff, Talb Court House; James Boon, Greensborough; Thomas & William Boon, Denton; Solomon Brown, near Denton; Seely Bun(?), preacher; Nathan Baily, Caroline; Francis Baker; James Bateman; John Bush; John Bennett; Henry Clift; John Crowder, care of Jacob Gibson; James Clayland; Peter Denny; Griffin Davis; John Dougharty; Richard Denny; William Dawson; Thomas L. Emory & Co; Capt Bartholomew Ennalls; Henry Ennalls; James Earle Jr; Archibald Foster; James Freeman; Stephen H. Fowle; Charles Goldsborough, Horns Point; Mrs. Caroline Goldsborough, Cambridge; Mrs. Catharine Goldsborough, Talb; Capt Jesse Harding, Dorset; Thomas Hicks, near Cambridge; Dr. Edward Harris; John Harrison; Thomas Harrison, Broad Creek; William Hambleton; Dr. Stephen Theodore Johnson; Miss Lydia Johnson, living at Mr. Bullit's; Thomas Jackson, Greensborough; John Jones, near Easton; Solomon Lowe; Capt James Lloyd; James Lows/Laws/Lowe(?); John Lamb; William V. Murray; Daniel McDonnald; William Melville, care of Peter Ferguson; Isaac Moore, Broad Creek Hundred; Robert Neall; John Nabb; Philip Rigby; Capt Thomas Smith; John Smith; William Stevens; James Stevens; William Skinner; Solomon Shearman, Dorch Co; Miss Hannah Sheppard, near Caroline; Thomas Lee Shippen; Samuel Swan; Mrs. Troth, Easton; Dr. Littleton Townsend; W. T. Wederstrandt; William Wheatley, North West Fork

203. ESHM Jul 11 1797/Celebration at Snow Hill at the house of Ezekiel Wise/ Died Friday last after a long illness, Capt James Ayres of this town/Levin Pollitt, sheriff Worc Co, has committed to his custody a negro man who says his name is George and belongs to John Yellott, Harf Co

204. ESHM Jul 18 1797/James Booker and Levi Seirs running as a packet, the schooner Susan, Easton to Balt/James Bowdle, Talb Co, collector of assessments

205. ESHM Jul 25 1797/John Doughertydenies the rumor that he conveyed property to defraud creditors/Land for sale near The Hole in the Wall, adj land of the Poor House - John L. Bozman, Talb Co/Arthur Whiteley, Fishing Creek, Dorch Co, offers reward for negro man, Joe, age about 36/House for sale near Hole in the Wall - S. Sherwood, Talb Co/Tract for sale about 2 miles from Lockerman's Mill - James Sullivane, New Market/Robert Traverse cautions persons from taking assignment on a bond he passed to James Tucker of Dorch Co/Died Sun last of a paralytic stroke, George Tilghman son of honourable James Tilghman of QA Co/Thomas Stevens exec of Catharine Jenkins/P. Beaston & Hannah Hickson, Lockerman's Mills, admin of James Alexander, late of Dorch Co, dec/H. Edmondson seeks overseer

206. ESHM Aug 8 1797/For sale the late res of the subscriber, James Steele, on Nanticoke River, adj seat of John Henry/William Skinner requests payment of debts/Two farms for lease in Black Water, within 5 miles of Cambridge, by James Price or apply to Dr. James Sulivane, New Market/Farm for rent, 3 miles from Easton; apply to William Hayward or R. Chamberlaine

207. ESHM Aug 15 1797/James Sulivane, Dorch Co, offers reward for negro man Wallis, age about 23/Amasa Robinson, Oxford Neck, Talb Co, admin of William Paddison, late Dorch Co, dec, and admin of Sarah Paddison widow of William Paddison, late of Dorch Co/Store house for rent now occupied by James Wilson, Washington & Dover St, Easton - Samuel Baldwin, Easton/Mills and tavern for rent on Hunting Creek, Dorch Co; also farm on Chicknicomico river where John Hedson formerly lived - John Eccleston, Dorch Co

208. ESHM Aug 22 1797/Tan-yard, currying shop & dwelling house in Easton for rent - John Matthews/Chancery case regarding lands in AA Co and Somerset Co

of William Adams, dec/Jeremiah Bromwell overseer of Poor House, Talb Co/James
Clayland to petition under the insolvency act

209. ESHM Aug 29 1797/John Nabb Jr submits an open letter to the perpetrator
of rumors that he mismanaged the wheat crop of Mrs. Elizabeth Lloyd, including a statement from Simon Smyth who examined the wheat stacking and shocks
in the field and saw no danger of loss/Chancery sale of house in Cambridge
fronting on High St of Patrick Kelly, late of Dorch Co - J. E. Gist, trustee,
Cambridge/A petition to be submitted to authorize sale of about 25 a. of woodland near Combridge, formerly property of John Blair, dec, for the benefit of
his children, all in a state of minority/James Grace, Talb Co, to petition
under the insolvency act

210. ESHM Sep 5 1797/Proposed petition to allow Dorch Co to purchase property of late Joseph Dawson, dec/William Everngam, Hunting Creek, offers reward
for apprentice lad, Charles Lecompte, age about 19/William Hemsly, my son ...
induced to go to Europe for a short period - William Hemsley, Easton/Owen
Kennard, Easton, admin of James Tilghman/George Wilhean, Princess Ann, offers
reward for Negro wench, Nell, age about 20, bought from Isaac Henry, atty at
law, early in 1796; she ran away from Welchgun creek near the mouth of
Nanticoke. John Henry owns her brother & others of her family. Said to live
at one Mr. Windows, a few miles from David Smith's, 7-8 miles from Vienna/
House for sale in Cambridge - John Bradshaw

211. ESHM Sep 12 1797/Died Mon night 28th ult, Thomas Boon of Denton/Died Fri
morning last, Dr. James Wilson, Talb Co/B. M. Ward, Talb Co to petition under
the insolvency act/Elisha Stewart Talb Co to petition under the insolvency
act/Thomas Nicols, Federalsburgh, Caroline Co, seeks calker to calk a brig of
about 140 tons

212. ESHM Sep 19 1797/Races at New Market - John Stevens/House of William
Gibson, late of Caroline Co, for sale - Elizabeth Gibson, Thomas Baynard/
Samuel Handy to petition as exec of William Handy, dec, to sell his land in
Snow Hill, Worc Co/Farm of late James Tilghman for sale near Head of Wye, QA
Co, which was part of estate of Richard Bennett Lloyd, dec, occupied by
William Richmond; apply to William Tilghman, Philadelphia or William Hemsley
near the premises/To petition to cut a ditch at the head of Unicorn Branch in
QA Co on a tract called Cleaves Rambles to Harmatage - John Clawson, James
Dudley, William Walker, John Fogwell Jr, Unicorn

213. ESHM Sep 26 1797/Horatio and John Edmondson exec Pollard Edmondson, dec/
G. R. Hayward to hold public sale at his farm in Bailey's Neck of horses,
sheep and hogs/John Barton, Caroline Co, offers reward for apprentice lad,
David Horner, age 19/William Barroll to petition for divorce from his wife/
Farm for sale on Kent Island, lately occupied by Dr. Jonathan Roberts/Job
Slacum, Dorch Co, offers reward for negro man, Sam, age about 35/Elisha S
Stewart to petition under the insolvency act

214. ESHM Oct 3 1797/Loran & son now opening in one of Col. Nicol's stores,
a variety of merchantize - Easton/Sale of 900 a., late the property of Joseph
Ennalls, Dorch Co - Skinner Ennalls/Ann Jenkins exec of Thomas Jenkins, late
Talb Co/Chancery sale at Mrs. Meeds Tavern in Centre-Ville: 1. tract called
Aulder Branch of 89 a. adj estate of Matthew Mason 2. tract on Long Marsh
called Roes Charm or Roes Chance, 49 a. now rented to Joseph Pippen; and at
Mr. Millington's Tavern, Tuckahoe Bridge 51 a. of a tract called Sylvester's
Addition adj land of Henry Nicolls - the above property being the estate of
the late Robert Browne - W. Richmond, trustee/Sale of horses, cows, hogs,
sheep and farm, formerly property of James Dawson, dec - Henry Nicols Jr/
Benjamin Jackson, Greensborough, offers reward for stolen mare/Chancery sale
on petition of Samuel Handy exec of William Handy, dec, to sell the land in
Snow Hill of George R. Wise which descended to him from his father William
Wise, dec - William Purnell, trustee

215. ESHM Oct 10 1797/Edward Harris admin to sell3 or 4 negroes, property of
the late William Dickinson, pursuant to order of Orphans' Court, Talb Co/
Samuel Wilson exec of Doctor James Wilson, to sell negroes, horses, oxen,
cows, sheep, and schooner laying at Skipton Wharf/Impey Dawson requests
payment of debts/G. I. Dawson requests payment of debts/Nathan Breerwood to
petition under the insolvency act/Chancery sale at the house of John Wright
of a tract called Smith's First Choice, about 200 a. in Dorch Co - William
Purnell, trustee/Chancery sale at house of Mrs. Calhoon the estate of Ephraim
Calhoon, dec, near the head of St. Martin's river, Worc Co - William Purnell,
trustee

216. ESHM Oct 17 1797/William Hindman has lost a bank note of 500 dollars in
Easton/House for rent in Easton occupied by James Price - Peter Sharp/Sale of
horses, ... Joseph Martin, the Trappe/William Perry, near Easton, offers
reward for negro man, Jim Beswick, age about 20, born Kent Co Md near Werten
Creek where his father still lives/Arthur Bryan exec of Richard Grason and
widow Mrs. Ann Grason, QA Co, dec/Letters remaining at P.O. Easton: Philip
Abell, care of Capt Robert Martin; Capt John Bush; David Barrow; Abraham
Bishop, Cambridge; Joseph Bruff; William Bruff; Richard B. Bennett Bewley;
Thomas Barnett; Mrs. Lurania Bruffit, near Cambridge; James Barnes; Thomas
Boon, Denton; James Boyle; Thomas Catrup; Capt Moses Calhoon, Bay Side; Messrs
Crain & Moore, Hunting Creek; John Cunningham; John Cane, Hole in the Wall;
Henry Clift; William Dawson; John Dougherty; Thomas Elliott; Henry Ennalls;
Solomon Fritritsey, minister; Levin Frazier, Dorset; Thomas Foster, Dorset;
John Green, collector of the revenue, 3d division, 3d survey; Woolman Gibson,
Miles river; John Genn, Choptank Bridge; Valentine Green, Hillsborough; Thomas
Hadaway, St. Michaels; Mrs. Margaret Harris; Adorins Harison; Thomas Hicks,
Caroline; James Hanson, Denton; Henry Haskins; Thomas Jenkins, Camden; Henry
Johnson; Henry King, Pokamoke; Robert Lewis; Edward Lecompte; John McLaren;
Susanna Matthews; John Murray; Stephen Miers, Roe's Cross Roads; John Mitchel
Jr, Dorset; Edward Mills, Ennalls Ferry; John McCara, care of Peter Ferguson,
Cambridge; Capt John Nabb; Walter W. Norman, Pig Point; John Pertt(?), ship
carpenter, Denton; Thomas Parrott, Easton; James Swigett, Caroline; William
Skinner; Edward Stevens; Mrs. Stevens, Cambridge; William Smith, Tuckahoe;
Guy Store; Ross Thompson, Caroline; Henry Thompson, Caroline; Decker Thompson,
Caroline; James Thomas, Talb; Miss Nancy Vickers; Robert Wilson; Dr. James
Wilson; Henry Waggaman; Thomas White/William Akers, Thomas Helsby, admin of
John Watts, late of Talb Co, to sell his dry goods and furniture/James
Sherwood requests payment ot estate of Philip Horney, dec/Benjamin Jackson
offers reward for stolen mare

217. ESHM Oct 24 1797/My wife Elizabeth having eloped from my bed and board
... Samuel Jackson Jr/Tavern for rent at the Hole in the Wall now occupied by
John Mullikin; apply to John R. Bromwell/Ann Ellis, Talb Co, wid of Robert
Ellis to petition the General Assembly for wages due her dec husband who
belonged to the 2nd Md Regt

218. ESHM Nov 7 1797/Property for rent now occupied by John Vickers,
subscriber, at Lewis Town, Talb Co/Baynard Wilson admin of William Loveday,
late of TAlb Co/Died at BAlt Sun 29 Oct, James Hull, merchant of Easton

219. ESHM Nov 14 1797/Sheriff's sale at New Market of the property of James
Sulivane, taken in execution of the suits of William Barclay, Somerwell and
Dugind: Hickory Ridge Plantation of about 320 a., Addition to York,
Littleton's Last Shift and the tract, New Market of 220 a. - John Tootell,
sheriff

220. ESHM Nov 21 1797/Benjamin Williams, Lemon St, Balt, offers reward for
negro girl, May, about 15 yrs, raised on the Eastern Shore by Capt Balke; her
mother lives on the Eastern Shore near Mr. Brown or Miss Hutchinson/On Thurs
night the 9th inst, the barn of Henry Bullen, Miles River, was entirely

consumed by fire/Died 20 Nov John Turner, Talb Co, after a long illness/P. Blake admin, to sell property of the late Charles Blake, dec at the farm lately occupied by Benjamin Ryland/John Blake exec of William Blake and admin of William Martin/Peter Edmondson, Dover Ferry, Talb Co, seeks overseer/R. Earle, Easton, admin of Michael Earle, late Cecil Co/George Bailey, druggist & apothecary, now opening at Washington & Dover St Easton

221. ESHM Dec 5 1797/S. Nicols requests payment to Henry Nicols & Joseph Parsons, dec/Died Saturday fe'night at his seat in Dorch Co, Capt Edward Noel, in an advanced age/Chancery sale at Snow Hill of the real estate of Joshua Townsend, dec, dwelling house where Rev David Bell lives, adj Snow Hill Town; pt of tract called Salem; lot adj Jonathan Hutchison & William Selby; pt of lot whereon Capt Thomas Hall lives adj Francis Rosse's lot; woodland called Dumfries adj Patrick Waters' land - William Whittington, trustee. Mary is the wid of Joshua Townsend

222. ESHM Dec 12 1797/Lots for sale: 1. in possession of John Parrot on road from Hole in the Wall to Island Creek 2. adj lands of William Berry near Hole in the Wall and occupied by Henry Delahay - and other lands - John L. Bozman/Arthur Bryan, Head of Wye, offers reward for negro man, Ned, age about 40

223. ESHM Dec 19 1797/William Atkinson, Easton, requests payment of debts/ Died 17 inst after a short illness, Daniel Robinson of this co, a single person/Sale of horses, sheep, cows at late dwelling plantation of Benjamin Parvin - Samuel Troth

224. ESHM Dec 26 1797/Sarah Turner exec of John Turner, late of Talb Co

225. ESHM Jan 2 1798/Letters remaining at P.O. Easton: Jane Blair, Cambridge; John Blake, Wye Neck; Solomon Brown, near Denton; Mary Barry; Thomas Bruff; Robert Bruff; James Bateman; Robert Bewley, bricklayer; Charles K. Bryan, Cambridge; Henry Banning; Dr. James Bordley; James Bowdle; Manaen Bull, Broad Creek; Richard Barnaby Junr; John Boyer, Cambridge; Henry Clift; Crane & Moore, Dorset; Sarah Collister; Lydia Cox; John Corrie, Tuckahoe Bridge; James Corrie, Tuckahow Bridge; James Condon, Cambridge; Peter Cornis, Cambridge; Charles Dickinson; James Dawson; Sarah Dawson; Thomas Dawson; James Davan; Joshua Driver; Peter Denny; Charles Emory; John Erskine; John Edmondson; William Frazier; Henrietta Frazier; Samuel Gossage; Charles Gibson, Caroline Goldsborough; Thomas Gordon; Baillay Gaddes; John Heynes; Thomas Harrison; William Hoffman; Robert Hay, St Michaels; Solomon Higgens, merchant; Edward Higgins, merchant; William Hayward; George R. Hayward; James Hull; Dr. Andrew Hall; Thomas Hughlett; Isaac Smith Isaacs; Dr. Stephen T. Johnson; John Jones; Rosannah Kelly care of Capt Ewing; Lodge No. 5, Easton; Lodge No. 5, Cambridge; John Leonard; Jacob Loockerman; Robert Lewis; William Lowry; James Muir, Easton; George Martin, Choptank Bridge; Thomas Oldham Martin; John Mullikin; Benjamin Massey; Samuel McKean; Levin Marshal; Tristram Martin; John Mosock, blacksmith, Cambridge; Tilton Newcome; Tristram Needles; Mr. Newman; William Nelson, Caroline; James Nabb; Robert Neale; Samuel Nicols; John Othoson; Samuel Poor; John Pirtt, shipcarpenter, Denton; Abner Parrot; James Price; Amasa Robinson; Henry Somerville; Dr. John Smyth; Simon Smyth; Levin Speddin; Speddin & Martin; Perry Spencer; William Spencer; Peggy Stevens; Alexander Stevens, Dorset; James Sulivain; Joshua Taggart; Dekar Thompson; Rees Thomson; John Thomas, Head of Wye; James Thomas, near Trappe; Mary Vallant, Deep Neck; George H. Wagner, near the West Branch of Delaware river; Rev Charles Wheeler; William Wilson; Robert Wilson; James Wainwright; Dr. Edward White; Ludwick Wainer; John Young, Tuckahoe/Tract for sale in Talb Co adj lands of Peter Edmondson at Dover Ferry formerly occupied by Richard Glover of Dorch Co and by him transferred to Philip McManus, at present the property of the McManus heirs - John Edmondson, near Easton

226. ESHM Jan 9 1798/Richard Trippe, Bailey's Neck, Talb Co, offers reward for mulatto man, Ned, age 29/Peter Sharp detained in Balt by ice/Firday 29 ult negro man, property of Mrs. Dunn, Kent Co, was executed at ChesterTown for rape/Edward Markland has just opened his English school at the house occuped last year by Samuel Clayton in Easton

227. ESHM Jan 16 1798/Chancery sale by John Elder Gist, trustee, of house in Cambridge, property of Patrick Kelly, dec; order served on Thomas Woolford

228. ESHM Mar 6 1798/Thomas Cuthcart refuses to pay on certain of his notes won of him by gaming/Partnership of Charles Gully & Thomas Cuthcart dissolved/ Amos Robinson, Oxford Neck, exec of Daniel Robinson, late of Talb Co/George Baily has just received a quantity of clover seed and medicines/Sarah Troup, Easton, has house for rent/Joseph Turner exec of George Dudley/William Boon, Denton, exec of Thomas Boon/George Dawson admin of Impey Dawson, late of Talb Co, dec

229. ESHM Mar 13 1798/Sale at the late dwelling house of Woolman Gibson, dec, of Talb Co, including his mill & mill seat - Jacob Gibson, agent/Sale of estate of General John Cadwalader, Kent Co, Md, called Shrewsbury Farm, about 1900 a. - Archibald McCall Junr

230. ESHM Mar 20 1798/Edward Cox, sheriff Talb Co, offers reward for men who broke the gaol of Talb Co: Charles the property of William Perry, age about 30; Will, the property of Nicholas Martin who has been seen in Dorset Co; a white man, Jacob Townsend, age about 24, formerly fifer for the company in Easton, supposed to be lurking about the Clash's near Ivy Town, as he lived with Rachel Armstrong last year. Deliver to Samuel Swann, gaol keeper or the sheriff/John McCulloh and Edward Pannell, Princess Ann, exec, to hold sale in the store house of the late James McCulloh, dec/Whereas I, William Hughlett, did some years ago purchase from Joseph Sedwick Dixon, lands in Caroline Co ...(responds to accusation the he obtained lands improperly)/Nicholas Watts, Ferry Neck, offers services of horse, Brilliant, to stand at William Watts', Easton and Mr. John Kersey's, Bay-Side/William Bond intends to remove from Easton this year/Chancery sale of tracts in Somerset Co, named Labour in Vain & Beard Tree Ridge of 220 3/4 a. which were conveyed by Col. John Done to the late John Denwood - John Wilkins, trustee/William Meluy requests payment of debts/William Goldsborough admin of Mary Ann Goldsborough

231. ESHM Mar 27 1798/Philemon H. Able, near the Trappe, offers the services of his horse, Escape, sold to Able by William Lyles, wit: Enoch M. Lyles/James Bowdle collector of the tax for Talb Co/Bowdle & Needles have declined their business

232. ESHM Apr 10 1798/Mr. O'Duhigg, a french gentleman, intends to open a dancing school at Easton/David Kerr, Easton admin of Jacob Gibson, late of Talb Co, dec/Robert Ewing at Vienna is selling lands on Nanticocke river adj lands of David Smith/William Chambers who intends to leave this place in a few weeks, requests debts be paid/Edward Harris admin of William Dickinson, to sell at Queens-Town a negro boy of the estate/James Corrie admin of John Corrie late of Talb Co, dec/Farm for lease on Wye River, 1 1/4 miles from Robert Williams' and Gibson's mill - Thomas Carslake

233. ESHM Apr 17 1798/James Clayland insolvent debtor/700 a. for sale on Wye River - C. T. Wederstrandt, QA Co/James Ringgold selling the property he now occupies in Chester-Town/Joshua Kennard, Centre-Ville Mills, QA Co, has horses for sale/Chancery case: Charles Lecompte and John Tootell against John Willy, Thomas Willy (infant who lives out of state) and Amelia Willy, heirs of Pritchet Willy of Dorch Co regarding land: Marsh Pasture and The Meadows/ Chancery sale of real estate of Robert Brown by William Richmond/Noble Wright dec, exec of Edward Wright, late of Dorch Co/Edward Harris admin of Robert Baxter

234. APM Mar 26 1793/Thomas Bruff, gold & silversmith, Chestertown/Peter Kirkwood, gold & silversmith, Chestertown, in the shop where Mr. Piper formerly lived/Sale of woodland on the main road from Chestertown to Chruchhill, pursuant of the last will of John Brown dec - John Lambert Wilmer, QA Co/Elizabeth Scott admin of Dr. John Scott, Chestertown/William Worth has opened a boarding house in High St, Chestertown

235. APM Apr 2 1793/James Claypoole resigns as Justice of the Peace of Kent Co/S. Wilmer of Edward, Worton, requests persons indebted to Richard Graves, dec, to make payment/James Ringgold senr, Kent Co, offers reward for negro woman, Hagar, age about 21

236. APM Apr 5 1793/Interrred on Sun in Christ Church burying-ground the remains of David Hall, eldest son of William Hall, painter, in the 19th year of his age

237. APM Apr 9 1793/Sale of a negro boy by James Wroth, Chestertown/Liberty (horse) will stand at the subscriber's mill - S. Wilmer

238. APM Apr 12 1793/Bajazet will stand at Daniel Perkins's mill - Richard Ricand

239. APM Apr 16 1793/Mr. Curley advertises to the ladies and gentlemen of Chestertown and vicinity that he is opening a dancing school at William Mansell's

240. APM Apr 19 1793/Partnership of Gerrish & Saunders dissolved; in the future this paper will be conducted by Robert Saunders Junr

241. APM Apr 23 1793/Members of the Abolition Society will meet at the Methodist Meeting House, Chestertown - Abraham Ridgely, sec'y/Daniel MacCurtin sec'y to Washington College Visitors and Governors/Household furniture for sale by Simon Wilmer of Edward and William Graves, Worton

242. APM Apr 26 1793/Jonathan Hodgson, Chestertown is taking a few boys to board and lodge/John Thompson, QA Co, has a threshing mill/Sale of 200 a. lying upon Red-Lion Branch QA Co adj lands of Joseph Comokin in tenure of Mr. Johnson; also 120 a. pt of tract, Harris's Rambles, lying on road from Dixon's tavern to Dover and about 1 mile from Thomas Rolph's - William Garnett/William Embleton at Howel's Point Kent Co Md, offers reward for negro man, Phil, age about 40; his wife is free, living on the plantation of Joseph George or at his sister's who lives at or near Sandtown.

243. APM Apr 30 1793/"...my wife Margaret Holding has eloped from my bed and board - John Holding "

244. APM May 3 1793/Samuel T. Wright, QA Co, exec of N. S. T. Wright QA Co/ Joel Brown has set up a hatting business in the shop lately occupied by Joseph Hodgson at Dover

245. APM May 10 1793/Died Tues evening last, Richard Willis in Kent Co/Sale of a lot at Head of Chester adj lands of Dr. John Thomas & Joseph Wilkinson; apply to William Thomas or John Fox, Centreville

246. APM May 17 1793/Died 25 Apr after a long and lingering illness, Dr. Zabdiel Potter of Caroline Co in the 46th year of his age/Packet from Chestertown to Balt - John Constable and James Piper, Chestertown/...my wife Ann Newman has eloped from my bed and board - Daniel Newman

247. APM May 24 1793/Anthony Philbin from Balt has opened a dry goods store lately occupied by Simon Wilmer/Daniel Hoffman, Chestertown, offers reward for an apprentice boy, John Wilkins, about 19 or 20, 5 feet 3 or 4 inch high, well

set, dark curled short hair

248. APM May 31 1793/Thomas Worrell, clerk of the commissioners of the tax for Kent Co

249. APM Jun 4 1793/Samuel Beck junr, Chestertown, to open a singing school

250. APM Jun 11 1793/Chancery sale at James Ralph's, Chestertown (2 lots) - Martha Gould, trustee

251. APM Jun 21 1793/Benjamin Chambers, clerk of Levy Court, Chestertown/ Philip Reed exec of Richard Willis/John M. Moore, John Bolton, Chestertown, admin of John Bolton, late of Chestertown/Sale of 508 1/4 a. on Corsica Creek in sight of Centreville - James Earle, Chestertown/Benjamin Walmsley has commenced a cartwright business and ploughmaking business in Chestertown opp Thomas Bruff's

252. APM Jul 5 1793/Letters remaining at P.O. Chestertown: Thomas Bruff; Ann Cobourn; Daniel Denning, Kent Co; Isaac Elbert Kent Co; William Elben; Sidney George; Daniel & James Groome, Langford's Bay; Matthew Hawkins care of Robert Anderson; RichardHealy, Kings-Town, Queen Ann's care of Samuel Rochester; Jean Hicks care of Widow Kemp; John Kay on board the ship Mary Ann; James McClean; Susanna Medford; James or Thomas Maslin or John Lamb, Kent Co; Francis D. Pastorius on board the Mary-Ann; James Ringgold; George Raisin near Chestertown; George Skirvin, Chestertown; Elizabeth Thompson, Chester river; John Weathered near Chestertown; Simon Wilmer near Chestertown; Bazilla Yewell; all letters are directed for Chestertown except thoses noted./James Piper, Chestertown, to remove to Balt Town;to rent his dwelling house, store houses, and granary/David Hull, Chestertown has a good assortment of saddlery/Susanna Dugan, Abraham Ridgely, admin of William Dugan, late of Chestertown, dec

253. APM Jul 9 1793/John Lamb the 3d carrying on the saddle manufactory at the sign of the Saddle in Market-Street, a few doors above Water-street

254. APM Jul 16 1793/Wants to purchase a number of negroes - Thomas Alexander Cecil Cross Roads

255. APM Jul 19 1793/M. Boudier, painter, now in Washington College, will teach drawing to such person of both sexes as are desirous of learning it - 10 dollars a guarter in which he will give 24 lessons/Chandeliers from Cape Francois as low as one Guinea per pair - J. Curley, Chestertown/Rebecca Dunn, Chestertown, admin of William Dunn Kent Co, dec

256. CGM Jul 26 1793/Meeting at Mr. Worrel's tavern to consider contributing to the relief of the unfortunate inhabitants of Capt-Francois/John Scott denies making a toast opposing the President of the U. S. for the 4th of July/ "A citizen" makes a charge against Rev. Colin Ferguson/Thanks to Mr. Dumoulain for his generous donation to the pensioners under my care - W. Biggs/Nathan Smyth, Stephen Smyth, exec of Hynson Smith, late of Kent Co/A lot for sale by James Yardsley, Church-Hill, where he now lives/A ball at Mr. Mansel's; the subscriptions remain open at Mrs. Dunn's

257. CGM Jul 30 1793/Lots for sale adj Georgetown Cross Roads; apply to William Manwill near the Cross Roads - Philip Reed/"Any person who is in the possession of a small book, bound in blue leaves, intitled 'Baron Steuben's Instructions to Young Officers," with the name of William B. Raisin, or the subscribers name written therein, are requested to leave it at the office of the subscriber, Philip Reed"

258. CGM Aug 9 1793/Wheras my wife Ann Taylor hath eloped from my bed and board ... John Taylor/James Blackiston, insolvent debtor/Thomas Ringgold finds his domestic busines "deprives me of the pleasure of being a candidate at the

next election..."/Donaldson Yeates, Turner's-Creek requests settlement of accounts regarding his dry goods business

259. CGM Aug 13 1793/Died Sun 4th inst at Chesterfield QA Co on the 16th yr of her age Miss Eliza Browne, the eldest dau of the late Robert Browne of Queen-Ann's/Benjamin Porter, Sasafras Neck, Caecil Co, offers reward for strayed horse/Sheriff's sale to be held at the Market-House in Chestertown of the land belonging to Kinvin Wroth Junr, lying in Kent Co on road from I. U. Church to Worton

260. CGM Aug 30 1793/Jere. Nicols, mouth of Langford's Bay, Kent Co, states "appeared at this place a swarm of Hessian Flies, so numerous as to cover the whole of my farm: they were of all sizes, from a gnat to the largest house fly, their course was to the southward."/Committed to the jail of Kent Co a negro man who calls himself Jack, age about 30 - Philip Reed, Sheriff/Isaac Dawson, Chestertown, has removed to the house lately occupied by Rebecca Dunn as an Inn, in Market-Street, opp the Church, where he carries on the Hatting Business/ Thomas Deford junr, Chestertown, requests payment of debts/300 bushels of wheat, property of William Maxwell, late of Kent Co, dec, to be sold by sheriff/ Jonathan Hodgson, Chestertown, requests payment of debts; also to let tavern and stage house where he now lives/Joshua Vansant, Head of Chester, admin of Thomas Lord, dec

261. CGM Sep 3 1793/Robert Wright not a candidate for the ensuing election/ To rent house - William McKenny, Chestertown/James Rolph, Chestertown, to open night school

262. CGM Sep 13 1793/Died Wed last about 7 o'clock in the evening, Mrs. Elizabeth Worrell wife of Thomas Worrell of this town in the 26th year of her age; she left a husband, infant dau and numerous relatives and acquaintances/ At a meeting of inhabitants of Chestertown it was resolved that William Slubey, James Smith, Capt John Nicholson, John Sturgis, John Lorain, James Piper and Tobias Ashmore would be the committee of Health and Inspection ... whereas expenses have already been incurred in the burial of Mrs. Cully who is supposed to have died of the aforesaid disorder, and other expenses ... resolved that Daniel McCurtin to be appointed to collect from the inhabitants such sums as may be necessary ... Samuel Chew, chariman, Chestertown/To let tanyard at the Head of Chester now occupied by William Glasgow; apply to Wilson & Hoopes at the Head of Chester or to the subscriber in Phila - Joshua Gilpin/Robert Walmsley Junr, Sassafras Neck, Caecil Co, offers reward for stolen horse

263. CGM Sep 17 1793/John Lynch who will continue in Kent Co for 3 weeks, invites those who have clocks that stand need of repair to leave them at Thomas Worrell's tavern/Edward Ireland forewarns person from harboring his negro man, Caleb/Charles Hackett, watch and silver smith business in Chestertown/Isaac Connell, Bay side, Kent Co, offers reward for negro woman, Easter, age about 40, formerly property of Robert Meeks

264. CGM Sep 20 1793/Samuel Chew replaced by Doctor Andrew Wisenthal as chairman of the Chestertown meeting. Resolved that David Hull and William McKenny be added to the Committee of Health & Inspection ...Resolved that Capt. Philip Reed, Philip Chaplin, Daniel McGinnis and James Rolph to enroll persons capable of bearing arms...(to prevent the spread of yellow fever)/ Thomas Little admin of John Little, dec

265. CGM Sep 24 1793/Sale in Worton Neck at the late dwelling house of William Betts dec, farming utensils, cows, oxen - Thomas Betts, admin/John Newell, Stillpond, to petition for a road leading from the main road that leads down Stillpond-Neck, over the head of Stillpond-Creek, until it shall intersect the main road at the head of Churn-Creek

266. CGM Sep 27 1793/John Cuff, Chestertown, offers reward for stolen mare

267. CGM Oct 1 1793/James M. Anderson and Abraham Ridgely, Chestertown, requests payment of debts

268. CGM Oct 4 1793/Died Wed morning in an advanced age, Mrs. Sarah Beck consort of Samuel Beck of this county/Chancery sale of property of Thomas Smyth, insolvent debtor, to be held at the house of John Rolph in Chestertown, the lots in Chestertown except at present subject to the life estate of Mrs. Arnold wife of John Arnold dec; also 500 a. in Kent Co - James Ringgold, trustee requests settlement of debts to Thomas Smyth or Thomas Smyth and Sons

269. CGM Oct 8 1793/Died Sun morning last in this town Miss Peggy Kirkwood, a young lady/Sale of 770 a. in Sassafras Neck, Caecil Co, known as Hall's Island. Francis H. Rozer, P.G.Co/William Glasgow has removed from Head of Chester to Georgetown, to the tan-yard belonging to Mrs. Wright where he means to carry on the tanning business

270. CGM Oct 15 1793/Drawing lessons by Mr. Boudier at Charles Farrow's opp the play-house/Mr. Cotelle will open a night's Franch School, Chestertown/ Lands for sale: Lance's Addition and Kinnamont's Outlett in Caroline Co, Dawson's Neck in QA Co, New Port and New Port Addition in QA Co; apply to Reuben Gilder, Balt or James Kent merchant QA Co/Samuel Sutton, Kent Co, offers reward for negro fellow, Andrew, age about 22/Sale of sole leather - David Crane/William Burneston, Chestertown had removed his goods to the store house lately occupied by James Piper/Letters remaining at P.O. Chestertown: Major James Clayland, Chestertown; John Sothern, Churchhill; Rev Mr. Jenkins, Newtown; Edward Wright, Kent Co; Darius Gambel, Kent Co; John Ireland, Kent Co; Margaret Roseter, Roe's Cross-Roads; William Ponder, Kent Co; Peter Flodwill, Chestertown; Betsey Scott, Chestertown; Daniel Clancey, Chestertown; William Anderson, Chestertown; Archibald Foster, Hunting Creek; Zerobabel Hughs, Buck-Neck; Samuel Folwell, Chestertown; James Spur, Kent Co; John Armstrong, Church-hill; John Dugan junr, Chestertown; Joseph Everitt, Kent Co; Andrew Spur, QA Co; James Butcher, Church-hill

271. CGM Oct 18 1793/Rachel Apsley responds to a report circulated through the county wherein she is charged with the death of Edward Apsley. Witness: Rachel March; also a statement by John Groome/Sale at Shipping Point in Quaker Neck, horses, cows, farming utensils - Francis Maslin

272. CGM Nov 1793/Partnership of Perkins and Ward dissolved - Ebenezer Perkins Junr, Kent Co/Mark Ward warns that Ebenezer Perkins was premature in the above advertisement; partnership not yet legally dissolved/Sale of house-hold furniture at the house Mr. Wroth in Chestertown - Robert Kent

273. CGM Nov 5 1793/Chancery case - Elizabeth Spier and William Thomas against George Turner, Eleanor Turner and Martha Turner, heirs of Margaret Turner dec; tracts in Kent Co: Cun Whitten or Came Whitten and Chance, Bottom Meadow adj lands of William Wilson and Ephraim Vansant - James Ringgold/Sale at the late dwelling house of William Eccleston, dec, horses, cows, sheep, hogs, negroes - Samuel Eccleston/Samuel T. Wright, QA Co, exec of N. S. T. Wright to sell his lands in QA Co and Kent Co Del/James Piper, Balt, requests payment be made to him or to John Bolton, Chestertown/Chancery sale of the estate of William Copper, late of Kent Co - Darius Copper, Charles Neal,

-46-

Kent Co, trustees/The Volunteer Company of Chestertown and its vicinity are
requested to meet at the usual place of parade on Saturday next ... Philip
Reed, Capt. Vol. /Starling Thomas announces the prize for a horse race/House
number 89 in Chestertown for sale - Apply to John Sutton or Isaac McHard

274. CGM Nov 12 1793/Died Fri last in Kent Co, Mrs. Sarah Ringgold, consort
of James Ringgold Senior/Sale on the farm where the subscriber now lives,
horses, cows, sheep, hogs, and farming utensils - William Coleman/Chancery
decree to approve the sale of real estate of John Gleaves, dec, by Nathaniel
Comegys and John Scott, be approved/Committed to the jail of Kent Co, negro
man, Denis; he says he belongs to Richard Bassett of Delaware/Samuel Crouch,
exec of William Dooley, late of Kent Co, dec, to sell house of William Dooley
in Chestertown/Samuel Gould, near Church-hill, offers reward for negro man,
Simon, age about 32

275. CGM Nov 15 1793/James Tilghman, William Tilghman, Chestertown, exec of
James Tilghman, late of Chestertown, dec/Elijah Cole, near Middltwown in St.
George's Hundred, Delaware, offers reward for stolen mare

276. CGM Nov 22 1793/Died 15th ult at his seat near Port-Tobacco, John
Hanson senr aged 84. He left a very worthy woman languishing on her sick
bed with whom he lived in a married state 61 years: they brought up many
respectable children/Died Sat 19th ult at his house in P. G. Co, Doctor
Richard Burgess, aged about 34 years/Sale of property in Chestertown, at
present occupied by William Worth, at upper end of High Street. Apply to
Doctor Worrell, Chestertown/John Anderson, QA Co, requests the return of
borrowed books

277. CGM Nov 26 1793/Sale at the dwelling house of the subscriber near
Massy's Cross Roads of negroes, horses, cows, sheep, hogs, and farming
utensils - Daniel T. Massey/John Waltham, Henry Stewart, Kent Co, exec of
John Stewart, late of Kent Co, dec

278. CGM Nov 29 1793/Died Sun last in the 59th year of his age, Alexander
Crabbin and on the Monday following his youngest son aged 14 years/Henry
Holtzman, Chestertown, has removed to High Street opposite to Messrs. Lorain
and Arnott's Store where he carries on the boot and shoe making business

279. CGM Dec 13 1793/Elizabeth McClure admin of Thomas McClure/Sale of the
farm near Easton pursuant to the last will of William McCallum late of Talb
Co, part of Mount Hope, part of Proprietary Manor - John Needles exec/
Charles Farrow, cabinet and chair maker, has removed his shop into High
Street, opposite to Starling Thomas's tavern

280. CGM Dec 17 1793/Bonds lost; if found please leave with Jonathan
Hodgson, Chestertown/Mary Van Dyke offers reward for the discovery of the
person who "broke open my Granary and stole from thence a quantity of wheat."

281. CGM Dec 31 1793/Chancery sale of tracts in Kent Co, late the property
of William Hanson, dec, tracts which the deceased purchased of Robert Little
- Simon Wilmer of Edward, trustee, Kent Co

284. ESHM Apr 24 1798/Edward Turner, Head of Wye, admin of John Allen Reed, late of Talb Co, dec/Joseph Dawson, Easton, requests information on mislaid subscription papers for contracting the payment of an assistant bailiff for this town/J. E. Muse, Cambridge, has farms for rent/Thomas Baxter, Kent Island, offers reward for negro man, Philip Seney, age about 27

285. ESHM May 1 1798/Married Sun 22nd ult, John Harwood, Talb Co, to Miss Mary Brewer of Annapolis/Daniel Nichols, near Hunting Creek, Dorch Co, seeks a tanner & currier/James Parrott admin of William Parrott, late ot Talb Co/ Miss Ann Smith, milliner, late from Balt, to open shop at Mrs. Mary Dawson's in Easton/Richard Newman, Easton, offers services of horse, Young Bazet, raised near Easton whose sire Old Bazet was owned by John Jones, near Easton, wit: Edward Wilkins/Peter Willis exec Joshua Willis, late Dorch Co, dec; Peter Willis requests claims against estate of Charles Willis, late of Caroline Co, be made to him or to Joshua Willis/Letters remaining at P.O. Easton: Samuel Baldwin; Thomas & William Boon, Denton; Anthony Boyle, Talb Court House; Robert Bewley, bricklayer; William Burtt, Caroline Co; Andrew Colbreath or Thomas Higgison, care of Dr. Tootel of Dorch Co; James Earle; Mrs. Sarah Ennalls, Dorch Co; John Field, Easton; Charles Goldsborough, Horn's Point; Peter Gordon, Cambridge; Mary Glenn, Caroline Co; Mrs. Greentree, Easton; Henry Haskins; Robert Hay; James Hanson, Denton; John Kealachan, care of Thomas McBurney, Easton; Hugh Lindsay; Nathan Ladday; John McLaran; Benjamin Mullican; Solomon Martin; George Medford; Joseph R. Neal, Denton; Robert Neale, near Easton; William Potter; Dr. Nathaniel Potter; Mr. Prince; Messrs. Speddin & Martin; Edward Stevens; Thomas or Adam Smith, state of Virginia, near Talbot Court House; Doctor John Smith; Horace Smith; James Stanley; Sheriff of Dorch Co; William Skinner; William Thompson; Ross Thomson; Mrs. Nancy Truitt, St. Michaels; Samuel Wilson, Head of Wye; James Wainwright; Hugh Work; John Woods, Easton

286. ESHM May 8 1798/On Fri last 4th day inst, died after a painful and perfect resignation in the 54th year of his age John Tibbels of this co/James Willson junr, Easton, requests debtors of Byus & Willson to make payment to himself or Samuel Casson/Benjamin Hatcheston, sheriff Kent Co, has committed to gaol, a negro man, Squire, who says he belongs to Thomas Law of Federal City/Ann Barton, mantua-maker from Balt, living in Dover St opposite Mr. Goldsborough's office

287. ESHM May 15 1798/Died John Logan on Wed evening last, merchant of this town/Henry Ennalls, Dorch Co, has 700 a. for sale between Cambridge & Ennalls Ferry

288. ESHM May 22 1798/Meeting in Centreville of committee of James Tilghman, Joshua Sweeney, Joseph Hopper Nicholson, Richard Tilghman Earle and William Carmichael to prepare a letter to the President of the U. S./John Henry exec of Richard Kennard, late of Caroline Co, requests payment of debts to him or Henry Coursey of Choptank Bridge

289. ESHM Jun 12 1798/Married Sun last by Rev Bowie, Dr. Nathaniel Potter of Caroline Co to Miss Kitty Goldsborough of Talb Co/Bennett Wheeler, Easton, admin of John Logan/W. Dawson, Miles River Neck, offers reward for negro woman, Esther, age about 25, with 2 yr old boy; husband is Phill Seney, a sawyer who belongs to Thomas Baxter, Kent Island

290. ESHM Jun 19 1798/Edward Cox, sheriff Talb Co, offers reward for white man, John Bootman, who escapted from gaol

291. ESHM Jun 26 1798/Alexander Maxwell, Eliza Maxwell, Caroline Co, admin of William Gibson, merchant late of Caroline Co, dec/Negro man, George Buly, age about 20, who says he was sold by John Tubman, Dorch Co, to a North Caroline man, is confined at gaol in Easton/Mrs. Williams has received the

whole of her London Spring Fashions (millinery)/Peggy Nichols admin of Major
Joseph Nicols Caroline Co to hold sale at Federalsburgh of a variety of
merchantdize/Samuel Swan, living at North West Fork, offers reward for negro
Dick, age about 25, lately purchased of William Goldsborough of Talb Co/Sale
of farm adj lands of Capt Christopher Birckhead a few miles above Chancellor's
Ferry - John Goldsborough, Cambridge

292. ESHM Jul 3 1798/Jean Green admin of Valentine Green, dec, to hold sale
at Hillsborough, Caroline Co, all the goods & merchandize remain on hand/L.
Bowdle admin of Henry Bowdle, late of Talb Co

293. ESHM Jul 10 1798/Died Thurs last Edward Cox, sheriff of Talb Co/Arthur
Bryan, Head of Wye, offers reward for negro man, Dick, age about 45, a water-
man formerly in the service of Mr. Pace & Jacob age about 20/Patrick Mullikin,
Head of Island Creek, Talb Co, offers reward for negro man, Perry, age about 20

294. ESHM Jul 17 1798/Samuel Thomas, Talb Co, offers reward for negro man,
Frank, known as Martin Needle's Frank/Letters remaining in P.O. Easton:
Josiah Bayly, Cambridge; Thomas & William Boon, Denton; William Boon, Denton;
Thomas Boon, Denton; William Berry, Talb; Charles Bryan, Cambridge; Richard
B. Bewly; Capt John Bush(?); Henry Bowdle; William Bruff jun; James Booker;
John Bennett; Jonathan Bunnel, New Market; Samuel Barrow, Tuckahoe; John Voss
Baker, Gilpin's Point; Samuel Baldwin; Rachel Barnes, to be left with granny
Grace, the midwife; Edward Cox; James Crig, Cambridge; Robins Chamberlaine;
John Cottman jun; John Carrie; Michael B. Carroll; B etsy Cheasly; Petter
Denny; David Duff; James Dawson; General Eccleston; John Eccleston, Cambridge;
Doctor Samuel Elbert; Joseph Everitt; Robert Ewing; Charles Emory; Solomon
Frazier, Cambridge; William Goldsborough, Cambridge; Catharine Goldsborough,
Talb; Thomas Goldsborough; Mathew Griffith; Obediah Garey; Margaret Gardiner;
Isaac Horsey; Solomon or Thomas Jones, Talb; Nicholas Killum; Moses Lecompte,
Cambridge; John Laverty, care of Peter Redhead; Robert G. Livingston; Jacob
Lockerman; Solomon Lowe; Dr. John Murray; William B. Martin; Thomas O. Martin;
Daniel McDonald; John Maclane; Rachel Mingo; Joseph R. Neele, Denton; Tristram
Needles; John Price jun, care of J. Earle; Thomas Parrott; Ritty Pamphelion,
Oxford; William Perry; William Robertson Cambridge; Edward Roberts; John
Roberts; James Steele; Henry Steele; William Skinner; James Shaw; Samuel Swan;
Simmons & Harper at the Nine Bridges; Samuel Stevens, care of M. Wainer; Ross
Thomson; Dekar Thompson; Lloyd Tilghman; Sherwood; Edward Turner; Ezekiel
Vickars, Dorset; The Vestry of St. Peter's Parish; The Vestry of St. Michaels
Parish; Joseph Wilkison; Cornelius West/John Sheppard, gold & silver smith
has opened shop in the house lately occupied by Messrs Bowdle & Needles in
Easton/Denwood Turpin, Somerset Co, to petition under the insolvency act

295. ESHM Jul 24 1798/Moses Allen, Talb Co, has plantation for sale, 3 miles
from Easton/Chancery sale of farm on which Major James Clayland now dwells
which John Gibson, trustee, sold to him for benefit of creditors of James
Clayland/R. Chamberlaine, Balt, offers reward for negro man, Jesse, age about
24, formerly property of Adam Muir, sold in Balt by Thomas Baily, supposed to
be in neighborhood of James Muir's near Vienna

296. ESHM Jul 31 1798/Land for sale 4 miles from Cratcher's Ferry, Dorch Co,
adj lands of David Smith - John Reed/George Baily, druggist & apothecary/
Jonathan Benny watch & clock maker, has opened shop in house fromerly occupied
by Greenbury Goldsborough as an office/James Earle junr has lots in Easton for
sale/Peregrine Tilghman, Talb Co, offers reward for horse strayed from farm
of Henry Nicols, near Easton/Houses for rent in Lewistown, Talb Co - John
Vickers/John R. Bromwell, offers reward for negro man, Isaac, formerly property of Joseph Haskins of Easton

297. ESHM Aug 7 1798/Married Thurs last at Perry Hall on St. Michaels River
by Rev Doctor Bowie, William Bedingfield Smyth to Miss Mary Hindman Perry

-49-

daughter of Hon'ble William Perry/Samuel Poor to petition under the insolvency act/Mary Cruckshank, Joseph Hynson, Mary Hynson, to apply to Kent Co Court to mark and bound the tract, Jamaica in Kent Co

298. ESHM Aug 14 1798/On Thurs morning last was found the body of Francis Lambdin, Talb Co, who drowned the evening before near the shore of the Eastern Bay, opposite his own house on the Bay-side; he left a wife and several children/Thomas Tongue, Herring Bay, AA Co, offers reward for negro man, Abraham, age about 38; he has been in Talb Co; changed his name to Samuel Lloyd; his wife Maria was liberated by Richard Dudley and now lives on Mr. William P. Clarke's farm, lying on Tuckahoe Creek..."I am informed that he is frequently employed by Henry Durdan of QA Co/Samuel Nicols, Easton, offers his services in the commission line/William Rose requests debts be paid to partnership of Rose & Jocobs/Farm for rent where late Doctor Kemp formerly res; apply to Samuel Barrow, Hillsborough, or Doctor Baynard Wilson on the premises

299. ESHM Aug 21 1798/Died 14 inst in the 23rd year of her age after a tedious illness, Mrs. Elizabeth Goldsborough wife of Charles Goldsborough junr of Dorch Co and daughter of Hon. Robert Goldsborough   buried in St. Paul's burying ground/Rev Bishop Claggett will attend White Marsh Church on 2 Sep to administer the confirmation/Alexander Smith, Vienna, Dorch Co, offers reward br strayed mare/William Boon, Denton, to let a dwelling house in Denton/House for rent in Denton, well calculated for a tavern and store - John A. Sangston, Denton/John Thomas junr, sheriff Talb Co, has committed to gaol negro man, Charles, who says he was fromerly property of Mrs. Nancy Clayton, Northumberland Co, Va and late in the possession of Capt John Crawley, same Co/Thoams Townsend, near the Oak, offers reward for strayed mare

300. ESHM Sep 4 1798/James Nabb Talb Co, offers reward for negro man, Paris/ House for rent in Easton, Mark Benton, Kent Island, QA Co; apply to Charles Gulley, Easton/Henry Hollyday, Talb Co, seeks overseer/H. Waggaman, Cambridge, to let planation above New Market/Involved in political argument in Caroline Co are Edward Oldham Clark; Charles Frazer; Joshua Seney; Lemuel Purnell; William Chambers, QA Co; Jona Brady; Ross Thompson -"a drunken school master;" Henrietta Price, Caroline Co; Andrew Price; James Brown; Richard T. Earle/ Catharine Jackson has opened a school in Easton opposite the printing office/ Peter Redhead, Easton, surviving partner of James Hall, to petition under the insolvency act/Thomas Walter, Vienna, to petition under the insolvency act/ Daniel Swiggett to petition under the insolvency act/Thomas Nicols, Federalsburgh, candidate for the General Assembly

301. ESHM Sep 11 1798/James Wilson junr to petition under the insolvency act/ James Magoffin has bee assigned goods, books, bonds etc. of the firm of Byus & Willson/Died Tues evening last after a severe illness, Thomas Oldham Martin, atty at law, age 25 yrs last July/Mary Harrison admin of Richard Harrison, dec, Talb Co, near Tuckahoe Creek to sell property by order of Orphan's Court of AA Co/Benjamin Garnett & Joseph McHard, Church Hill, QA Co, to petition under the insolvency act

302. ESHM Sep 18 1798/John Edmundson, Talb Co, candidate for General Assembly/ John Vickers, Talb Co, candidate for House of Delegates/William Stenson comments regarding the political conversation of Joshua Seney & George Finley in Stenson's store/Married Sun evening last by Rev Bowie, James Wilmor, merchant of Centreville to Miss Nancy Emerson of this town/Thomas Hardcastle to petition to open navigation in Choptank river from Choptank Bridge at Greensborough to mouth of Thomas Goldsborough's branch/Nathan Gregg Bryson & Roney to petition under the insolvency act/George Medford, John Gale, Rasin Gale to petition for public road from Worton manor (formerly property of Richard Lloyd, dec) to main road leading from Worton Neck to Centre-Ville/ Richard Rochester, QA Co, to petition under the insolvency act/Ann Ellis to

petition for payment for services rendered by her late husband, Robert Ellis
who belonged to the 2nd Maryland Militia Regt/Joseph Phillips admin of William
Phillips, late of Dorch Co/Samuel Stevens has just opened saddlery & harness
making business, Easton, opposite Solomon Corner's Tavern in Washington St

303. ESHM Sep 25 1798/James Hubbert Dorch Co to petition under the insolvency
act

304. ESHM Oct 2 1798/John L. Bozman hiring overseer for his farm at Third
Haven/Levin Birckhead selling horse and whisky at the store of James Birckhead/
Ebenezer Handy to petition under the insolvency act/James Wright makes state-
ment regarding the previous statements of Joshua Seney and George Finley at
Mr. Stinson's Store/Patrick McIntier, Wye Mill, offers reward for information
on the person who burnt down his house and granary/600 a. on Choptank river
between Cambridge and Ennall's Ferry for sale; plat may be seen at John E.
Gist's or Thomas Coleston's - Henry Ennalls, Dorch Co/Farm for rent in Caroline
Co adj lands of Isaac Purnell where Samuel Townsend now acts as overseer -
John Hughes, living near Miles River Ferry/John Warfield, QA Co, to petition
for relief under the insolvency act

305. ESHM Oct 9 1798/George Parker to petition to alter divisional county
road leading from Parker's Mill to Salisbury/Jacob Gibson to bestow corn on
poor widows of Talb Co through John Thomas at his house or mill (upper end of
county), William Lowery (lower end of county), Thomas L. Haddaway or Capt H.
Banning (Bayside) and William Rose (Easton)/Miniere, Easton, offers reward for
French, negro boy, Nelson, age about 15/John Harwood selling plantation where
he now lives adj Kingstown/Nancy Powell, Kings' Creek, admin of Howell Powell
junr, late Talb Co

306. ESHM Oct 16 1798/John W. Harrison, Talb Co, offers reward for two negro
men: Perry Caulder, age about 27, and Daulph Cornish, age about 22/Died Fri
last after a sudden illness at her dwelling in Oxford in the 66th year of her
age, Mrs. Elizabeth Peacock/Whereas my wife Scarborough has eloped from my
bed and board in 1792, since which time she has has 3 children by other men, I
will petition for divorce - Charles Heron, Dorch Co/Regarding a previous
notice for insolvency, I beg to inform the public that the aforesaid is Coln
Ebenezer Handy of Salisbury S. C. - Capt Ebenezer Handy/Henry Banning exec
Mrs. Peacock, Oxford

307. ESHM Oct 23 1798/Zebudiah Gregory notifies all persons having wood or
rails in his wood to take it away immediately; all persons are to bring a line
from me to receive the wood except for Samuel Edmondson/Storehous for rent,
lately occupied by James Birckhead & borther/Died Joshua Seney, QA Co, Sat
last; remains were interred at Church Hill on Mon following/Letters remaining
P.O. Easton: George Ash; Henry H. Allen, Dorset; James Ayres; John Bennett;
Miss Ayers; Thomas Bruff; James Bowdle; William Bishop; Mrs. Susan G. Bordley;
Nancy Clark (a black woman); Mr. Corner (a carpenter); John Crowder; The
Oxford Company; James Corsute; Thomas Cook; James Catrop; Christopher Driver;
Charles Downes; Peter Denny; Sarah Dawson; Mary Emory; Capt Samuel Elliott;
Charles Fleharty; Capt Joseph Farland; Hugh Flannagan; George Finlay; Charles
Gibson; Thomas Goldsborough; John Green; William Humphreys; John W. Harrison;
James Henegan; William Hindman; Ross Thomson; Francis Lambert; Patience
Lordmore; Capt Charles Lecompte; Isaac Logan; George Martin; Nicholas Martin;
Thomas Martin; William Malvol; Alexander Morrison; Tristram Needles; Isaac
Purnell; Henry Paritt; Dr. Potter; Perry Parret; Dr. Joseph Price; Rev.
Nicholas Pomp; John Roberts; Mitchell Russum; William Skinner; Thomas Stevens;
Joseph E. Sullivane; John Stevens; John Tillotson; James Toben; Richard
Tilghman, 5th; Col. John Vickers; Arthur Whitely; William Whitely; Rubin
Withgott, Dorset; Samuel Wilson/Chancery sale of plantation on north side of
Minikin River, Somerset Co which includes tracts: Moore & Cacett -

Littleton Dennis, trustee/Emory Sudler to petition under the insolvency act

308. ESHM Nov 20 1798/John Bowie will open grammar school in Easton/Races at New Market - Denwood Hicks, John Stevens/Charles Baker asks creditors, "Why will you run me to the enormous expence you have done, while I am making every honest measure to raise the cash ..."/Nimrod Maxwell, living in Kent Co Del, near Black Swamp, offers reward for horse strayed from Mrs. Hardcastle's mill near Tuckahoe Bridge/Joseph H. Nicholson candidate for House of Representatives of U. S./John Goldsborough junr candidate for House of Representatives/ Robert Elliott to open school in Easton/John Muir selling his plantation, 2 miles from Vienna/Plantation for rent of Charles Goldsborough junr, Cambridge, at the mouth of Hunting Creek, Caroline Co whereon Thomas Waddell is now overseer/John Tripp holding sale at the Trappe of a variety of dry goods

309. ESHM Nov 27 1798/Elizabeth Pickering & John Roberts admin of Robert Pickering, late of Talb Co

310. ESHM Dec 4 1798/Jesse Hopkins, taylor, has removed his shop in Easton opposit Doctor Moore's & nearly opposit Mr. Prince's Tavern in Washington St/ Samuel Barrow, Hillsborough, exec of Dr. William Kemp, to sell 4 negroes left as legacies to his daughter Eliza Kemp/Charles Baker, Chancellor's Point, requests payment of debts/House for rent lately occupied by Solomon Cornor in Easton as a tavern together with billiard table, stables-William Cornor/ Thomas Barnett of Dorch Co has plantation for sale in Dorch Co at Drawbridge/ Michael Ryan to epen school near John Thomas of Wye

311. ESHM Dec 11 1798/On Fri last Jacob Alborn, barber, of this town, terminated his existence by a pistol-ball through his head; the cause is unknown/ Whereas my wife Rosanna has eloped from my bed and board for some time and since cohabitted with other men ... I will petition for divorce. Stephen Christopher

312. ESHM Dec 18 1798/Died Mon 17th inst Edward Needles of Talb Co/Chancery sale of farm in Kent Co, late the res of John Turner, dec - William Spencer, trustee

313. ESHM Jan 29 1799/500 a. in Westmoreland Pa for sale - John Bush, Boolingbrook/Mary E. Goldsborough, Charles Goldsborough junr, Robert H. Goldsborough, exec of Robert Goldsborough, late of Talb Co/John Singleton, Talb Co, seeks teacher for small children/Negroes for sale - Perry E. Noel, Easton/William Watts junr, offers reward for strayed mare near Easton/John Lorain junr calling for subscriptions to fund fire engine/Apple brandy for sale - Francis Sellers, Hillsborough/James Rosberry, QA Co, near Rod Lyon Branch, offers reward for negro man, Phill, age about 32/Edward Lloyd forewarns persons from shooting on his land/Samuel Thomas reports items put on board Easton Packet, owner unknown

314. ESHM Feb 12 1799/Vestrymen of St Peter's Parish: John Singleton, Thomas Hayward; Edward Stevens; Samuel Chamberlaine; Samuel Nicols; Thomas Stevens; John Goldsborough - Joseph Jackson, Rector/Tristram Needles exec of Edward Needles, admin of John Needles, and William McKellum, late of Talb Co

315. ESHM Feb 19 1799/Luther Martin states opinion regarding the re-election of the acting sheriff/Farm for sale in the bottom of Dirty Neck, Talb Co, known as Long Point; apply to William Shield on the premises/Farm on Harris's Creek owned by Joseph Caulk, dec, to be sold-Henry Banning, Hugh Sherwood of Huntington, John Kersey, Wrightson Lambdin, as authorized by Talb Co Court/ Sale of 551 a. of plantation of John Muir, Dorch Co, seized at the suit of the U. S. - Jacob Graybill, Marshall, Balt/Chancery case - William Williams versus Ann, Sarah, and Dorothy Bozman, involving the sale of tracts: More & Cacett

316. ESHM Feb 26 1799/William B. Smyth admin of William Perry, Talb Co; Perry E. Noel intends to leave Easton; to sell house on Washington St where he now

-52-

esides/James Marchant senr offers reward for negro man, Tom, age about 23

317. ESHM Mar 5 1799/Sale of 540 a. in Caroline Co opposite Kingstown on Choptank river - John Dickinson, Talb Co

318. ESHM Mar 12 1799/Letters remaining at P.O. Easton: Thomas Abbott, Easton; John Bowers, near the Trappe, Talb; Brown & Holbrook, Choptank; Luranna Bruffit; John Craig, Dorset: Sarah Carsy; Charles Cox; James Catrupp; Elizabeth Coghlars at Ennalls Ferry; Henry Downes; Elizabeth Downes; Mathew Doyle; Capt Robert Dawson; James Dawson; Joseph Dawson; Michael, Benjamin or James Dorsey in Talb; Charles Emory; John Edmondson; Capt S. Farland; Solomon Frazier; Thomas M. Forman; James Goldsborough; Thomas Goldsoborough; Charles Gibson; John Green, Cambridge; Benjamin Hanson; Robert Hay; Charles Holland; Jacob & E. Handy; Richard Hayward; William Hamilton; Mathew Hawkins; Joseph Hanreckson; John Kain; Matthew Keane; William Knox; John Lindsay; John Laverty; Capt James Lloyd; Solomon Martin; Henry Martin; Tristram Martin; Nancy Marshall; Patrick McIntire; John Mullican; James Mackelvenney; The Master & Warden of Lodge No. 5; John Martin Needles; Andrew Orem; John Patterson; John Proud; Elijah Priget; Richard Patterson; John Purnell; Stephen Purnell; William Perrin; Samuel Quimby; William Robertson; Peter Rea; John Reed; Richard Sherwood; Richard E. Smith; Capt Thomas Smith; William Sewell; John Sanders/Daniel Trippe admin of Paul McIntire, dec, Dorch Co/George Noble exec of Nehemiah Noble, late of Talb Co, requests claims be presented at the Old Mill or Baley's Tavern/William Boon admin of Thomas Boon, late of Caroline Co dec/William Dimond admin of Sarah Kent

319. ESHM Mar 19 1799/Died Sat last after a tedious illness, Henry Bowdle of this town/Mary Moore, Thomas Robertson, Outerbridge Horsey, admin of William More, late of Cecil Co, dec, request creditors to meet at Mary Moore's on Bohemia Manor/Renting front of house of late Dr. Noel; inquire of Joseph Talford, Easton

320. ESHM Mar 26 1799/Levin Keene requests persons indebted to estate of Benjamin Keene of Transquaken, dec, to make payment/William Hindman, selling his dwelling plantation

321. ESHM Apr 2 1799/Tract for sale formerly property of Henry Parrott, dec, - William S. Bond; Married Sun evening last by Rev Bowie, Edward N. Hambleton to Miss Polly Sherwood, both of Talb Co/Thomas Bruff to operate in all branches of the dentist business/James Chaplain, Loftus Bowdle, admin of Henry Bowdle junr, late of Talb Co/John M. Anderson selling farm where he now lives on Fishing Creek, Dorch Co/For sale farm of Samuel Nichols 3 miles from Easton

322. ESHM Apr 9 1799/Second-hand phaeton for sale - Samuel Hopkins, Easton/ James Earle Denny, near Easton, offers reward for negro man, Peter, age about 25

323. ESHM Apr 16 1799/School teacher needed at Buck-Town, Transquaken, Dorch Co - John Scott/Lorain & Son, Easton, intending to leave Easton in a short time, will sell goods at reduced prices/Cor. Lee offers services of running horse, Trimmer, begotten by Richard B. Hall's Eclipse; Trimmer is the brother to James Lyle's Mides(bred by Jack Darnall), also brother to C. Bowen's California; Trimmer bred by Col. W. Lyles of P. G. Co

324. ESHM Apr 23 1799/Married Sun last by Rev Bowie, Robert Banning to Miss Susan Thomas, both of this co/Notice is hereby given to all those persons of Easton and its vicinity, between the ages of 18 and 45 years, who compose part of the 4th regiment, that Monday the 29th instant is appointed for them to assemble at their usual place of Parade - The Drum will give notice at 2 o'clock, and the Roll will be called precisely at three o'clock, when all absences must expect to be fined agreeable to the law. John Coats, Easton/ Whereas a certain James Byus, dec, late of Dorch Co, did execute a deed for

tract, Black Water Range, which was never recorded, to petition to have title confirmed -Richard Tubman

325. ESHM Apr 30 1799/William S. Bond admin, to sell in St. Michaels, all personal estate of Massey Fountain, late of Talb Co, dec

326. ESHM May 7 1799/"On Wednesday evening 1st inst was overset in a squall of wind, between the Fort and Fell's Point, a schooner, belonging to Captain John Morling, from Wye River, in which where Messrs. William Hindman, Henry Carter, William Keats, Patrick McIntire and daughter, a negro woman and a negro lad belonging to Mr. Hindman, and the Captain and his two men. We are sorry to inform our readers, that of this number Messrs. Carter and McIntire, the negro woman and free negro man were drowned were drowned; the others were providentially saved."/Married Sun last by Rev Bowie, Richard Trippe to Miss Mary Ennalls, both of Talb Co/Thomas Robinson, near Oxford Ferry, to run a packet from Easton to Balt commanded by Capt Thomas Pamphilion

327. ESHM May 14 1799/Chancery sale of tracts in New Market area: Littleton's Last Shift, Addition to York, New Market, property of James Sullivane, mortgaged sometime ago to Messrs. Bingham & Gilmor - Robert Harrison, trustee/ George Noble, Head of Wye, offers reward for hired white servant man, William Matthews who stole a horse

328. ESHM May 21 1799/Married at White Marsh Church by Rev Jackson, Tristram Martin to Miss Polly Oldham/Samuel Sherwood, Hole in the Wall, offers reward for negro man, Harry, who has for some time kept a free bright mulatto woman named Alfe Short; reward also for negro woman, Bet, sister to Harry and Bet's husband, Jim Steel who is property of Mr. G. Goldsborough/Sale of the estate of Doctor Samuel Cooper on Tuckahoe Creek the tracts: Hampton and pt Rich Range adj lands of William Hayward and Edward Turner in the heart of the fisheries; pt of Dudley's Choice and pt of Strawbridge adj land of William Hayward and George Willson; apply to Samuel Coats, Thomas Morris, Elliston Perot, surviving exec of Samuel Cooper dec in Philadelphia or Tristram Needles at Kings-Creek, Talb Co/Lloyd Nicols, Talb Co selling Plain-Dealing lands/ Letters remaining at P.O. Easton: Margaret Anderson, Easton; Josiah Bailey, Cambridge; James Birckhead, New Market; Thomas Bright, Easton; Col. P. Benson; William Boon, Denton; Mrs. Lovisa, Caroline; W. Cramer, Easton; Thomas Currie, Easton; Major Daniel P. Cox or John Nabb, Talb Co; James Condon, taylor, Cambridge; John Dawson, Talb Co; Joseph Douglas, Federalsburgh; John Edmundson, Easton; Ann Edmondson, Caroline Co; James Earle; Charles Emory, Easton; Furguson & Reed, merchants, Cambridge; Jacob Fowle, merchant, Easton; John Goldsobrough, from Easton; John E. Gist, merchant, Cambridge; Obediah Garey, Talb Co; Charles Hodson, Cambridge; Thomas Harrison, St. Michaels; James Harcastle, Caroline; John Jenkinson, near Easton; Lawson Lee, Kent Co; Lodge No. 5, Cambridge; Lodge No 18, Cambridge; Lodge No 6, Easton; Corbin Lee, Talb Co; Richard Mansfield; Patrick McNeal; Thomas McKeel; Mr. McDonnald, Cambridge; Henry Martin near Easton; Samuel Nicols, Talb; Henry Nicols, Easton; Hon. William Paca; Nicholas Pope, Easton; Isaac Purnell near Snow Hill; Henry Steele, Dorset Co; James Shaw, Easton; Master John Seney at Mr. Emory's Easton; Dr. William Thomas, Easton; James Vansandt; George Ward; Henry Waggaman, Cambridge; James Wainwright, Easton/William Thomas who formerly read Physic with Dr. Thomas has commenced practice of Physic in Easton; he lives at Mr. William Thomas's & keeps his shop where Doctor Noel formerly had his.

329. ESHM May 28 1799/Property of Charles Goldsborough junr, Cambridge, for sale

330. ESHM Jun 11 1799John Vickers has house for sale in Easton/Thomas Walters insolvent debtor, Dorch Co

331. ESHM Jun 18 1799/Married Tues last by Rev Rigg, Dr. John Irwin Troup to

Miss SallyHemsley of QA Co/John Harwood, trustee for creditors of Peter
Redhead/Elizabeth Millis, Cambridge, exec of Edward Millis, late of Dorch Co/
Broke jail, Charles Baker of Talb Co, committied for debt/Chancery sale of the
estate of Mrs. Mary Dickinson wife of John Dickinson, Dr. William Thomas and
Turbut Harris - all the estate devised by James Dickinson of Talb Co, John
Edmondson, trustee - to be sold to discharge mortgage by Mr. Dickinson to the
late James Chamberlaine of Talb Co. Also to be sold if above sale insuffic-
ient to meet debts, the dwelling plantation of Stephen Darden of Talb Co/
Chancery sale of tract in QA Co near Head of Chester, property of Thomas
Coursey, late of QA Co of 624 a. - Robert Ruth/Benjamin Drew, Cambridge,
offers reward for two negro brothers: Levin, age about 16 and Cuff, age about
18, purchased of James Goldsborough of Talb Co/Andrew Price, Greensborough,
Caroline Co, offers reward for John McDowell (carpenter & joiner)who ran away
and stole a set of tools; he once worked with Mr. West in Talb Co; he supposedly has a father living near Vienna, Dorch Co/James Beatie reports a stray
horse coming to his res about 11 miles from Easton, on road leading to Centre-
Ville/Solomon Bartlett to petition to establish a road from a little village
called Federalsburgh "to my mills for the benefit of the publick's going to
and from said mills, to cross the swamp called Ivy Swamp, and to lead into
the county road near the corner of Thomas Watkins' plantation."

332. ESHM Jun 25 1799/To let a farm in Tulley's Neck within 6 miles of Centre-
Ville, late the property of Col. George Baynard, dec - Stephen Lowry/W.
Patton, Talb Co, near the head of Tuckahoe Creek, offers reward for negro lad,
Faddis Garland, age about 17, once the property of Traverse Garland, dec,
has one brother and two sisters in Miles river Neck and another brother and
sister, near Head of Wye

333. ESHM Jul 2 1799/Alleged American from Maryland detained on board British
ships of war, for want of sufficient documents to prove their citizenship:
John Coop, James Clouds, Samuel Campbell, James Hobbs, James Henry, George
Higginbottom, Robert Jackson, Enock Jenkins, George Longford, Jonathan Maton,
John Paranavis, Charles Story, John Williams/Simon Wilmer exec of John L.
Wilmer, late Kent Co and admin of Catharine Brown late QA Co

334. ESHM Jul 16 1799/Farm for rent in Caroline Co adj lands of Isaac Purnel;
apply to John Hughes near Miles River Ferry/Matthias Bordley, Wye River,
offers reward for young negro man, Jem Merick, formerly owned by Capt Henry
Coursey; his father, Old Merrick, lives between Kent Island Narrows and
Greenwood's Creek on a place belonging to Capt Coursey/S. Elbert, Easton,
offers reward for apprentice boy, William Madray, age about 19

335. ESHM Jul 23 1799/Emory Sadler insolvent debtor, QA Co/Samuel Baldwin
admin of Jacob Alborn, late of Talb Co, requests persons indebted to estate
to make payment to Samuel Clayton/Letters remaining P.O. Easton: William /
Atkinson at Bartholomew Ennall's, Cambridge; Margaret Andison, Easton; William
Burtt, Choptank river; Stanly Byus, Eastern Shore of Maryland; Christopher
Birckhead; James Birckhead; Thomas Bright, Easton; Thomas J. Bullit; Charles
K. Bryan, Cambridge; William Boon, Denton; John Dawson, Denton; James Earle;
Benjamin Elliott, St. Martins; Mrs. Henrietta; M. Frazier, Caroline Co; Rev.
Joseph Flood, Cambridge; Ferguson & Read, Cambridge; John Fleming Easton;
Jacob Fowle; Capt Greenbury Griffin, St. Michaels; Charles Gibson; Obadiah
Garey, T lb Co; John E. Gist, Cambridge; Thomas Harrison, Broad Creek; Thomas
Hardcastle, near Easton; Robert Hay, St. Michaels; James Hardcastle, Caroline
Co; Christopher Harrison, Cambridge; Charles Hodson, Cambridge; Alexander
Kinney, Easton or if not there in Baltimore, America; William Meluy or in his
absence, Samuel Edmondson, Easton; Thomas O. Martin; Patrick McIntire; Mr.
McDonnald, Cambridge; Henry Nicols, Easton; Thomas Nicols, Federalsburgh;
Peter Redhead, Easton; Edward Roberts, Talb Co; Peter Rea, Cambridge; John
Reed, Cambridge; William Smith, Tuckahoe Bridge; James Shaw; Henry Somerville,

Cambridge; Joseph Sulivan, New Market; William Thompson, blacksmith, Easton; Thomas Weaver; George Ward, Cambridge; Henry Waggaman, Cambridge

336. ESHM Jul 30 1799/Samuel Sawn, Easton, offers reward for negro man, Abe, age about 40, formerly the property of Mrs. Blake, QA Co, but has always lived in Talb Co; his wife is at Samuel Chamberlaine's near Oxford; he also has acquaintances at Henry Nichols and Samuel Nichols in Talb Co/Senah Busick admin of William Keene, late of Dorch Do, dec, requests persons to settle accounts against the estate with John Brohann on Slaughters Creek

337. ESHM Aug 13 1799/Died Fri last Mrs. Anne Roberts, amiable consort of Edward Roberts of this co/Lots for sale, property of St. Michaels Parish - Hugh Sherwood, Wrightson Lambdin/James Steele to petition to set aside condemnation of part of a lot of his in Cambridge, laid off for a street called Spring St/Chancery sale at John Keene's Tavern, Church Hill, the real estate of Jonathan Seney, late of QA Co, dec, farm adj lands of late Joshua Seney dec - Mark Benton, trustee/Nathan Breerwood insolvent debtor, Dorch Co/John Lorrain, junr, Easton, intending to remove to Philadelphia in a few weeks

338. ESHM Aug 20 1799/Sale of real property of Charles Blake, dec, lying in QA Co; apply to Peregrine Blake, living on premises or to Richard T. Earle at his office in Centre-Ville/Samuel Poor insolvent debtor, Somerset Co

339. ESHM Sep 3 1799/Rembrandt Peale, portrait painter, Easton and vicinity for a short time/Joseph E. Muse has property on Transquaken River, Dorch Co for sale/John Stanford, Cambridge, to petition under the insolvency act/ Medford Andrews, Dorch Co, by reason of three years sickness to petition under the insolvency act/Peter Townsend to petition under the insolvency act/Farm for rent, now in tenure and occupied by James Barrow, Head of Wye; apply to Robert H. Goldsborough, Myrtle Grove

340. ESHM Nov 5 1799/Letters remaining P.O. Easton: Thomas Abbett, Cambridge; Thomas Barnett, Cambridge; Daniel Byrne near Miles river; James Berry; Michael Bateman; Mrs. Elizabeth Beatty; James Bowdle; James Condon, Cambridge; Cassandra Corse; Edward Clayton; John Currie; Thomas Coward; Eli Covington; Benjamin Denny, Denton; John Dawson, Denton; John Dashiell, Broad Creek; William Ennalls, Cambridge; James Earle; Miss Ann B. Fauntleroy; Mrs. Catharine Forsyth; Mrs. Henrietta Maria Frazier; Ferguson & Reed, Cambridge; Stephen H. Fowle, Trapp; Mrs. Mary Gordon, Miles river; Mrs. Hamilton's Theatre, Cambridge; Thomas Hardcastle; Mrs. Margaret Johns; Moses Lecompte, Dorch Co; Simon Light, Caroline Co; Hugh Lindsay, Cambridge; Thomas Leonard; John Leonard; Captain Mitchell, Cambridge; William Meluy; John Mullikin, Eben. Newton, Cambridge; William Oxenham, near Denton; Samuel T. Orme, near Trappe; John Pirtt, ship carpenter, in Denton; Patty Pickering; Francis Parvin; Nicholas Pope; Thomas Robertson, Oxford; Mr. Ray; Captain Isaac Spencer, 9th Regiment Infantry; Robert Speddin; Capt James Trippe, Cambridge; Joshua Taggart; Samuel Troth; Nathaniel Talboot, Caroline Co; William Walker, Caroline; John Wollin, Little Choptank; Samuel Willson, Head of Wye River; Charles Goldsborough, junior, seeks overseer for estate of Mrs. Elizabeth G. Ennalls of Dorch Co and also her plantation at Shoal Creek/T. Loockerman announces races to be held at Hunting Creek, Caroline Co; Nathaniel Smithers, Kent Co, Del, Catharine Smither, Caroline Co, exec of Alexander Robertson, late of Caroline Co, dec, and John Robertson, late of Caroline Co, dec/ Benjamin Skinner to petition under the insolvency act/William B. Martin, Cambridge, offers reward for negro woman, Milly, age about 22, went off with a mulatto man who has a sister in Philadelphia/Edward Lecompte admin of Mrs. Lecompte, late of Talb Co, dec/D. Smith, Dorch Co, offers reward for negro woman, Cloe, age about 40 and her daughters: Milly, age about 12 and Rosetta, age about 9; her husband James Green, age 40, passes in Dorch Co as a freeman; he has a pass to work for himself from Dr. James Sulivane and Robert Sulivane, son of the deceased living in New Market/Farm for rent where subscriber,

Peter Denny, now lives, about 3/4 miles from Easton/ Deserted from Head-Quarters at Havre de Grace on the night of the 10th inst. the following soldiers: John Thomas, born in Talb Co, 20 yrs of age, 5 ft 11 1/2 inch high, grey eyes, brown hair and light complexion; William Barnes, of the same county, 20 yrs of age, 5 ft 6 1/2 inch high, black eyes, brown hair, and light complexion; Edward Clash of the same county, 21 yrs of age, 5 ft 5 inch high, dark eyes, dark hair, and dark complexion; Purnel Baily of Somerset Co, 22 yrs of age, 5 ft 8 inch high, blue eyes, sandy hair, and dark complesion; Moses Cox of the same county, 18 yrs of age, 5 ft 8 inch high, dark eyes, light hair and fair complexion. They took with them their uniforms, knap-sacks and blankets. - The above reward (50 dollars) ...Isaac Spencer, Richard Earle, Captains, Head Quarters, 11 Sept 1799/A petition to be made for the Nanticoke Indians regarding the tract on the Nanticoke River, Dorch Co, known as Great Indian Town, sold by Mr. Junifer some years ago/Isaiah Dorman confined to gaol in Somerset Co for debts over 200 pounds, to petition under the insolvency act/ Joseph McHard, at this time a cripple and unable to work, to petition under the insolvency act/James Coursey to petition under the insolvency act

341. ESHM Nov 19 1799/Chancery sale of a tract lying in Caroline Co called Piney Point of Charles Vickers, late of Easton, dec, adj lands of Charles Blair and Thomas Valiant - Robert Moore, trustee/Dwelling plantation for rent in lower part of Talb Co, owned by Christopher Birckhead, dec, apply to James Birckhead, New Market/Mary Wainer admin Ludwick Wainer, late of Talb Co, dec

342. ESHM Nov 26 1799/Sheriff's sale of tracts in Tuckahoe Hundred, Talb Co: Vickers Triangle, Vickers' Necessity, Rich Range, Francis's Delight - taken in execution from John Vickers at the suit of Tristram Needles/House for rent and household furniture for sale - Charles Troup, Easton/Sale at the swelling plantation of the late William Perry, dec, on Miles River - William B. Smyth

343. ESHM Dec 10 1799/Lots for sale in Easton, between house occupied by Mr. Jackson and John Duncan's lot - James Earle junr, Easton/Henry Trice, Elizabeth Trice, admin of John Trice, Dorch Co, dec/Sale at his dwelling place on Wye River - Thomas Keats/Joseph & W. Haskins have just opened a store in Easton between Mrs. Trippe's & Mr. Nichols's stores/Sale at the late dwelling of Richard Arringdell of Talb Co, dec - George Parrott, admin/Sale of property of Jesse Hopkins, late of Easton, dec - Joseph Neale, Easton, exec/Thomas has a negro woman for sale/Philip Dickinson, Caroline Co, offers reward for negro woman, Memory, age 17/House for rent where Thomas Ball now lives/James Birckhead exec of Capt Christopher Birckhead, dec

344. ESHM Dec 17 1799/Samuel Swan has opened new tavern, sign of General Washington, Washington St/K. & W. Flint, sadlers, cap & Harness makers, Washington St. opposite Bullen & Roper's Tavern, Easton/Deserted from the rendezvous at Centre-Ville on the 31st of Oct past, a soldier named William Jolly, 21 yrs of age, 5 ft 5 inch high, black hair, grey eyes, swarthy complexion...John W. Hackett, Capt. 9th Reg'mt, U. S. Infantry/Plantation for sale on Transquaken River which the late Archibald Pattison pruchased of Bartholomew Ennalls; apply to Col. Robert Harrison, near Cambridge; Archibald Moncrieff exec Archibald Pattison/Sale by virtue of last will & testament of Mrs. Sarah Goldsborough at her late dwelling house near Oxford, negroes, household furniture, farmming utensils - John Singleton, exec

345. ESHM Dec 24 1799/Died Fri last Mrs. Margaret Kennard, the amiable consort of Joshua Kennard of QA Co/Chancery sale of real estat of Samuel Betsworth by Lambert Hyland, trustee to Thomas Jones

346. ESHM Jan 21 1800/Married by Rev Mr. Bowie, Robert Henry Goldsborough to Miss Henrietta Nicols daufhter of Col. Robert Lloyd Nicols of Talb Co/Died Wed 15th inst, Mrs. Elizabeth Elbert consort of Henry Elbert of Talb Co/

Henry Clift admin of John Clift, late of Talb Co/Sale of farm called Barker's
Landing near Easton by Henry Nicols junr/Robert Williams & Edward Roberts, Wye,
Talb Co, seeking person to keep an English School/Mrs. Sharp wishes to
commence boarding-house in Easton/Chancery decree to approve sale of real
property of by Robert Denny, trustee in Annapolis belonging to heirs of
William Adams/Andrew Orem requests payment of debts to John Vickers/John
Harwood has opened in the store-house, "sign of the Spinning Wheels," opposite
Mr. Joseph Hatkins and Mr. Samuel Nicole's stores, a small assortment of dry
goods/Polly Smith exec of Walter Smith, late of Worc Co/Zadock Long, Princess
Anne, offers reward for negro man, Jeremiah, about 45 yrs old, formerly owned
by Mrs. Dorson or Mrs. Brasscup of Easton and acted for them in a tavern as
hostler; he has changed his name to Ben Hammond and passes himself as a free
man and as such was employed by Mr. Thomas Pierson at Coxe's Mill about 8
miles from Easton/John Trippe, Easton, will accommodate 3 or 4 boys as
boarders next year/George R. Hayward offers reward for negro man, John, age
38 yrs/Nathaniel Davis, Nancy Johnson, Snow-hill admin of James Johnson, late
of Worc Co, dec/Reward for deserters by Isaac Spencer, Capt, Easton, deserted
from their rendezvous at Easton: James Dickinson, Abel Matthews, Greenbury
Clifton and Ben Philips, soldiers in the 9th U. S. Regt. Dickinson was born
in Talb Co and deserted around the 1st of June last; he is 19 yrs old, 5 ft
4 inch high with light complexion and brown hair. Matthews was born in
Somerset or Dorch Co; was enlisted at the World's End, in Dorch, and deserted
around 15 Aug last; he is 20 yrs of age, 6 ft high with ruddy complexion and
brown hair. Greenbury Clifton was born in Caroline Co and deserted 13 Dec
last; he is 21 yrs old, 5 ft 6 inch high, dark complexion, dark hair and grey
eyes. Ben Philips was born in Dorch Co and deserted on 1st inst; he is 17 yrs
old, 5 ft 3 inch high, has fair complexion, grey eyes and light hair/William
Chambers, Centreville, offers reward for negro man, Levin, 25 yrs, last seen
in the service of Thomas Rodgers of this co, formerly belonged to the late
William Allen of Worc Co; he has a mother in Easton who is free/Sale of estate
of Mrs. Sarah Goldsborough, dec, by John Singleton, exec

347. ESHM Jan 28 1800/Woolman Warner admin of Robert Warner late of Talb Co
dec/Deserted from rendezvous at Wilmington, Daniel Buckley, enlisted soldier
age 35, 5 ft 10 inch high, ligh hair, grey eyes, light complexion, cooper by
trade; also John Vanhorn, age 22, 5 ft 9 inch high, dark complexion, dark
eyes and dark hair/Robert Denny requests payment of debts/Died 20th inst Rev
Isaac Foster, rector of Coventry Parish in Maryland, leaving wife and four
children

348. ESHM Feb 4 1800/Letters remaining at P.O. Easton; John M. Anderson, near
Cambridge; Mrs. Maria R. Anderson, near Cambridge; Elizabeth Baly, Miles
river; Charles Blair, Caroline; Peregrine Blake, Easton; James Booker; Thomas
Bright; Capt John Bush, Talb Co; Charles Daffin, Dorset Co; Joshua Driver,
Caroline; Anthony De Bonne; Miss Mary Ennalls, Blackwater, Dorset Co; John
Edmondson, Easton; Samuel Eason; Major T. M. Forman, Easton; Samuel D.
Freeman, Cambridge; John Fountain, senr, Caroline; John Goldsborough, Eastern
Shore; John Genn, Choptank Bridge; Greenbury Goldsborough, Oxford; Peter
Gordon, Cambridge; Hon. William Hindman; Thomas W. Loockerman, Hunting Creek;
Joseph Needles, Caroline Co; Andrew Robison, near Easton; Doctor Robert
Richardson, Trappe; William Stevens, Denton; John Smoot, Federalsburgh; M.
Skidmore Crammer, Denton; Mrs. Sarah Trippe, Dorch Co; Ross Thompson, Caroline
Co; Joseph Taggert, merchant, Easton; Mrs. Teagle, Easton; William Troth,
near Easton; Alexander Tolson, Caroline; James Wilson, Dorset Co

349. ESHM Feb 11 1800/James Roney insolvent debtor, Somerset Co/James
Duhamell admin of James Johnson, late of QA Co, dec/Application may be made
to Messrs Bullitt, Coats, Martin, Johnson, and Hammond for position as
professor in Easton Academy/Samuel Clayton acting exec for Mary Wainer
regarding the estate of Ludwick Wainer of Easton, sadler, dec

-58-

350. ESHM Feb 18 1800/William Hughlett and William Dill admin of Jacob Dill of Caroline Co, dec/Rebecca Thompson, Samuel Thompson of Church Hill admin of Doctor Samuel Thompson, dec, of QA Co

351. ESHM Mar 4 1800/Thomas W. Loockerman heir at law of Mrs. Sidney Loockerman of Caroline, dec/Sale of houases of Charles Vickers, dec, located on Hanson St/John Hitch admin of Joshua Hitch, dec, to sell his property in Rockawalkin, Somerset Co/John Betts, Kent Co, Md, insolvent debtor

352. ESHM Mar 11 1800/Isaac Atkinson, Somerset Co, near Lower Ferry, Wicomico, offers reward for negro man, Clem, age about 25 yrs/P. Beaston, Henry Travers, Ebenezer Newton, Thomas Hicks, Dorch Co, trustees of Amity School

353. ESHM Mar 18 1800/Sale of 200 a. in Dorch Co situated on Transquaken River about 4 miles from drawbridge by Thomas Daffin, Caroline Co

354. ESHM Mar 25 1800/Nathan G. Bryson insolvent debtor of Somerset Co/ William Meconekin exec of John Meconekin, late of QA Co, to sell tract called Addition at head of Wye mill stream/Robert L. L. Nicols offers reward for stray cow, bought from James E. Denny/Requesting information from the neighborhood of Vienna regarding the execution of a power of attorney in 1795 by John Clifford & wife, Isaac Wharton & wife, and William Rawle of Philadelphia; the power of attorney was given to a gentleman whose name is not recollected; it was recorded by the late Mr. Henry

355. ESHM Apr 1 1800/Nicholas Watts has a full-bred horse who will stand for mares at James Slaughter's, James E. Denny's, J. Rose's near Dover Ferry, Richard Dudley's near Lewistown, John Roberts' Mill Farm and William Watts junr near Three Bridges/Hyland Gears insolvent debtor of Kent Co Md/Medford Andrews insolvent debtor of Dorch Co/William Haddaway has just started a new stage, from his ferry 21 miles below Easton, to Easton/George Baily, Easton, has just received from Philadelphia fresh garden seeds

356. ESHM Apr 15 1800/Joseph G. Daffin, Cambridge, offers reward for negro girl, age about 18/Philemon H. Able, near Trappe, has horse for standing/ Loftus Bowdle, acting admin of Henry Bowdle, late of Easton, dec/Thomas J. Bullitt candidate for presidential elector/William Sharpe insolvent debtor of Talb Co/Thomas Bruff, dentist, now at Easton/John Goldsborough junr, Easton, has supply of plank for sale/Partnership of Harrington, Crawford & Boyer at Greensborough is dissolved

357. ESHM Apr 22 1800/Robert Dixon and Levin Charles, insolvent debtors of Caroline Co/Chancery decree - Creditors of Nicholas Mace, dec, immediate exhibit of claims against the estate/Sale of farm lying in Tulley's Neck, QA Co by Joseph Price, Head of Wye/Elizabeth Millis admin of Edward Millis, Dorch Co, dec/Owen Kennard, Easton, to sell 5 negro men/Elizabeth Marshall, Benjamin Wailes, admin of John D. Marshall, late of Worc Co, Pitt's Creek Hundred/Peter Hopkins, Easton, plans to run schooner, the Nancy, as a packet from Easton to Balt, once a week/Letters remaining at P.O. Easton: Joseph Bewly, head of Wye River; Nathan Basset, Choptank; Isaiah Bell, Dorch Co; Nathan Bradley, Dorch Co; Capt John Bush; Mrs. Grace Brooks; William Benny; Mrs. Mary Coarsea, to be left at Mrs. Dickinson's, Easton; Mr. Daffin, care of Mr. H. Nicols, Easton; Robert Dodson, St. Michael's; James Dodson, St. Michael's; Thomas Dodson, St. Michaels; Peter Elliott, Cambridge; John Edmondson; Capt William Frazier, near Easton; Cole Fields, Easton; John Goldsborough junr; Greenbury Goldsborough; Lot Genn, Caroline Co; Thomas Goldsborough, Bell-Air; Thomas Hayward, near Easton; Doctor Hall; Henry Haskins; Miss Ann Helm; Mrs. Ann Hingson, Dorch Co; Col. Robert Harrison; Charles Harper, Dorch Co; Mrs. Margaret Johns; Solomon or Thomas Jones; William Kennedy, care of Mrs. Trippe, Easton; James Mace, Dorch; Tristram Needles; Mrs. Christianna O'Donnell, Easton; Samuel Ormes; Miss Kitty Pearce; Elisha Pelham; James Pursley; Dr. Walter Perkins;

Peter Redhead; Solomon Robinson; Levin Simmons; Mrs. Mable Smith; Peter Smack, Kent Island; John Stephens junr, Kent Island; John Stevens, New Market; Joshua Taggart; Doctor Devreaux Travers; Michael Tulley; Thomas Tibbles or Charles Gibson; James Wilson junr; William Woods; John Walker

358. ESHM Apr 29 1800/Thomas Wing, Caroline Co, living near Dover Ferry, offers reward for negro fellow, Benjamin, age 40, formerly belonged to William Perry of Talb Co

359. ESHM May 6 1800/Joshua Kennard at Centreville has assortment of Black Walnut planks for sale/John R. Bromwell forewarns persons from traveling through his lands/William Wilson, Caroline Co, near Denton, offers reward for apprentice boy, Foster Manship, about 11 yrs old/Jacob Loockerman, Easton, offers reward for stolen mare

360. ESHM May 13 1800/Richard E. Waters, near Princess Anne, Somerset Co, offers reward for negro man, Will, about 24 yrs old/George Medford, Joseph Rasin, Mary Rasin, Kent Co, admin of George Rasin, late of Kent Co, dec/Joseph McHard insolvent debtor, QA Co

361. ESHM May 20 1800/Died Sat night last, Major Daniel Powell Cox of Talb Co/Chancery sale of realestate of John Brown, Somerset Co, dec, to be held on the premises near William Russum's, Barron Creek, John Leatherbury, trustee/ Samuel Brookes insolvent debtor, QA Co

362. ESHM May 27 1800/Doctor R. Richardson, Trappe, has assortment of medi- cines/Jeremiah Bromwell, Easton, candidate for sheriff/Samuel Elliott, near Cambridge, offers reward for stolen horse/Joseph McHard, Margaret McHard, admin of Morrise Ellers, late of QA Co, dec/Thomas Keats' house in Easton may be rented by applying to Doctor Robert Moore in Easton; Mrs. Keats has taken a house at Park Lane & Calvert St, Balt, and offers to accommodate boarders

363. ESHM Jun 3 1800/Ebenezer Saunders, late post master, at Georgetown Cross Roads, Kent Co Md, was indicted at the circuit court, held at Annapolis, for secreting and embezzling a letter directed to Mr. John Chew, of Chestertown, and for stealing out of the same ten post bank bill of one hundred dollars each...found guilty,... to receive thirty-nine lashes and seven years imprison- ment at hard labor/Rosanna Marshall admin of Levin Marshall, late of Dorch Co, dec/Robert Sharp Harwood candidate for sheriff, Talb Co/Sale of 180 a. in QA Co adj Doctor Edward Harris and Jacob Seth by Edward Carey, QA Co

364. ESHM Jun 10 1800/Sale of tracts in Dorch Co near Blackwater Bridge: Widow's Lot, Partnership, Staplefort's Privilege, Merchant's Outlet, Hartford, Hog Range, Levin's Discovery, Standford's Desire, Parson's privilege by John F. Mercer, West River/Frances Carson, Chruch-Hill, QA Co, offers reward for negro man, Will, age about 26/Doctor William Thomas to practice medicine in Easton next door to Mr. Taggart's store, having attended three last winters the medicinal lectures at the University in Philadelphia/Tavern of Thomas Prince, Easton, known as Fountain Inn is for sale/James Willson junr insolvent debtor of Talb Co

365. ESHM Jun 24 1800/Nominating committee for selection of delegates to the General Assembly: Nicholas Hammond, Henry Banning, Henry Martin, James Goldsborough, Ennalls Martin, John Dickinson, Henry Johnson, John Fisher, William Hambleton, John Kersey, Henry Nicols, James Dudley/Sale of two farms in QA Co, one in part occupied by Capt Henry Coursey; sale to be held on the upper farm adj William Tilghman's; apply to John Harrison, living near the head of Marshy Creek, Christopher W. Carradine, Head of Corsica Creek/Chancery sale at Mr. Vanhorn's store at the head of Church Creek, Dorch Co to sell tracts: Chance, near the head of Church Creek and Tootells Adventure - Catharine Kallender, trustee/Mary Andrews admin of Russell R. Andrews, late of Droch Co, dec/Hugh Sherwood of Huntingdon and John Thomas, candidates for

-60-

sheriff, Talb Co/Henry Tate, QA Co to petition under the insolvency act/
Chancery case: Conrad Theodore Wederstrand, George Vanderford, Henry Carter,
Andrew Pearce and Edward Chatham versus heirs of Thomas Coursey

366. ESHM Jul 1 1800/Chancery Court in Somerset Co relative to the real
estate of William Adams, dec; one of the parties is Andrew Adams/Chancery sale
at Mr. Vanhorn's store at the head of Church Creek, Dorch Co of the tracts,
Chance and pt of Tootell's Venture, Catharine Kallender, trustee/Charles Troup
of Easton has placed his books and papers in the hands of John Harwood,
merchant of Easton/Luther Martin gives opinion regarding election of sheriff/
Thomas James Bullitt candidate for presidential elector

367. ESHM Jul 8 1800/Mr. Generes to open dancing school in Easton; subscript-
ion papers will be left with Doctor William Thomas and Mr. Kerr/Male servant
wanted - Joseph G. Daffin, Cambridge/Letters remaining in P.O. Easton: Henry
Arnett, Dorset Co; Miss Sophia Bullitt, Easton; William Bowers; Stanley Byus;
Jacob Bromwell, Talb Co; James Byus, Eastern Shore; William Blake, Miles River
Neck; Dr. George Baily; Samuel Brown, Easton; John Beard, Dorch Co; Peregrine
F. Bayard, Denton; Christian Baxter, clock & watch maker, Easton; John Craig;
Collins Carey; Thomas Cook, Hook Town; Henry Downes; Joshua Driver; Mr.
Daffin; Charles Dickinson; John Edmondson, Easton; Charles Emory; Lieut Levi
G. Ford, Denton; Cole Fields, Easton; William Frazier; John Fleming, Easton;
Robert Findelater; Mrs. Mary Gordon; Miss Esther Gregory; Matthew Greentree;
Capt Edward Griffin, Dorset Co; Thomas Harrison, Broadcreek, Talb Co; Robert
Hay, St. Michaels; Dr. Edward Harris; Widow Hendricks; Jonathan Jones,
Cambridge; Cornelius Johnson, Caroline Co; Solomon or Thomas Jones; Capt Levin
Jones, Cambridge; Negro John, who calls himself John Parrot at the Hole in the
Wall; The Honorable General Lloyd; Stanley B. Lockerman; Mrs. Prudence
Lambdin; Robert Moore; Thomas Oldham Martin; Richard Mansfield; Henry Nicols
junr; William Needles, Caroline; John Patridge; John Regester; Jeremiah
Rhodes; Levin Stevens; Edward Stevens; Robert Spedding; Major Peregrine
Spencer; Henry Troth; Mrs. Mary Webb; William Whiteley; William Weaver/Nathan
Newton requests accounts be settled against the estate of Joseph Nicols, late
of Caroline Co

368. ESHM Jul 15 1800/John Goldsborough junr answers public accusations made
by Jacob Gibson at the Trappe/Thomas Martin, Dividin Creek, Talb Co, offers
reward for negro lad, Job or Joe, age about 19; he may use the name of Elisha,
Daniel, or Davey Dixon since he may have obtained a copy of manumission from
me of the above negroes who were manumitted by Mary Martin of Talb Co/Joseph
Neall exec of Jesse Hopkins, late of Easton/Tract for sale on Chicknamicomico
River at Drawbridge, Dorch Co by Thomas Barnett

369. ESHM Jul 22 1800/James Dudley candidate for sheriff, Talb Co/Two farms
for rent in Hunting Creek, Caroline Co, one now occupied by William Walker,
the other by Isaac Whittington - Charles Goldsborough junr/Ezekiel Wise,
clerk, Snow Hill, gives notice that the Presbyterian Church of Snow Hill will
petition for incorporation.

370. ESHM Jul 29 1800/Died at Cambridge Sat 19 inst in his 51st year of his
age, Doctor Charles Troup, late of this place...patron of literature/"On
Monday the 21st instant, a challenge passed from Mr. Perry Driver, to Mr.
William Stevens, both of Denton, whcih was accepted and the parties, with
their seconds, (Doctor Henry Helm, second of Mr. Driver, and James Porter,
Esquire, second of Mr. Stevens) instatntly went into the Delaware State, in
order to effectuate the same. The parties on the ground behaved with becoming
firmness, and having exchanged a shot, and insisting on another, the seconds
interfered, and brought about a happy reconciliation."/4th of July celebration
at Denton by Federal Republicans - oration by James M. Broom, Esq; entertain-
ment by Mr. Denny; Major Joseph Richardson appointed president and Christopher
appointed vice-president/Henry Buckley candidate for sheriff, Talb Co/

Elijah Wooters and William Canckes request settlement of claims against the estate of James Barwick, late of Caroline Co, at the dwelling house of Benjamin Denny, Denton

371. ESHM Jul 29 1800/Philemon Willis candidate for sheriff, Talb Co/Land for sale in Caroline Co by William B. Smyth, Miles River, Talb Co, 1 1/2 miles from Dover Ferry on both sides of Dover Road; apply to Captain William Frazier of Caroline Co or John Sprouse who lives on the premises/Richard Earle, Easton, gives notice to the legal representatives of Aaron Parrott, late a private in the 9th Regiment of Infantry, that he has money belonging to said Parrott

372. ESHM Aug 5 1800/Purnell Porter gives notice that inhabitants of Worc Co will petition for public road/Packet from Easton to Balt run by Samuel Sherwood & Robert Spedin/Schooner, The Kitty, available for employment; apply to Thomas Townsend junr or James Benson, both living near the place called the Oak, Talb Co

373. ESHM Aug 12 1800/Mary Willoughby admin of Job Willoughby, late of Dorch

374. ESHM Aug 19 1800/Thomas S. Denny and William Rose request that anonymous writer of article criticizing their conduct in the General Assembly come forward/James Porter, Denton, candidate for General Assembly

375. ESHM Aug 26 1800/Eliza Troup, Cambridge, exec of Charles Troup,   :' physician, late of Dorch Co/Isaac Purnell, Caroline Co, to petition to erect grist mill in Caroline Co near where Thomas Hardcastle, late, built a new bridge, to be turned by the Choptank waters/Samuel Nicols, Easton, merchant

376. ESHM Sep 2 1800/"...elegant new mansion of Major Waggaman, Dorch County, struck by lightning and set on fire Thursday night last, ...the building was considerabley injured - An house of Mr. John Smoot at the cross roads near Cambridge, and the wind mill of G. R. Hayward Esq. of this county were struck during the same gust. Providencially no lives were lost."/House for let now occupied by Mrs. Elizabeth Thomas - William Stevens, Trapp/Samuel Tenant offers reward for negro lad, Sam, age 18, brought from Hartford Co/James Lucas QA Co, offers reward for negro boy, Pert, age about 14/Hatfield Wright, living near North West Fork Bridge, offers reward for apprentice boy, Eli Anderson, orphan son of James Anderson of Kent Co, dec

377. ESHM Sep 9 1800/John Singleton, Talb Co, exec of Mrs. Sarah Goldsborough/ The debatingsociety of Princess Anne gives reasons for expeling Thomas W. Handy, physician/Levin Stevens, Collector of Talb Co assessment/Tan-yard for rent in Easton, now in the occupation of William Atkinson - John Stevens

378. ESHM Sep 16 1800/Samuel Nicols, secretary of Eastern Shore of Maryland Jockey Club/Inhabitants of Dorch Co to petition for public road from the end of the road made by John Williams and Thomas Coulston, to intersect the Blackwater Road/Farm owned by C. T. Wederstrandt for sale, on the branches of the head of Wye River/George Skirvin, secretary of Chester-Town Jockey Club, announces upcoming races on 9 Oct/Sale of horses, cattle and sheep by Solomon Frazier/John Vickers to petition under the insolvency act/Robert William candidate for sheriff, Talb Co

379. ESHM Sep 23 1800/Thomas Stanford, Dorch Co, to petition under the ʲⁱ insolvency act/Charles Ricketts and Benjamin Skinner, insolvent debtors of Kent Co Md

380. ESHM Sep 30 1800/Thomas White, Somerset Co, to petition under the ᵢ insolvency act/Married Thurs evening last by Rev Mr. Bowie, Mr. Govert Haskins, merchant of Balt, to Miss Leah Eccleston of Talb Co/T. Bruff, dentist, to be at Centreville on Wed, before his removal to Federal City/Thomas P. Smith, Easton, gives notice to James Porter regarding a note that is due/For sale - late dwelling plantation of Rev Thomas Gordon of Talb Co, dec, situated on

Bolingbroke Creek - Thomas Gordon junr/Charles Goldsborough, near Potts' Mill reports a stray horse/John Colston, Dorch Co, to petition under the insolvency act

381. ESHM Oct 7 1800/Elisha Rigg, St. Paul's Parish, QA Co, seeks teacher/ Robert Green, Dorch Co, to petition under the insolvency act

382. ESHM Oct 15 1800/Died Sun week last, James Birckhead, merchant of New Market/Died Tues evening last, Joseph Neale of this town/John Harwood will accommodate 4 or 5 boys as boarders/William Gore, Talb Co, to petition for divorce from his wife, Margaret Gore

383. ESHM Oct 21 1800/William Boyman, Somerset Co, to petition under the insolvency act/Lauder Mister and Milly Ross, Dorch Co, offer reward for two negro men/Letters remaining at P.O. Easton: Mary Adams; Elizabeth Buley; Peggy Bowdle; Tristram Bowdle; Larrence Battle; John Bullin; James Ball; Capt William Bond; Rev Mr. Bolton; Rev William Bishop; Daniel Cain; James Calhoun; Thomas Cook; Charles Cook; Henrietta Maria Chamberlaine; Robert Chamberlaine; Solomon Clark; Mrs. D. Dickinson; Charles Dean; Becky Dulin; John Erskine; Rev Thomas Foster; Obadiah Garey; John M. O. Hartnett; Robert Hay; Joseph Hopkins; Edward Harris; Rev William Hardisty; Peggy Heymell; Andrew Johnston; William Lowry; Thomas Mathews; Robert Nash; Lloyd Nicols; Capt Abner Parrott; Andrew Price; John Rust; Adam Robbins; Nancy Smith; Robert Spedding; Thomas Stevens; John Simpson; William Skinner; Daniel Sullivan; John Smoot; Kendal Smack; Joshua Taggart; Lloyd Tilghman; Nathaniel Talbott; John Titus; Thomas Wainwright

384. ESHM Oct 28 1800/Died Sun evening last after a long and tedious illness, Peter Webb of Talb Co/Married Thursday 23d inst at the seat of Mrs. Anna M. Chew on Wye River, John Philemon Paca, Esq. to Miss Juliana Tilghman, dau of Richard Tilghman, Esq. of Chester Town/Francis Neall and James Neall exec of Joseph Neal and admin of Jesse Hopkins; James Neall to carry on the cabinet and chair making business at the shop lately occupied by Joseph Neal, dec/ John Howard to petition under the insolvency act/Sale at dwelling house of Jeremiah Colston, late of Dorch Co, dec, by Henry Colston acting admin/George Handy, sheriff Princess Anne, reports confinement in jail of negro Sam who states he was raised in this county (Somerset) and sold sometime ago by George Revill to Henry Carlton of Georgia, currently owned by Thomas Harrison who lives about 16 miles from Washington, N. C./Joseph Everitt, QA Co, to petition under the insolvency act

385. ESHM Nov 11 1800/Chancery sale by John Thomas of land mortgaged to James Armstrong by William Turner, dec/William Bozman, Somerset Co, to petition under the insolvency act/John Colston and Thomas Stanford, both of Dorch Co, to petition under the insolvency act

386. ESHM Nov 18 1800/Died Thurs morning 13 inst wife of Benjamin Barrow of Talb Co and on the Friday following her husband died/Died Thurs morning last John Sheppard of this town/Christopher Cox, QA Co, offers reward for stolen gelding/Tristram Needles admin of William McCallum to sell several of his houses on Washington St/Robert Sulivane, Clement Sulivane, New Market, exec to hold sale on the farm where Capt Christopher Birckhead formerly lived, estate of James Birckhead, dec

387. ESHM Dec 2 1800/Harrison Dickinson admin of Peter Richardson Dickinson, late of Caroline Co/John Webley, hairdresser, has removed his shop to his dwelling house in Dover St, Easton

388. ESHM Jan 6 1801/James Roper, Easton, has opened a tavern in the house formerly occupied by Mrs. Troth at the sign of the Sheaf of Wheat adj the public square in Easton/S. Swan has removed to the house lately occupied by

Dr. John Trippe, where he continues keeping tavern at the sign of General
Washington/Chancery sale of real estate of Levin Wailes, dec, in Somerset Co
- James B. Robins, trustee/Negro confined in Somerset Co jail, who calls
himself Thomas Jackson, age about 24; says he was a freeman, raised in
Middlesex Co, Va/George Baily has given up his shop to Doctor Moore/Henry
Ozman,Bolingbroke, forewarns persons from hunting on the farm owned by William
M. Catrop at Chancellor's Point/Henry Travers exec of Hannah Hickson, late of
Dorch Co/Levin Noble admin Isaac Smith, dec, Caroline Co, requests settlement
of claims at the house where John Nicols now lives at North West Fork Bridge

389. ESHM Jan 13 1801/Henry Nicols junr, Easton, contemplating to remove from
the state, offers for sale property near Easton name Galloway/Thomas Mullen,
Kent Co Md, insolvent debtor/Letters remaining at P.O. Easton: Thomas Abbott;
George Armstrong; John Bullin; John Bush; Israel Bringhurst; Gilbert Bigger(?);
Perry F. Byard; Robert Butler; Daniel Cain senr; James Chires; Thomas Cook;
Sovreign Dawson; John Edmondson; Michael Flax; Sarah Franklin; Peregrin
Garnett; Abza Geben; Thomas Goldsborough; Mary Gordon; Matthew Greentree; Jane
Gray; Thomas M. Goldsborough; Col Haversham; Job Haskins; John Haddaway; John
W. Harrison; Dr. G. W. Miller; Richard Martindale; John McDaniel; Thomas
Ozment; Abner Parrott; George Patton; Florah Parrott; John Quimby; William
Russon; William Sharp; Cyrus Sharp; Ann Swan; Levin Spedden; Clement Sulivane;
Hugh Sherwood; John Sheppard; Fronetter Thomas; Lloyd Tilghman; Lewis Turner;
Joshua Taggart; Richard Warsham; John Willis; Solomon Young/Letters remaining
at P. O. Cambridge: Dr. James Tootle; William Elbert; Peggy L. Brady; William
Melvin; John Neill; Daniel Smith; Thomas Lord; Solomon Frazier

390. ESHM Jan 20 1801/Chancery sale of real estate of William Moore, late of
Cecil Co, dec, seized, part of Bohemia Manor by Isaac Horsey, trustee/Robert
H. Goldsborough, Miles river, offers reward for negro Stephen, age about 24;
he has a wife who is a free woman living on William Hayward's land on Miles
River

391. ESHM Jan 27 1801/Died Fri last at his seat in this place William
Goldsborough/James Clayland junr, Attorney for Charlotte S. Clayland,
Centreville admin of Jacob Clayland, merchant, late of QA Co/Daniel Perkins
admin of William Biggs, late of Kent Co, request claims against the estate be
made at the office of James Houston in Chester-Town

392. ESHM Feb 3 1801/Samuel Barrow exec of Dr. William Kemp, late of Talb Co/
John Fleming admin of James Hull, requests claims be made at his shop in
Easton

393. ESHM Feb 10 1801/Married Thurs 22 inst by Rev Reefe, Thomas Curtis,
merchant of Princess Anne to the amiable Miss Sally Elzey of Somerset Co/Died
Mon 2nd inst Miss Polly Clayland, eldest dau of John Clayland, Talb Co/Died
Thurs morning last after a tedious illness, Arthur Bryan of Talb Co/John
Dougherty, Talb Co, reports a stray black horse

394. ESHM Feb 17 1801/Joshua Taggart has clover seed for sale/Sarah Jones
and Thomas Jones admin of William Jones to sell his personal property at the
farm of Benjamin Parrott, taylor, laying between Easton and Dover Ferry/John
Bowen, Easton, has hired an assistant in the instruction at his academy/Robert
Moore has opened a hat manufactory in Easton under the inspection of Benjamin
Parrott, at the shop lately occupied by Samuel Hopkins, nearly opposite Thomas
Princes's Tavern/Benjamin Skinner, silversmith, has opened his shop adj Samuel
Baldwin in Easton/Thomas Daffin, Caroline Co, request creditors of Charles
Daffin junr, dec, Caroline Co, to attend at Denton with their claims.

395. ESHM Feb 24 1801/Married Thurs 12 inst by Rev Bolton, James Price,
Easton, to Miss Mary Richardson, dau of Col Richardson of Caroline Co/Married
Sun following, Samuel Nicols, merchant, of Easton, to Miss Eliza Smyth of Kent
Co/Died a few days ago Matthew Tilghman of Kent Co/Died on 12th inst, Dr.

Henry Hayward of Havre de Grace after a lingering illness/John Kellie, Easton, intending to decline his business, offers his stock of goods at reduced prices/ James Price, Reg'r, requests person entitled to letters of administration of the estate of Nehemiah Noble, late of Talb Co to come forward/Notice that shares in the Chesapeake and Delaware Canal are offered for sale at Mr. Kennard's store, Easton, James Earle junr, Owen Kennard/Daniel Fiddeman gives notice of the sale of lots near the church in St. Michaels/William Farrell junr, attorney in fact for Ann Meeds, admin of James Meeds, late of QA Co

396. ESHM Mar 17 1801/Died Tues last at Mr. Joseph Tilford near this place, Miss Elizabeth Franks, buried at the burial ground of the people called Methodists

397. ESHM Apr 14 1801/Married Tues 31 ultimo, by Rev Bowie, Littleton Gale, to Miss Peggy Holliday of Talb Co/Married Wed last by Rev Jackson, John Leeds Kerr of this town to Miss Sally Chamberlaine dau of Samuel Chamberlaine of Oxford/John Thomas to sell lot in Easton opposite Samuel Yarnall's store

398. ESHM May 5 1801/James Coursey insolvent debtor of Caroline Co/Mary Noble admin of George Noble, late of Talb Co, requests claims be made to John Fisher of Talb Co/John Jones surviving admin of James Troth

399. ESHM May 12 1801/Gabriel Duvall, P. G. Co, offers reward for negro fellow Harry who was born in QA Co in the family of the late Richard B. Lloyd and has a brother and other relations there; he calls. himself Henry Wallace/ Edward Bromwell, senr; Oxford, offers services of his horse, Sloan/John Jones surviving admin of James Troth, dec, to sell house where John Mullikan now lives, property of the dec/John Harwood, trustee for the creditors of James Wilson of Easton/Letters remaining at P.O. Cambridge: Benjamin Pallengell; Peter Gordon; Sewell Howeth; John Watson; James Read; William Lindsay; Thomas Vickars; John Stevens; John Harrington; Robert Kersey; Peter Redhead; Thomas Barnett; Ezekiel Richardson; William Trippe; Robert & Clement Sulivane/Levin Ballard admin of John Dove late of Somerset Co/Sale in Dorch Co of 400 a. formerly sold by John Murray to Alexander McIntire - Thomas Barnett, Dorch Co

400. ESHM May 19 1801/William Sharp insolvent debtor, Talb Co/George Anderson now has at his store, formerly occupied by Messrs. Anderson & Mudic, a general assortment of wet & dry goods (Chestertown)/Chancery sale of real estate in Somerset Co, late the property of William Adams/Joseph Cummins requests claims against the estate of Henry Anderson, late of Dorch Co, dec

401. ESHM May 26 1801/Farms in Caroline Co for lease: 1. now in the tenure of Charles Blair at the head of Fowling Creek 2. occupied by D. Jones 3. ccupied by J. Rumble

402. ESHM Jun 2 1801/Joseph Farland, Bay-side, Talb Co, offers reward for two negro men: one calls himself Jacob Thomas, age about 28, and the other is Ralph Bantom, age about 35 who has a sister (Jacob's mother) and a brother. Jacob has a wife at Fells Point at Philip Sherwood's and has a mother and brother at Capt Richardson's near St. Michaels. Both men were bought from Captain Robert Rolle about 2 1/2 yrs ago

403. ESHM Jun 9 1801/William D. Thomas, Head of Wye, seeks teacher

404. ESHM Jun 16 1801/Reward for deserter, David Collison, a recruit who enlisted 8th of last month, born in Caroline Co, 22 yrs old, 5 ft 7 1/2 inch high, grey eyes, black hair, fair complexion, by trade a blacksmith - R. Chamberlaine, 1st U. S. Reg't Artillerists & Engineers, Commanding at Easton/ Ann Auld admin of Samuel Auld, late of Talb Co/Baynard Wilson requests claims against estate of William Loveday, Talb Co, dec/Levin Ball admin of Sarah Stephens

405. ESHM Jun 23 1801/On Saturday fe'night Charles Goldsborough ESQ. died at

his seat in Dorch Co called Horn's Point/John Kersey requests payment on bonds left to him by late Impey Dawson/Chancery sale of land of James Tilghman junr late of Talb Co, situate near the head branches of Miles River/David Lamb admin of Ann Vansant, late of QA Co (granted by Orphans' Court of Kent Co)

406. ESHM Jul 14 1801/George Purnell admin of Samuel Gunn, late of Worc Co/ Farm for sale on branch of Third Haven Creek near Peach Blossom, now occupied by Henry Smith; apply to Joseph Haskins, Easton, or Graham, Haskins and Co, Balt/Esther Waters and Peter Waters, admin of Patrick Waters, late of Worc Co

407. ESHM Jul 21 1801/Tract for sale called Retaliation, property of William Stevens junr in Caroline Co - Benjamin Willmott

408. ESHM Jul 28 1801/Robins Chamberlaine insolvent debtor of Talb Co/Anne Goldsborough admin of Charles Goldsborough/Chancery decree approving sale of property of James Clayland by John Gibson

409. ESHM Aug 4 1801/Died Mon 3rd inst, Mrs. Rebecca Hammond, consort of Nicholas Hammond of this town/lands for sale in QA Co, pt of Dawsons Neck where present tenant is Philip Porter and pt of Hawkins' Pharsalia where the tenant is Isaac Boggs and pt of Margaret's Hill where the tenant is Richard Baker, farm for sale in Talb Co called Long Point occupied by Jacob Gibson and tract called Heworth where the tenant is John Arrandale - by Joseph Haskins attorney for Messrs. R. Gilmore, William Patterson and J. Dall, Easton

410. ESHM Aug 11 1801/Doctor Mace offers his services - at his shop or at dwelling house of Thomas Lockerman, upper Hunting Creek Mill, Caroline Co

411. ESHM Aug 18 1801/Died Thurs last after a long and painful illness, John W. Harrison of Talb Co

412. ESHM Aug 25 1801/Died QA Co 13th inst, Colonel Arthur Emory, occasioned by a fall from his horse; he was Presiding Judge of the Orphan's Court of QA Co for a number of years; he was advanced in years/Samuel Sylvester, QA Co, to petition under the insolvency act/John Goldsborough, Howes Goldsborough, living near Cambridge, offer reward for three negroes: Jonathan, age about 30, Sylvia, age about 17, Sall, age about 2 years younger than Sylvia her sister/Brick dwelling house lately occupied as a tavern at St. Michaels by Samuel Harrison, for let/Samuel McMaster gives notice that the Presbyterian Congregation in Pitts Creek Hundred, Worc Co, to petition to be incorporated/ Chancery case: Daniel Cain versus John Earle, heir at law of Benjamin Earle regarding the sale of Upper Heathworth in QA Co

413. ESHM Sep 1 1801/Died on Wed morning last, after a long and painful illness Mrs. Ann Emerson of this town and on the following day her remains were attended by a large and respectable concourse of citizens to the burial ground of White Marsh Church/Coachee and horse for sale - Dr. Thomas Willson, near Queens Town/Chancery sale of real estate of William Moore, late of Cecil Co/ Francis Rosse to petition under the insolvency act

414. ESHM Sep 8 1801/Richard Denny, Deep Neck, Talb Co, offers reward for negro man, Harry, age about 19/Woolman Hewey, Miles River, offers reward for horse which strayed from the farm where Jonathan Hewey now lives/James Benson offers for sale the schooner Susan/Nicholas Mace admin of William Mace and Nicholas Mace, late of Dorch Co, dec/Lot for sale in Nanticoke Manor, Dorch Co, previously sold to Richard Waters by state of Md/Easton Academy lately under the direction of Rev John Bowie; in consequence of his death it will be opened under the direction of Charles Emory and Thomas Bowie - John Coats, chariman of the Standing Committee/Amos Warren Talb Co to petition under the insolvency act

415. ESHM Sep 15 1801/Died Sat last, Thomas W. Lockerman, Caroline Co/S. W. Pitt candidate for Delegate to the Assembly/George Truitt, John Holland, exec

Jonathan Hucheson, late of Worc Co/John Goldsborough, Cambridge, offers farm for sale a few miles above Chancellor's Point Ferry adj land of the late Capt Birckhead and Tristram Bowdle; apply to subscriber or John Goldsborough junr at Easton/Chancery Sale of land of James Johnson, late of QA Co, dec, at Mr. S. Sparks' Tavern, Church Hill - includes farm where George Willson now lives, a parcel adj lands of Charles Burgess and Allin Hollingsworth - John Duhamell, trustee

416. ESHM Sep 22 1801/James O'Bryon for Elizabeth Carradine admin of John Carradine, late of QA Co/Joseph Ennalls admin of Nathaniel Manning, late of Dorch Co/Ebenezer Perkins to petition under the insolvency act/William Hughlett, Spring Mills, offers mills for sale in Kent Co Del, 3 miles from Frederica/Robert Rolle, Dorch Co, to petition under the insolvency act

417. ESHM Sep 29 1801/Overseer wanted for estate of Mrs. Elizabeth G. Ennalls of Dorch Co - Charles Goldsborough/Mitchell Russum, secretary, announces upcoming races at Easton/Robert Anderson, Chestertown, partner in the House of Anderson & Murdic, to petition under the insolvency act/Thomas Gordon to petition under the insolvency act/Houses in Easton for sale, occupied by Charles Gulley, Peter Redhead, John Jefferies, William G. Killum, Thomas P. Smith, William Bromwell - Benjamin Willmott/James Bowie admin of Rev John Bowie

418. ESHM Oct 6 1801/Married Sun fe'night, Thomas H. Goldsborough, Talb Co, to Miss Maria Thomas dau of Honorable James Thomas of Annapolis/Margaret Walker admin of Thomas Wynn Loockerman, late of Caroline Co/William Brown of Joseph, Kent Co Md, to petition under the insolvency act/John McLaran to petition under the insolvency act/Levin Parsons, Worc Co, to petition under the insolvency act

419. ESHM Oct 13 1801/Died John Roberts of Talb Co yesterday morning after a few days illness/It is reported that the famous Peter White for whom the Governor and Council have offered a reward of 200 dollars, was taken a few nights past in the vicinity of Denton, by the strategem of a man of his own color./Sale by Charles Blair, Caroline Co, on his plantation of some years back, known as Mr. William Stephen's plantation, of cattle, sheep, farm utensils, household furniture/Henry Martin, Talb Co, offers reward for dark mulatto boy, Phil, age about 15/William Cornor, Talb Co, to petition under the insolvency act

420. ESHM Oct 20 1801/Married Thurs last Robins Chamberlaine of this town, to Miss Kitty Blake of QA Co/Married Mon 19 inst William Atkinson of Talb Co to Mrs. Hannah Awlston of Kent/Thomas Bruff, Princess Anne, Somerset Co, offers reward for information on the thief who broke into his shop (gold and silversmith)/Woodland for sale adj Dr. E. Martin and Samuel Abbott on the head of St. Michaels Creek; apply to William Harris, living near the land - Henry Maynadier/Porperty of widow Stevens for sale; she is living at the place called Rich Bottom - horses, cattle, sheep and household furniture

421. ESHM Oct 27 1801/Ann Wright, Dorch Co, gives notice that the power of attorney previously given to David Woolford is null and void and all persons indebted to her or Messrs. Nathan, Edward and Noble Wright of Dorch Co are forewarned against paying any said debts to David Woolford/On Fri evening last Theadore Wederstran Esg. of QA Co unfortunately fell from a door into the area of Even's Tavern in Balt, which put a period to his existance in a few minutes thereafter./Henry Colston, Talb Co and Elizabeth Colston of Dorch Co, admin of Jeremiah Colston, late of Dorch Co, dec/Sophia Harrison, Talb Co, exec of John Wynn Harrison, dec

422. ESHM Nov 3 1801/Died 23 Oct, Col. Moses LeCompte, Dorch Co, member of legistlature for many years

423. ESHM Nov 10 1801/Teackle, Dennis & Teackle of Princess Anne offer extensive assortment of merchandize/John Smith admin of David Smith late of Dorch Co/James Trippe junr admin of Paul McIntire, late of Dorch Co, dec/James Tucker admin of Richard Tucker, late of QA Co, dec

424. ESHM Nov 17 1801/Chancer sale of real estate near the head of Chruch Creek, Dorch Co, late the porperty of Edward Wright, dec, and known as Addition to White Havan, also 12 lots of land westward of Fort Cumberland in Alleghany Co - Ann Wright, trustee/"...The dwelling house of John Kearsey, Esq, on the Bay-side of Talb unfortunately took fire on Thursday the 12th inst. and was entirely consumed with all its furniture."

425. ESHM Nov 24 1801/On Thurs 19th inst a funeral sermon was delivered by Rev Works over the remains of John Roberts, Esq. late of Talb Co; Mr. Works was then succeeded by Rev. Mr. Moore and the Rev. Mr. Sparks; Mr. Roberts was a representatvie forseven years, an associate judge.../William Lloyd Bewly, living in QA Co, near Nine Bridges, Caroline Co, offers reward for horse strayed from the pasture of David Robinson in Oxford Neck, Talb Co

426. ESHM Dec 1 1801/On Fri last Peter White, pursuant to his sentence, was executed on the commons near Denton. It is said that this unhappy man died truly penitent of all his crimes./Died Tues last Basil Sewell/Died same day William Applegate of Talb Co/Henry Downes exec of Robert Williams to sell dwelling plantation adj land of William Hindman and lands of the heirs of Dr. Wilson on Wye River/Mary Tripp to rent two houses on Harrison St, now occupied by Mrs. Sarah Dawson and William McGuire

427. ESHM Dec 8 1801/Chancery sale by William Barroll of real estate of William Sluby/Married Thurs last by Rev Rigg, Richard Tilghman Earle to Miss Polly Tilghman dau of Hon. James Tilghamn, all of QA Co/Married Sun last by Rev Rigg, William Dawson Thomas of QA Co to Miss Polly Dawson, eldest dau of William Dawson, Talb Co/Farm for rent on Bay-side adj John Kersey by Rachel Thomas, Oxford Neck

428. ESHM Dec 15 1801/Nathan Mills, Kent Co Del, offers reward for delivery of stolen horse to Matthias Clifton in Delaware

429. ESHM Dec 29 1801/Chancery case: Solomon Clayton and others versus James McCabe and others regarding will of Mary Elbert in which all her estate was devised to James McCabe fraudulent means; also sale to McCabe of two tracts in QA Co called Reward and Mackley's Addition/Chancery case: creditors of Joseph Johnson are requested to present claims to Joseph Briscoe, trustee

430. ESHM Jan 12 1802/Greenbury Goldsborough, Talb Co, near Oxford, offers reward for dark mulatto man, James Steel, age about 30

431. ESHM Jan 19 1802/Died Sat morning last Mrs. Mary Blake, consort of John Blake of this place and on the day following her remains were attended by a great concorse of her friends and acquaintances to the Methodist burial ground/Mrs. Mansell of Chester-Town Boarding School has engaged the services of Rev. Joseph Douglas as a teacher

432. ESHM Mar 16 1802/Henry Hicks gives notice of caution that"my wife Peggy Hicks has behaved in a disagreeable manner that I cannot live with her.../ Mary Hitch admin of William Elgate Hitch/For sale all the estate of John Mulliken, after the death of his mother now an aged and infirm woman, the valuable farm near Hole in the Wall where he died/Chancery sale of land mortgaged by Levin Dorman, Somerset Co, to William Adams same co in favor of William Cottman & wife within 6 miles of Princess Anne - Henry J. Carroll, trustee/Plantation for sale in Wye Neck, QA Co by John King Downes, Wye Neck/ Samuel Brown admin of William S. Bond, dec, Talb Co/Samuel Thomas and Nicholas Martin junr, Easton, have opened a granary at Skipton/Chancery sale of the real

estate of James Johnson late of QA Co by John Duhamell in which tracts,
Marlins Beginning and Smith's Field were sold to Samuel Richester and the
tract called Compulson was sold to James Rochester

433. ESHM Mar 23 1802/Philemon Downes asserts "that John Turner of Easton,
is a coward."/William Willson, Kings Town offers services of his horse Pilate
to cover mares/Lloyd Day offers reward for negro Harry, age about 21, formerly
the property of Richard Denny of Talb; he made his escape from the habitation
of James Crookshanks, near Chester in Kent

434. ESHM Mar 30 1802/Chancery sale of realestate in Princess Anne of John
Purse, late of Somerset Co, dec, Evans Willing, trustee

435. ESHM Apr 7 1802/Died Wed morning 31 inst after a short illness of 16 hrs
Mrs. Elizabeth Applegate, relict of William Applegate/Defending the character
of John Turner in a card game: Thomas Daffin Caroline Co, James Nabb; John
Troth, Talb Co; PhilipClarke, Caroline Co; S. Reyner

436. ESHM Apr 13 1802/Sale of land in accordance with the last will and test
of James E. Denny, late of Talb Co, 278 a. adj Thomas Hardcastle and James
Broady in Caroline Co and 141 a. adj Potts' Mill in Talb Co - Henry Banning/
Solomon Barrott has removed to Easton and taken the house lately occupied by
Solomon Lowe, now distinguished by the sign of General Washington, where good
accommodations can be had for man and horse/Died Mrs. Margaret Bowie on Sun
evening last after a illness of about 5 hrs; she was the relict of Rev John
Bowie, late of Talb Co/James Price, attorney for George Roberts admin of John
Roberts

437. ESHM Apr 20 1802/James Lowe admin of James Lowe

438. ESHM Apr 27 1802/Married at Friends Mtg House Thurs 22 inst, Robert
Bartlett to Miss Sarah Fairbank, both of this co/David D. Barrow, near Dover
Ferry, offers reward for negro woman, Cate, age about 30, formerly belonged
to Thomas Barrow, Talb Co, dec, afterward the property of Benjamin Barrow,
also dec; subscriber becam admin of Benjamin Barrow

439. ESHM May 4 1802/Died Tues night last around 9 o'clock, Mrs. Anne Denny,
relict of the late James E. Denny of Talb Co

440. ESHM May 18 1802/James Buchanan, Kent Co Md, offers reward for mulatto
fellow, Tom, age about 40

441. ESHM Jun 1 1802/Edward Bromwell junr, William Patton, William Cornor
junr, Samuel Swann, all of Talb Co, insolvent debtors

442. ESHM Jun 8 1802/Samuel Stevens, Dividing Creek, notifies the public that
Richard Lyon, Methodist preacher of Somerset Co perverts the truth regarding
his accusation of James Goldsborough and Joseph Martin/Sale of property called
the Oak on St Michaels river - Owen Kennard, Easton, for Lloyd Nicols/James
Bond has taken a warehouse on McElderry's wharf for storage and commission
business; apply to Christopher Hughes or the James Bond

443. ESHM Jun 15 1802/Denwood Hicks, secretary, announces forthcoming races
at New Market

444. ESHM Jun 22 1802/Chancery sale of tract called Little England on road
from Easton to Cambridge, adj James Sherwood and a lot in Easton presently
under lease to Henry Nicols and Joshua Taggart - John Edmondson, trustee

445. ESHM Jul 6 1802/Farm for rent in Caroline Co, 2 miles from Dover Ferry,
now in tenure of David Waddle - William Frazier/George Shanahan, Thomas
Townsend advertise the availability of schooner, Fair American/Chancery sale
of real estate of Edward Dawson, late of Caroline Co, at Collins Cross Roads,
the farm whereon Elijah Cremeen junr now lives, called Dawson's Hazard -

446. ESHM Jul 13 1802/Daniel Fedeman, regr St. Michaels Parish announces meeting of the Vestry

447. ESHM Jul 20 1802/Robert Elliott holding sale of some household furniture - "going to Europe in the fall."/Anthony Banning admin of Mrs. Anne Denny, dec, to sell her estate at Oxford

448. ESHM Jul 27 1802/Married 22 inst at Friends Meeting House in the Bay-Side, Robert Dixon to Elizabeth Fairbanks, both of this co

449. ESHM Aug 17 1802/On Wed 4 inst the degree of Doctor of Divinity was confirmed on Rev James Kemp of Md at Columbia College, N. Y./Cattle sale on farm called Four Square near Barwicksburgh - John Goldsborough junr

450. ESHM Aug 24 1802/120 a. for sale on Miles River 1 1/2 miles from St. Michaels, late the property of Thomas Ashcroft, dec - Henry Banning, Hugh Sherwood, Perry Spencer, William B. Smith, John Dawson, Commissioners/John Fleming exec of Edward Halsey, late of Talb Co

451. ESHM Nov 2 1802/Died a few days ago in QA Co, William Brufe, merchant of Balt

452. RSM Mar 24 1801/Meeting of Commissioners of the Tax for Talb Co, Thomas Benning, clerk/Sale of 500 a. in Dorch Co at Chinamacomaco drawbridge and 400 a. across the river, formerly sold by John Murray to Alexander McIntire - Thomas Barnett, Dorch Co/White B. Smith, Federalsburgh constructs hanging and raising windows; those in upper end of Caroline, who may have a wish to have them hung in the new mode (without weights or springs), by a line to the care of Mr. Charles, innkeeper, at Denton, will be immediately attended to./ William Farrell junr, attorney for Ann Meeds admin of James Meeds, late of QA Co/House in Centreville to be sold, at present occupied by James Wilmer; apply to John Thompson within 3 weeks or afterward to David Nichols Centreville/Josiah Samuel offers reward for negroes: Levin, age about 30, formerly property of Mr. Chamberlain of Easton; James, age about 21, formerly property of Thomas Marsh Foreman; John, age about 25, formerly property of William S. Chandler of Balt/Benjamin O'Brian, Centreville, offers reward for a red Morrocco pocket book last between Mr. Roper's Tavern in Easton and John Clayland's gate/Farm for sale whereon George Gilbert now res, lying in QA Co, bounded on the south by lands of Col. Peregrine Tilghman, Sweatman Forman, and Mrs. Antonia Carmichael - seized and taken in execution as the property of William Carmichael at the suit of Thomas Worrell admin of John Ferrell - to be sold by Henry Costin, late sheriff of QA Co at Church-Hill/Thomas Daffin requests creditors of Charles Daffin junr of Caroline Co to attend at Denton for settlement

453. RSM Sep 7 1802/Died Sat evening last after a short illness, James Rose, only son of William Rose of this co; he has left a wife and two small children to lament his death/William Bromwell, Easton, continues to carry on the sadling business/Martin L. Haynie, Thomas Bayly, Somerset Co, to petition for the sale of real property of Doctor Ezekiel Haynie, late of Somerset Co, dec

454. RSM Sep 14 1802/Four mares for sale, Edward Coursey, Easton/Houses for rent, occupied by Mr. P. Willis, T. Harper, I. Atkinson - Samuel Baldwin

455. RSM Feb 22 1803/Celia Partridge, Dorch Co, admin of Jonathan Partridge, late of Dorch Co/William Croney admin of Joseph Blake, dec, Talb Co

456. RSM Mar 15 1803/Died Sun night last, James Cooper res of this co/ Elizabeth Sewall, Bayside, forewarns person from harbouring 2 negro men, Tom & Ambrose, sawyers by trade

457. RSM Aug 2 1803/Ann Sharp admin of Solomon Dickinson, Talb Co

458. RSM Aug 16 1803/Zebulon Hollingsworth's barn struck by lightning at Elk Landing and destroyed

459. RSM Dec 13 1803/Died Sun last in this town, Master Nathan Wright of QA Co, from taking a great draft of water after a severe exercise at play

460. RSM Jan 17 1804/Married Tues last in QA Co, William T. Wrgiht to Miss Betton, both of QA Co

461. RSM Jun 19 1804/Married 17 ult by Rev Walker, William Bowers to Miss Sarah L. Lamb, both of Kent Co/Married Sat 2nd inst by Rev Ralston Samuel Stevens junr of this co to the agreeable Miss Eliza May dau of Col. Robert May of Chester Co Pa/Married Mon 4th inst by Rev Keens junr, James Hammond of QA Co aged 64, to the agreeable and much adminred Miss McClement of Del aged 20/ Married Sun last, Thomas Robinson to Miss Elizabeth Crey, both of this town

462. RSM Jul 1804/Letters remaining at P.O. Easton: Thomas Abbott; Richard Adams; John Blake; Edward Burke; Mrs. Mabel Barns; Henry Bullin; Rev Francis Barkley; Dr. James Bordley; Brian & Roney; Miss Matilda Chase; Thomas Clarke; Joseph J. Cartrite; M. Chamberlain; Joshua Driver; Philemon Dickinson; William Dunn; Solomon Dickinson; James Delahay; Peter Johnson Downs; Pere Driver; James Edmondson; Charles Emory; James Earle junr; John Etherington; Robert Edgell; Joseph Farling; H. M. Frances; John Goldsborough; Charles Goldsborough; Thomas Godwin; Greenbury Goldsborough; William H. Goldsborough; John Hains; William W. Haddaway; Joseph Hutchins; Samuel Harrison; Thomas Harper; John Higgins; P. W. Helmsley; Robert Harrison; E. N. Hambleton; William Haddaway junr; Rev J. Jackson; Mrs. Silver Johnson; Rachael Kemp; Col. Richard Keene; Mrs. Rich. Keene; Dr. Samuel Y. Keene; Sally Kemp; Rev James Kemp; William Lowrey; Stanly B. Loockerman; John Lamb; Mrs. F. T. Loockerman; Thomas Monally; Richard B. Mitchell; Miss Mary Markland; Richard Martindale; James Nabb; E. L. A. Pelham; Mrs. E. Pamphilion; Lemuel Purnell; Mrs. Primrose; William Patton; James Price; John Quimby; Edward Roberts; Sally Ratcliff; Robert Speddin; Phil. Sherwood; Lydia Sherwood; Samuel Swan; Joseph Stingester; James Stanlee; William Sands; Mrs. A. M. Smyth; Richard Sneath; John Shannon; Hugh Sherwood; William Stant; Jenifer Taylor; Mrs. Eliza Thomas; William Tibles; Charles Twiford; Dekar Thompson; Joshua Taggart; Thomas Vickars; George Walker; Daniel Whelan; Thomas Wing; Hugh Work; Henry Wright; Samuel Willson; Stephen Young/ Henry Nicols junr, Talb Co, trustee for Samuel Nicols, insolvent debtor of Talb Co; creditors may settle accounst with Bennet Wheeler or Hall Harrison or Henry Nicols/Patrick Kennard exec of Philip Everitt, late of Kent Co Md/ For sale - merchant mill and farm in the Head of QA Co - John Campbell, Bridge -Town, Kent Co

463. RSM Jul 10 1804/Married Fri evening last by Rev Francis Barckley, Josiah Polk junr of Somerset Co to Miss Rebecca Troup of this town/John Comegys, Kent Co, admin of Abraham Millan and Daniel Greenwood, dec/Samuel Thomas, Easton Point, Talb Co, offers reward for negro man, Ralpher, formerly property of Mrs. Hollyday, near Easton; he is about 30 yrs old/Chancery sale by James Brooke in the use of John and Henry Page against John Chew and St. Ledger Meeks/Front room of house occupied by Mrs. Mary Dawson for rent by Impey Dawson/John Kemp exec of George F. Dawson/Letters remaing at P.O. Chestertown: Levi Alexander; Mrs. Frances Andrews; Moses & Aron Ashley; Mrs. Sarah Ambers; Elijah Beck; Hasea Beckley; James Bradshaw; Joseph Blackiston junr; Mr. Borrall; George Corell; John Campbell; James Cruckshanks; Hezekiah Cooper; John Collins; Nathaniel Davis; James Eagle; Joseph Everitt; Thomas Edwards; Mrs. Margaret Fletcher; Sweetman Ferman; James Frisby junr; Mrs. Nancy Gibson; Thomas Gale; Miss Mary Hamel; Thomas Hynson; John Heron; Judy Holland; Mathew Hawkins; Upton S. Heath; Mrs. Isabella Jones; Samuel Keene junr; Richard Keene; John Leatherbury; Richard Mitchel; Alexander Maxwell; James Melton; William Newman; Miss Maria Nicholson; Jeremiah Nicols; Joseph Pennington; John Paley; Daniel Pirkins; James Ross; Mrs. Mary Rasin; Henry Ringgold;

Joseph Simmonds; Thomas Smith; James Stoops; Henry H. Stuart; William Thomas; Mrs. Anna Trulock; Philip Taylor; Marmaduke Tilden; Richard Tilghman; Rev Simon Wilmer; George Way; David Whiteing/Letters remaining at P.O. Centreville: James Bateman; Perigrine Blake; Mathias Boardley; Richard Collins; Mr. Cuiso; Mrs. Charlotte Clayland; Reynolds & Clarke; John Davis; Miss Nancy Edward; Richard J. Earle; Charles Emory; Mrs. Elizabeth Fiddeman; Mrs. Polly Harris; Benjamin Hatcheson; Mrs. Holliday; Richard Harris; Benjamin Hall; Mrs. Anna Honey; Miss A. M. Kent; James Hindle; Samuel Kerr; Samuel Keene; James Kerr; David Lucas; Daniel McGinnis; Hugh McAllister; Haley Moffitt; Charles Neale; Benjamin Obryon; James Pryor; Jacob Pearce; John Patrick; John Southrose; John Scrivener; Thomas Sharp; Peter Seth junr; Jessee M. Sherwood; Thomas Smith; William Taylor; Mrs. Anne Tilden; Sam. S. Voorhees; Mrs. Ann Warfield; Henry Weeden

464. RSM Jul 17 1804/Married Thurs last by Rev Stockett, John B. Campbell aged 20 yrs to Mrs. Jane Armstrong, both of QA Co/Robert Dixon admin of Joseph Dixon, late of Caroline, dec/Thomas Kersey has houses for rent near Easton/ James Pursley, Miles River Neck, wants a place either as a teacher or clerk to keep accounts

465. RSM Jul 24 1804/James Nicholson and George Attwood, Centreville, running two schooners as packets from Centreville to Balt/William and Thomas Atkinson admin of James Cooper, late of Talb Co/William Clayton, secretary of the Centreville Academy

466. RSM Jul 31 1804/Aaron Merchant, overseer for Edward Harris's farm QA Co, near Seth's Mill, offers reward for negro lad, Dick, age about 18, who has relations on the Bay-Side with a Mr. Harrison/William Lowrey to let house where he now lives in Trappe/Chancery sale by Solomon Scott of property which was mortgaged by George Baynard to Henry Pratt; Chancery order to be served on William Todd or published in newspaper

467. RSM Feb 12 1805/Married Sun evening 2d inst by Rev S. Wilmer, Dr. John Maxwell to Miss Elizabeth Redgrave, both of Kent Co/Died Mon 4th inst Mrs. Leah Bayly consort of Josiah Bayly, Cambridge

468. ESHC May 17 1791/Sale of prop of Moses Ringrose, dec, at Col Lloyd's farm called Hamonds where dec did dwell - Arthur Bryan admin/Edward Vidler makes bricks/Arthur Bryan offers reward for three man slaves who ran away from the farm of John Beale Bordley, near Chestertown: Harry, age about 30; Jim, age about 20; Jim age about 25

469. ESHC May 24 1791/John S. Crapper, Dorch Co, reports that Eli Smoot, a young gentleman in Capt John Smoot's family was cruelly and inhumanly murdered by a negro man, property of Capt John Smoot, named Will. He has obtained a pass that Francis Waters, Somerset Co, gave to one of his negro men called David. It is expected that he will make for the neighborhood of Warner Mifflen of Delaware/Partnership of Thomas Hughlett & son, Choptank-Bridge dissolved/ business relative to partnership will be settled by William Hughlett-who continues to do business at the same place and stores/James Vansandt, Easton, seeks apprentices to carpenters & joiners business/William Perry selling young negro woman; apply to Col. William Richardson, Caroline Co or Samuel Swan in Easton/B. M. Ward gives notice that George Biscoe did, in the year 1786, fraudulently obtain a note for about 20 odd pounds, which note has been assigned to Spedden Bromwell

470. ESHC Dec 27 1791/Peter Gordon exec of Archibald Patison, late of Dorch Co/Henry Martindale & Thomas Hicks admin of Michael Melooney, late of QA Co, dec/Chancery decree requests creditors against Thomas Kalendar, Dorch, to present their claims/Henry Darby, William Clay - New Castle and John Chambers Caecil Court House announce new stage line from Philadalelphia to Easton by

way of Caecil Court House and New Castle Del

471. ESHC Jul 24 1792/John L. Bozman renting plantation on which Tristram
Martin now lives, lying on Third-haven in Talb Co/For rent - Walnut Ridge
Farm near Chester Mill, QA Co; also farm near Tuckahoe Bridge, Talb Co where
James Plummer now lives; apply to Robert Lloyd Nicols, Talb Co/Managers of
lottery to dispose of land in Dorch Co and Annapolis: John Davidson, James
Shaw, John Randall,of Annapolis;Col. Uriah Forrest, Colonel William Deakins,
of Georgetown; Colonel Peter Chaille, Capt Levin Handy, Worc; Gustavus Scott,
Alexander Douglas, William S. Bond, Dorch; Samuel Chamberlain, William
Hindman, Talb; Colonel William Richardson, Peter Edmondson, Caroline; James
Hollyday, QA. The property has been deeded to subscribers (Gabriel Duvall and
William Campbell) by Clement Hollyday for the purpose of redeeming certain
notes/Forming a society of builders - Cornelius West, James Benson, James
Vansandt/Letter to editor from Susanna Greentree (Mr. Greentree is not at
home.) regarding incident involving Jacob Gibson in shearing some of her sheep
by accident/William Winstandly regarding the above sheep shearing incident/
Jacob Gibson correct a letter regarding Samuel Tannant, William Mason, and
Thomas Coward/Joseph Huzza riding as a post from Easton to Dover Del/Nicholas
Watts announces his horse Brilliant at Joseph Denny's in Dirty Neck on Fri; at
John Kearsey's, Bay Side on Sat; Francis Morling's below Easton on Mon & Tues
and at James E. Enny's just above Easton later part of Tues/A lot for sale on
Miles River, Talb Co by James Barrow/Chancery sale of tract called Pearl,
property of Walter Meeds, dec, in QA Co, about 1 1/2 miles from Calliester's
ferry on Chester River, by James Scott, trustee

472. ESHC Dec 23 1800/Died in this town on 15 inst Kendal Flint, saddler/
William M. Catrop will sell at his farm near Hook-Town the remaining part of
the property which was taken from Isaac Chambers/George Baily informs the
public that hs has given up his shop to Dr. Moore who will carry on the
business under the firm of Moore & Bailey - drugs, medicines, dyes and paints;
Dr. Moore will leave Easton near the commencement of the new year - in case of
his absence those indebted may pay Doctor Moore/Hugh Work has a store house in
the Trappe for rent/Richard Martindale requests settlement of debts to the
estate of Ludwick Wainer, late of Easton/Mrs. Keats to open boarding school
for 12 young ladies at Mrs. Blake's Farm about 1 miles from Centreville/
Charles Emory exec of John Sheppard, late of Talb Co/Alexander Innes, a hatter,
was some time ago on board the constellation frigate, and was in 1798 in
Norfolk Va; he has not been since heard of. Anyone knowing of his situation
would please communicate it by post to Robert Innes junr, merchant, Easton Pa/
Lauder Mistor and Milly Ross, Dorch Co, offer reward for two negro men/Samuel
Swan, Easton, seeks cook, waiter, hostler, and waggoner for hire/John Harwood,
Easton, will accommodate 4 or 5 boarders

473. ESHC Aug 28 1798/Thomas Nicols, Caroline Co, Federalsburgh, candidate for
General Assembly/James Nabb, Talb Co, offers reward for negro man, Paris/
Houses for rent in Easton; apply to Charles Gulley, near the printing office
in Easton, or to Mark Benton, Kent Island/Henry Hollyday, Talb Co, wants an
overseer

474. ESHC Dec 11 1798/Senah Busick admin of William Keene, Dorch Co; all
indebted make immediate payment to John Brohann, on Slaughter's Creek/Letters
remaining at P.O. Easton: William Atkinson, at Bartholomew Ennalls's, Cambridge;
Margaret Andison, Easton; William Burtt, Choptank river; Stanley Byus, Eastern
Shore of Maryland; Christopher Birckhead, Maryland; James Birckhead; Thomas
Bright, Easton; Thomas J. Bullitt; Charles K. Bryan, Cambridge; William Boon,
in Denton; Thomas Curtis, Easton; John Dawson, Denton; James Earle; Benjamin
Elliott, St. Martins; Mrs. Henrietta M. Frazier, Caroline Co; Rev Joseph
Flood, Cambridge; Fergus & Reed, Cambridge; John Fleming, Easton; Jacob Fowle,
Maryland; Capt Greenbury Griffin, St Michaels; Charles Gibson; Obadiah Garey,

-73-

Talb Co; John E. Gist, Cambridge; Thomas Harrison, Broad Creek; Thomas
Hardcastle, near Easton; Robert Hay, St. Michaels; James Hardcastle, Caroline
Co; Christopher Harrison, Cambridge; Charles Hodson, Cambridge; Alexander
Kinnery, Easton, or if not there Baltimore; William Meluy or in his absence
Samuel Edmondson, Easton; Thomas O. Martin; Patrick McIntire; Mr. McDonald,
Cambridge; Henry Nicols, Easton; Thomas Nicols, Federalsburgh; Peter Redhead,
Easton; Edward Roberts, Talb Co; Peter Rea, Cambridge; John Reed, Cambridge;
William Smith, Tuckahoe Bridge; James Shaw; Henry Somerville, Cambridge;
Joseph Sulivan, New Market; William Thompson, blacksmith, Easton; Thomas
Weaver; George Ward, Cambridge; Henry Waggaman, Cambridge/Emory Sudler,
insolvent debtor/Matthias Bordley, Wye River, offers reward for Jem Merick,
young negro man, formerly the property of Capt Henry Coursey; his father, Old
Merick, lives in a place belonging to Capt Coursey, between Kent Island
Narrows and Greenwood's Creek/Simon Wilmer exec of John L. Wilmer and admin
of Catharine Brown/William S. Bond admin of Massey Fountain

475. ESHC Dec 16 1800/Inhabitants of Dorch Co to petition for a public road
from end of road made by John Williams and Thomas Colston, to intersect
Blackwater road

476. ESHC Jan 4 1803/Public sale at farm called Thomas one coachee and horse,
cows, horses, oxen and farming utensils by Charles Goldsborough exec of
Rebecca Goldsborough, dec, Pleasant Valley/In consequence of a report that
Peter Denny, Esq. was accessary to the late cowardly attack of Jacob Gibson
upon my person, I (at the request of Mr. Denny) hereby declare my belief in
the innocence of Mr. Denny relative to the above mentioned report. J. Cowan/
Richard Stanfied, Easton, trustee for creditors of Samuel Swan

477. ESHT Apr 5 1791/Subscribers are appointed to erect a court house and
gaol in QA Co and intend to meet at Chester Mill, QA Co - Henry Pratt, Robert
Walters, Solomon Clayton, Philip Fiddemon, Thomas Caradine

478. ESHT Mar 3 1801/Herring Fishery situated on the waters of Great Choptank
known as Wing's Landing for rent; apply to Miss Elizabeth Alcock, living near
the fishery or to the subscriber, David Woolford, living near Cambridge/Robert
H. Goldsborough exec of William Goldsborough/Lots for sale near the Church in
St. Michaels by order of the vestry, Daniel Fiddeman

479. ESHT Mar 10 1801/John Lowe admin of James Lowe of Talb Co/Elizabeth
Willis admin of William Willis, Talb Co/By authority of representatives of
Thomas Alcock, late of Caroline Co, I offer to rent the Herring Fishery on the
waters of the Great Choptank

480. ESHT Mar 24 1801/Married Sun 15 inst by Rev Bowie, Dr. William B. Keene
of Caroline Co to Miss Betsy Clayland of Talb Co/Ann McIntire admin of Patrick
McIntire, late of Talb Co/William Lambdin, living in Bayside, Talb Co, offers
reward for mulatto man about 18 to 20 yrs old who was purchased from Capt John
S. Blake, Mouth of Wye/Sale of building and property by James Ritchie,
Salisbury/Sale of 400 a. in Dorch Co by Thomas Barnett of Dorch Co, formerly
sold by John Murray to Alexander McIntire

481. ESHT Mar 31 1801/Thomas Field offers dry goods for sale opposite New
Market House, Easton/Edward Martin admin of Nicholas Martin/Joseph Telford,
Easton, intends to make a voyage to the West Indies/Daniel Knock, Kent Co, Md,
to petition under the insolvency act/John Wilkins admin of Jesse Holland

482. ESHT Apr 21 1801/Richard Newman has commenced running a stage between
Centre-Ville and the City of Washington by way of Queen's-town, Shirk town and
Broad Creek, Kent Island to Annapolis, twice a week/John Ward & John H. Price
to petition under the insolvency act/John Earle Denny, living near Wye-Mill,
QA Co, offers reward for yellow negro girl name Cate about 17 yrs old/Sale of
plantation of Arthur Bryan of Talb Co, dec, by William Bryan and Henry Hobbs
of Wye Manor, admin of Arthur Bryan/Elizabeth Meconekin admin of John Meconekin

offers reward for negro lad named Sam about 18 yrs old who was raised by Lewis
Derochbrune on Kent Island and lately the property of John Meconekin of near
Wye-Mill, QA Co/Letters remaining at P.O. Easton: Hugh Auld; Philemon H. Able;
Clement L. Breadey; Jacob Barney; James Booker; Nathan Basset; George Bailey
& Co; Rachel Carcekson, care of Parson Bowie; Oliver Cowan; Robins Chamberlaine;
Philip Corrigan; Dooris & Corrigan; James Dooris; Charles Emory; Samuel Elbert;
Samuel Edmondson; Michael Flax; William Frazier; John Ferguson; Peregrine
Granett; Thomas Goldsborough; Mary Gordon; Z. Gregory; Thomas Haney; Kitty E.
Hutchins; Edmund Hayward; Samuel Hopkins; John Lucas 3d; Edward Markland; Lucy
Morgan; Tristram Needles; Richard Pritchard; Parry Prouse; John Price; Thomas
Rob erts; Edward Roberts; Edward Stevens; William Stevens; Mr. Stevens, saddler;
John Seney; Mary Seney; Samuel Swan; D. Sulivane; Archibald Serrell; Joshua
Taggart; Sarah Troup; Mary Valliant; Anthony Wheatley; John Walker; William
Walker; Cornelius West; Edward White; John Young/Charles Goldsborough admin of
Mary Ann Goldsborough of Talb Co/Sarah Vickers offers reward for bay roan mare
strayed or stolen from her plantation in Talb Co/Leverton and Pardin have
commenced the coach making business at Bridge-Branch

483. ESHT Apr 28 1801/Married a few days ago, John Dickinson to Miss Loyd dau
of James Loyd of Talb Co/John E. Gist exec of Peter Webb, admin of Alexander
McCallum and admin of Hester McCallum, offers for sale the plantation in
Banbury, Talb Co, which the late Peter Webb purchased of John T. Birckhead/
John Councell admin of James Glandon of Caroline Co, to settle accounts at
Nine Bridges/Whereas Rouse Gray, Worc Co, did obtain a note of hand from Samuel
Polk, minor of Somerset Co, for $55 for which Samuel Polk has never rec'd
consideration/Thomas N. Williams admin of Layfield Collier/Lanta Wright and
John Bishop admin of John Wright of Worc Co

484. ESHT Jan 26 1802/William Richmond and William Bryan admin of Arthur Bryan
of Wye Manor/John Dickinson, Talb Co, offers reward for negro man Oliver about
25 yrs old/William Craft admin of John Bestpilete late of Dorch/Died on Tues
last 19th inst Mrs. Mary Yates, consort of Thomas Yates, of the city of Balt/
Sale of the mansion of the late Major Richard Chew AA Co/James Kemp, Castle
haven, offers reward for negro man, Jack, belonging to Edward Noel Cox/John
Roberts admin of Elizabeth Pickering late of Talb Co

485. ESHT Mar 9 1802/Samuel Brown admin of William S. Bond, late of Talb Co/
Samuel Thomas and Nicholas Martin Junr announce they have opened a granary at
Skipton on Wye River for immediate reception of wheat and corn/
Died Mon 1st inst, John Thomas, sheriff of Talb Co; Hugh Sherwood of Huntington
will be his successor/Richard Denny lost 80 dollars in Easton/John Hasset,
overseer, offers reward for negro man named Jack Holland, 38 yrs old, who ran
away from the farm of Mrs. Mary Wederstrandt near Wye Mill, QA Co; also Jack's
wife, Fanny, 36 yrs old; a girl Teresa commonly called Cresy, dau of Jack and
Fanny about 13 yrs old; a negro girl named Suck, Terresa's sister, about 10 yrs
old. They left their two small children, one age three and the other age 1 yr/
Solomon Scott, trustee, to sell dwelling house of John Partrick in QA Co in
Tullie's Neck and the real estate of the late Col. George Baynard, dec, that
was mortgaged to Henry Pratt lying in Tullie's Neck/Zacharias Roberts,
surveyor of QA Co, wants a single man who understands
arithmetic well/John Davidson, trustee, to sell interests of Joseph Massay and
John and Benjamin Comegys to tract in Kent Co called Partnership and Dungarnon,
Massey's Addition and a tract on which Richard Semans lived - to satisfy debt
on mortgage from Joseph Massey to John and Benjamin Comegys and a judgement
obtained by Frederick Grammar against Joseph Massey/William Winder admin John
Rackliff late of Worc Co/Real estate of James Johnson late of QA Co sold by
trustee John Duhamell

486. ESHT May 25 1802/Thomas Manning admin of John Manning late of Dorch Co/
Fri night last the dwelling house of Isaac Farrington of Somerset Co sustained

considerable injury by lightning - But what is particularly distressing in
this event is the loss of Mr. Farrington's son (a child) who became an instant
victim to the destructive spark/Died 13th inst Mrs. Elizabeth Rose consort of
William Rose resident near this place/Died Wed night last, after a tedious
illness, John Duncan, an old and respectable citizen of this town/Lambert W.
Spencer responds to accusations by B. Richardson that Spencer is a coward and
a liar; following this item is a notice by Richard Barroll of Chestertown who
states that Lambert W. Spencer is a coward and a paltroon/Chancery decree case
- James Corrie admin of John Corrie vs James Hindman and Parrett Clarke's heirs
in which creditors of Parrott Clarke are requested to make claims to chancery
court/John A. Smith admin of David Smith, late of Dorch Co/James Bacon admin
of Captain John Handy, late of Worc Co/Mathew Dorman admin of Nehemiah Dorman,
late of Worc Co/Mary Anne Rice exec of George Rice, late of Worc Co/Sale of
land mortgaged by Robins Chamberlaine to Anna Maria Holliday by John Edmondson,
trustee for creditors/Charles M. Bromwell of Talb Co applies for relief under
the insolvency act/James Buchanan of Kent Co offers reward for mulatto named
Tom about 40 yrs old, 5 feet, 8 to 10 inch high/Chancery case - James Lloyd,
William Bryan, William Hemsley, Thomas Carwelle, Philip Tayler and Simon Wickes,
complainants regarding the legal title of certain lands sold by James Lloyd,
the other complainant, which said lands were conveyed 20 May 1780 to James
Tilghman, now dec, from whom the estate has to the defendants who are his heirs
at law; the defendants: William Tilghman, Richard Millbank Tilghman, Harriet,
Caroline, Emily and Charlott Tilghman res out of the state of Maryland; the
other defendants are James, Elizabeth, Maria, Ann and Margaret Tilghman/Mary
Hitch admin of William Elgate Hitch, late of Somerset Co/Peter Medford of Dorch
Co applies under the insolvency act

487. ESHT Jun 29 1802/John Stevens Junr announces a new druggist shop next
door to the New Market house in Easton/Morgan Brown admin of Morgan Brown, late
of Kent Co/To sell real estate of Hessey Deford, heiress of Joseph Deford, late
of Talb Co, for the use of creditors of Joseph Deford, the house of William
Casson of Hillsborough and all the real estate of said Joseph Deford, being
part of a tract called Keld's Inheritance, about two miles from Tuckahoe Bridge
in Talb Co (William Jones lives on the premises)/Edward Bromwell sen of Oxford
offers reward for negro woman named Jinny with three children: girl 4 yrs old,
boy about 3 yrs old, girl about 4 months old, mulattos, supposed to be stolen
away by Jinny's husband, Richard Wilson, a free mulatto/Chancery case of John
Mace against Elizabeth Meddis regarding tract called Head Range conveyed to
John Mace father of complainant in 1771; said John Mace died in 1796; Elizabeth
Meddis res out of state. Tract situated in Dorch Co/Taxes due for 1801 on land
in Caroline Co: Mariah MacDearmont; John Turner's heirs - Abner Park; William
Elliot Greffiths heirs; Thomas Studham's heirs - Pratts Hope; James Cooke -
Baynards Cowpens; John Cheshire's heirs - house and lot in Denton/George
Shanahan and Thomas Townsend announce the launching of the schooner, Fair
American /Philip Richardson, trustee, to sell real estate of Edward Dawson of
Carolline Co for benefit of creditors at public sale at Collinses's Cross Roads
- the farm whereon Elijah Cremeen junr, now lives, fomerly the property of
said Edward Dawson, called Dawson's Hazard/Thomas Bruff of St Michaels offers
reward for negro woman, Precilla,\with girl about 6 yrs and a boy about 4 yrs;
Precilla is about 35 yrs, formerly lived in Caroline Co with John Valliant/
Rebecca Elbert and Henry Costine admin of Doctor Joshua Elbert late of QA Co/
Mary Barrow, living in QA Co, offers reward for negro man, Will, about 25 yrs
old, 5 feet, 6 or 7 inch high/Matts. Bordley, The Island, Wye River, offers
reward for Dick, mulatto lad about 17 yrs old, seen near Emmerson's warehouse/
Dr. John Stevens, junr, Easton; Ferguson and Reed, Cambridge; and James
Clayland, Centreville, offer valuable medicines for sale/Sale of real estate of
Charles Dickinson, late of Caroline Co, but now res at Nashville Tenn, lying

in Caroline Co between branches of Fowling Creek and Hunting Creek, divided by the main road; the first lot includes the farm where William Kelly now lives; 2nd lot includes the farm whereon Solomon Jones now lives; 3rd lot includes Manor Plantation of late Henry Dickinson - by William Richardson, atty of Charles Dickinson

488. ESHT Aug 3 1802/Sale of estate of Robins Chamberlaine known as Peach Blossom including that purchased by said Chamberlain of Mrs. Anna Maria Hollyday and by him mortgaged to Daniel Carroll of Balt Co/Tristram Needles admin of Samuel Bowman, late of Talb Co/Isaac Atkinson of Easton offers for sale, boot-legs, calf-skins, shoes, boots/Isaac Dreddin admin of William Boland late of Somerset Co/Chancery case - Hamilton and sons and others vs Frederick, Elizabeth, Henry and Mary Randall, heirs at law of Francis Randall, dec who died intestate leaving lots in Snow Hill, Worc Co to the defendants who are infants. Frederick Randall and Elizabeth Randall have removed out of the state

489. ESHT Aug 10 1802/Isaac Purnell of Caroline Co to petition to erect mill on the Choptank near the place where Thomas Hardcastle has built a new bridge/ William Marshall, secretary of New Market Races/Benjamin Denny, Carolline Co, offers reward for dark mulatto woman, Kate, 25-30 yrs old/J. E. Gist exec of Col. Robert Hanson of Dorch Co, dec, to sell his personal property including sett of black smiths tools/John E. Spencer, Centreville, offers reward for black man, Tom Short, about 50 yrs old, hired last year to Mr. Newman of Centreville

490. ESHT Sep 7 1802/Sale of farms of Richard Newman in QA Co, Meagreholm and Ashley; Mr. Levick lives on the premises. Also a farm in Caroline County called Hobbs Venture where Gallant Lamer lives

491. ESHT Sep 14 1802/Married Thurs last by Rev Price, Edward Roberts to Mary Tilghman of Talb Co/House for rent now occupied by John C. Stewart as tavern, with stalbes, by Thomas Stewart, Cambridge/Martin L. Haynie and Thomas Bayly, Somerset Co, to petition for the sale of the property of Doctor Ezekiel Haynie, late of Somerset Co/Edward Hall, QA Co, to petition under the insolvency act/ William Fitzue, living near the mouth of the Patuxant River, St. Mary's Co, offers reward for mulatto fellow named Nace, about 22 yrs old who crossed the Chesapeake Bay, landing at Meakin's Neck, Dorch Co, in company with two black fellows: Robert Wattson and John Hughes. They were seen at a methodist meeting near the place where they landed/Benjamin Craft, William Craft, Samuel Philips, Hugh Craft, all of Dorch Co, to petition to erect public road of our private road, beginning at a point on Chicmecomico Road to Nanticoke Riverside/David Shippey, Dorch Co, intends to petition under the insolvency act

492. ESHT Sep 21 1802/Thomas N. Williams admin of Layfield Collins, late of Worc Co; persons having claims appear at the Trapp in Worc Co/Farms for rent in Caroline Co at head of Fowling Creek, where Mr. Jones is tenant and the second adjoining the former where Mr. Rumble is tenant/Samuel Nicols, Easton, to sell farm near Easton occupied by John Clayland and house and counting room near Easton which he presently occupies/William Jones, Chester Town, to petition for release from debts/Richard Besswriks to petition for release from from debts/Daniel Deady, Balt, offers reward for mulatto slave name Bill Teen, about 28 yrs old, raised in this county by Edward Ridgley, dec, and after his death owned by James Edwards of Balt who sold him to Mr. Cromwell near Reistertown from whom I bought him/Samuel Veasey, Worc Co, to petition for divorce from wife Sally Veasey/John Campbell, Princess Anne, to petition for relief from debts/Elizabeth Townsend admin of Levin Townsend, late of Worc Co

493. ESHT Feb 9 1802/John Black, trustee, to sell real estate of Isaac Perkins, late of Kent Co, Md, at Benjamin Hatchison's Tavern in Chestertown, property on Still Pond Creek called Cannell's Point; a tract called Muddy Branch near

I. U. Church and the Quaker Meeting House in Kent Co; also tract called
Hackett's Farm near Chester Town; two a. of wood land adj Jesse Comegy's land
and Perkins's Mill pond in Kent Co/Henry Colston of Talb Co and Elizabeth
Colston of Dorch Co admin of Jeremiah Colston, late of Dorch Co/Property in
Somerset Co of following persons to be sold for taxes: William Adams' heirs -
Pt. Waley Chance, pt Waley Chance, pt Cramburn, pt Trouble, pt Windsor, Mill
Lot, North forhand, Marsh; Isaiah Dorman - Dorman's Discovery, Dorman's
Conclusion; Tubman Woolford - Thornton, Jessemine, Hackle, Thomas' Beginning;
Thomas Pollitt's heirs - Addition to Hog Yard; Joseph Cotro - a lot; James
Polk's heirs - 405 a., name unknown/Sale of land of Robins Chamberlaine, an
insolvent debtor of Talb Co, lately occupied by John Jones adj Easton/Sale by
Henry Banning exec of James E. Denny of land in Talb Co adj plantation called
the Fork between Easton and Centreville; also farm adj Thomas Hardcastle and
James Brodey in Caroline Co

494. ESHT Mar 2 1802/George Parratt exec of Slitter Parratt and admin of
Richard Arringdell, both late of Talb Co/Chancery sale of real estate of Maurce
Ellers

495. ESHT Oct 12 1802/Thomas Gordon to petition for relief from debtors/Henry
Coursey, QA Co, to sell 220 a. on Eastern Bay/James Dickinson to petition for
relief from debts/Married 25th ult by Rev Kemp, Capt Bartholomew Byus to Miss
Delia Noel/Married 10th inst, Joseph Haskins of Balt to Miss Henrietta Sulivane
of Dorset/Married 10th inst by Rev Wilmer, Jacob Loockerman to Miss Mary
Harrison of Dorset

496. ESHT Oct 26 1802/Sale at farm of Mr. Chamberlaine rented by Mr. Tilford
near Easton/Chancery case of William Slubey's creditors: Edward Wright, William
Embleton, John Warder & Co, Benjamin R. Morgan

497. ESHT Nov 16 1802/Samuel Hooper, Dorch Co, renting farm near Middle Town/

498. ESHT Dec 7 1802/Ezekiel Richardson, sheriff of Dorch Co, has a negro man
in gaol who calls himself William and says he was born free in Va/Chancery case
- John Hughes vs Bennett Bracco, grandson of John Bracco, and James Boker &
wife/Miss Mary Ann Fletcher who has acted as assistant in a school in Phila
offers instruction to young ladies of Easton/John Singleton exec of William
Walker, late of Talb Co/Elizabeth Townsend admin of Levin Townsend, late of
Worc Co/Richard Stanfield appointed trustee for the creditors of Samuel Swan
of Easton

499. ESHT Mar 1 1803/John Shanahan, Talb Co, offers reward for Daniel Haskins,
about 22 yrs old, yellow complexion/Chancery case - Claims of Edward Wright and
William Embleton are not established to the Chancellor's satisfaction/Richard
Butler offers reward for negro man named Saul, about 19 yrs old, who ran away
from owner about 10 miles from Hancock, on the Patowmack, purchased from Dr.
Daniel Sullivan of New Market/Real estate of John Purse sold by Evans Willing,
trustee/Chancery sale at Denton of pt of tract, Revival, in Tuckahoe Neck,
property of Anna, Susanna and Lydia Clarke, for the payment of debts of Parrot
Clarke/Chancery case - John Skinner and wife vs state of Md; creditors of
Thomas Groves dec of Talb Co notified to exhibit claims

500. ESHT Mar 8 1803/William Crane and Hester Crane admin of Richard
Blackiston, late of QA Co/George Grundy and Joseph Thornburgh, assignees of the
estate of Aquila Brown junr, bankrupt, will sell in Balt a tract called Sillen
on Kent Island; also a store in Balt/Chancery sale of real estate of Benjamin
Woolford dec, situated in Dorch Co on the head of Tabaccostick Bay, by Thomas
Loockerman, senr, trustee/Saddle horse for sale by Solomon Lowe in Aston

501. ESHT Mar 22 1803/Died Fri last, Capt Robert Ewing, an old and respectable
inhabitant of this county/John Campbell of Somerset Co, insolvent debtor, to

-78-

appear for interrogatories of his creditors/Samuel Collins, Dorch Co, admin of
Reubin Withgot, late of Dorch Co

502. ESHT Mar 29 1803/Died Fri morning last, Mrs. Abbott, consort of Samuel
Abbott of Talb Co/Benjamin Denny and Sarah Denny, Caroline Co, admin of Blanch
Lecompte, late of Caroline Co

503. ESHT Apr 5 1803/William Evans of QA Co, near Tuckahoe Bridge, offers
reward for dark bay horse stolen at Wye Mill

504. ESHT Apr 19 1803/James Parrott to apply for relief from debts

505. ESHT May 3 1803/Married Thurs last by Rev Jackson, Andrew Skinner to
Miss Betsy Harrison, both of Talb Co/Philemon Murphy, QA Co applying for relief
from debts/James Dudley, Talb Co, applies for relief from debts

506. ESHT May 10 1803/Robert Ewing admin of Robert Ewing, late of Talb Co/John
Burgess seeks relief from debts

507. ESHT Jun 21 1803/Died Sat 11th inst, after a short illness, Capt Peter
Sharp of Balt

508. ESHT Jun 28 1803/Married Tues evening last by Rev Jackson, Thomas Gordan
to Miss Anne Barnett, both of Talb Co/Chancery decree to sell real estate of
John Jones, who died intestate and father of Betsy Jones, Dorch Co, and Levin
and Harriot Jones, infants, res in Sussex Co Del/John Primrose, QA Co, admin
of George A. Primrose, late of QA Co/Chancery sale by Francis Sellers of
property of Hessy Deford of 1000 a., provided a copy of order is served on
William Owens, guardian of Hessy Deford/Sarah Ennalls exec of Henry Ennalls,
Dorch Co/John Shanahan offers reward for negro woman named Rhody, 41 yrs old,
who left with infant child about 6 months old; has husband at Hook-Town who
calls Scipio Haskins; she has other connextions at the honorable William
Hindman's and also a brother-in-law, Richard Haskins and a sister in Balt,
supposed to be living at Col. James Handman's/Thomas Monelly offers reward for
negro man, Tom, about 20 yrs old who ran away from farm called St. Joseph, Talb
Co/Thomas A. Fisher from Balt, Gold & Silversmith, has commenced business in
the shop formerly occupied by Joseph Bruff, Easton/Sale of real estate of
Robert Mace, late of Dorch Co, on the head of a branch that issues out of Black
Water River and less than 1 mile from the head of Church Creek - by John
Williams, trustee/Charles Blake, QA Co; Solomon Hopkins, Talb Co; Samuel Mills,
Dorch Co - all insolvent debtors

509. ESHT Aug 2 1803/John Wilkins admin of Jesse Holland, late of Somerset
Co/Apply to Eliza Troup to rent brick house on Washington St. now occupied by
John Harwood/Land for sale near Cambridge of Col. R. Harrison, dec, called
Appleby and Willow Vale, by John E. Gist, exec/William Winder admin of Isaac
Henry late of Somerset Co/Tilden's Farm for sale on Northeast Branch of
Langford's Bay - Jere. Nicols, Kent Co/Joseph Ennalls to petition to erect
grist mill on a stream situated on Secretary's Creek on Great Choptank, Dorch
Co/Edward Martin admin of Nicholas Martin late of Talb Co/Mrs. Primrose has
taken a house in Dover St where she will board and lodge boys attending the
Easton Academy/Stanly B. Loockerman watns overseer for his estate at Hunting
Creek/Land of Andrew Skinner Ennalls, late of Balt City, lying in Dorch Co
within 4 miles of Cambridge and now occupied by Samuel Cook - to be sold by
Leah Hicks Ennalls, exec/Thomas Field has dry goods for sale at the New Market
House, Easton/Ann Jones and John Jones admin of John Jones late of Talb Co/
Joseph Dodson admin of John Harrington late of Dorch Co

510. ESHT Nov 8 1803/Bruffitt Tall admin of George Brannick/Sale of tract
called Ill Neighborhood formerly the property of Lewis Daltrew, late of
Somerset Co, for use of creditors/Solomon Dickinson admin of Samuel Sharpe,
Talb Co/Ann Sharp and Solomon Dickinson admin of Peter Sharp, Talb Co

511. ESHT Nov 15 1803/David Kerr, Jr, has removed his store to the house
lately occupied by William Meluy at the corner of Washington & Dover Sts where
he offers an assortment of goods/Elizabeth Green admin of John Green of
Caroline Co/Mrs. Redhead - millinery, Easton

512. ESHT Nov 22 1803/Died Fri last at an advanced age, John Goldsborough of
Cambridge/Chancery sale made by James B. Robins, trustee of estate of Levin
Wailes of tract called Giles Lot in Worc. Co

513. ESHT Mar 13 1804/Ann Chaille admin of William Chaille, late of Somerset
Co/William Richmond admin of Thomas J. Seth, late of QA Co

514. ESHT Mar 27 1804/Andrew Hall and Samuel Nicols - insolvent debtors of
Caroline Co

515. ESHT Apr 3 1804/Nicholas Brice admin of James Brice to sell land called
White Marsh in Sassafras Neck, Cecil Co, estate of the late Col. James Brice
of Annapolis

516. ESHT Apr 10 1804/Died a few days passed, Francis Sellers, Caroline Co

517. ESHT May 15 1804/Died Fri morning last, Thomas Goldsborough, Talb Co; on
the day following his remains were interred at White Marsh/Died Sat last, Miss
Maria Chamberlaine, dau of Samuel Chamberlaine, Talb Co/Partnership of Peter
Ferguson & John Reid, Cambridge, dissolved/Committed to the goal of Dorch Co
by Thomas James Pattison, sheriff Dorch Co, a negro woman, Henny Roberts, who
has a child about 3 months old. She appears to be about 20 yrs old; says she
was raised near Salisbury and alledges she was free born

518. ESHT June 5 1804/Married 22nd ult by Rev Kemp, Charles Goldsborough to
Miss Sally Goldsborough, both of Dorch Co/Married 23rd ult, William Wilson to
Miss Mary Bowers, both of Talb Co/Died Wed 20th(30th?) ult, Mrs. Margaret
Hughes consort of Col. John Hughes of Talb Co/John Grason, living on Wye River,
QA Co, near Queens Town, offers reward for negro fellow, George, 18 yrs old/
J. C. Wilson admin of Samuel Wilson late of Somerset Co/Jeremiah D. Nicols of
Caroline Co, insolvent debtor/Plantation for sale in Dorch Co near the Bridge,
on the Chicknacomico River by John Rolle, near St. Michaels; William Trippe
near the premises will shew the land/James Holmes, Easton, has hackney stage
for hire; intends to run to Aker's Ferry on Thursdays. Mrs. Holmes has ladies
bonnets on hand/Sale of tracts: Dover, Dover Marsh or Lowe's Dover on Choptank
River, Talb Co, being part of the estate of John Winn Harrison, dec

519. ESHT Jun 10 1804/John Stevens has on hand, drugs, spices, dyes, medicines/
Thomas Prince denies allegations that he has purchased and transported negroes
to distant states

520. ESHT Jun 26 1804/Married Mon 18th inst by Rev Barclay, Dr. Davidson to
Mrs. Coursey, both of QA Co

521. ESHT Jul 31 1804/Married Sun 22nd inst by Rev Duke, George Bevans to Mary
Ogle dau of Benjamin Ogle of the city of Annapolis/George Ward, living near the
premises, offers to rent a tan-yard, 4 miles from Cambridge/Small farm for sale
near Hole in the Wall, now occupied by Francis Price/Chancery sale of real
estate of Richard Bright who died intestate, leaving his sister and brothers
of the half blood all of whom are full age except Basil who is a minor and
res outside the state. Thomas Jones, John Williams and others vs Betsy, Aaron
and Basil Street/Chancery sale of estate of William Adams, dec, house in
Princess Anne now occupied by Thomas Lawes, tract called Mill lot adj land of
Capt Robert Dashiell, to be sold by Lambert Hyland & Henry James Carroll,
trustees/Josiah Bayly, Cambridge, declines to run as delegate to Gen. Assembly/
Sale of tract, Broomly Lambeth by William Richmond, living near the premises or
to James Davidson, QA Co/Sale of farm on Greenwood's Creek, now occupied by
James Imbert; apply to James Ringgold Blunt near the premises or to

William Richmond, QA Co/Rent of house where Doctor Martin now lives by Joseph
Martin/Dwelling house where William Lowrey, Talb Co, now lives, to be let, as
he intends to leave this place by 1st of Jan/Z. Gregoryannounces that whereas
my wife Esther eloped from my bed & board without just cause in 1799 and since
has had a child by another man ...is to petition for annulment of marriage/
Plantation on which Robert Neall now lives is for rent - John L. Bozman/Nancy
Hunt admin of George Hunt, late of Talb Co

522. ESHT Aug 14 1804/Jesse Shanehan res near Easton, offers reward for negro
lad, Adam, 17 yrs old/Sale of farm in Blackwater, Dorch Co; apply to Samuel
Pill who lives adj to the subscriber, Joseph Martin, near the Trappe/The firm
of Joseph Martin & Co intends carrying on the tanning & currying business more
extensively the ensuing year/Charles Frazier and Thomas C. Earle, Centreville
in partnership to run boats between Centreville and Balt city with schooner,
Nancy & Jane, which they purchased of Capt Samuel Thomas of Easton

523. ESHT Sep 4 1804/Died Mon night, Mrs. Dorothy Richardson of Talb Co,
advanced in her age; she sustained affliction with patience and fortitude/
Died on the following evening after a long and tedious illness, Miss Harriot
Collister of Talb Co/Thomas and Samuel Wanewright inform the ;ublic that they
have begun the cabinet and chair-making business in the house formerly occupied
by James Holmes as a tavern/Sale of farm of Rev William Gibson and Mrs. Ann
Gibson, his mother, situated on Hunting Creek, Talb Co/Sarah Dickinson exec of
John Dickinson of Talb Co/William B. Smith, Perry Hall, has seed wheat for sale/
John Cook Stewart offers reward for negro man, Jim, who ran away from Cambridge/
Frances Palmer, now Frances Townsend, admin of John Palmer, late of Talb Co

524. RST Sep 21 1802/Rev Francis Barclay appointed Principal, Charles Emory
appointed Vice-principal and Edward Markland continues as professor of Easton
Academy/Philip Hardcastle, Kent Co, Del, to petition to open a road from "my
mills in Caroline Co to intersect the main road leading from Greensboro to
parson Keene's Cross Roads."/Levi Rue, Dorch Co, to petition under the
insolvency act

525. RST Sep 28 1802/Charles Blair, Caroline Co, to sell cattle at
Blairsborough/Philemon Willis candidate for sheriff of Talb Co/Sale to be held
at dwelling house of Col. Robert Harrison, Dorch Co, dec/Requesting settlement
of claims against estate of Thomas Fisher Webster, cabinet maker, late of QA
Co/Edward Barton, Caroline Co, offers reward for servant lad, Cain James, about
19 yrs old/James Colston admin of John Valiant Jr, late of Talb Co/Hester
Blackiston admin of Richard Blackiston, late of QA Co/John Hart of Balt
continues boot & shoemaking next door to Thomas Abbott's store/Sale of tract,
Broad Creek, Kent Island, along with ferry by Kitty E. Hutchinson, Belle View,
Kent Island/Sale at Peach Blossom by Joseph Telford and on the farm where
Joseph Telford now rents from Joseph Martin

526. RST Oct 12 1802/Sale of tracts by Joseph Haskins, atty for trustees of
the late Charles Crookshanks: Hawkins Pharsalia in Tully's Neck, QA Co, whose
tenant is Isaac Baggs; Dawson's Neck in QA Co whose tenant is Philip Porter;
tract called Heworth within a mile of Easton,
John Arandale/Plantation for rent by Peter Denny near Easton where Timothy L.
Price now lives/Thomas Pendigrast available for ditching and banking; a number
of hands will be kept in readiness/Letters ramaining at P.O. Easton: William
Akers; George Alborn; Louis Bush; Robert Benning; Thomas I. Bullit; William
Bryan; Susan G. Bordley; Grace Brooks; William Burtt; William Curtis; Thomas
Cook; Stephen Camper; Sally Camache; Thomas Chapman; Jacob Curtis; Jabez
Caldwell; James Dudley, Benjamin Dashiel; Thomas C. Dawson; Philemon Downs;
Henry Downs; James Earl; Rev Joseph Everite; John Edmondson; Robert Francis;
Thomas Flint; Joseph Finou; Thomas Foulke; William Flint; William Gibson;
Thomas M. Goldsborough; John Goldsborough; Thomas Goldsborough, Oxford Neck;
Charles Gully; Mary Ann Goldsborough; Samuel Harrison; Joseph Haskins;

John Harrison; John Hawley; Maria Hemsley; Benjamin Hopwell; Capt William
Haddaway; Thomas Hutchins; Isaac Holt; Capt Josiah Johnson; John Jump; William
Jordan; Rev Joseph Jackson; John Lucas; E. Mott; Dorcas Martin; Nathan McDonald;
James Nabb; Isabella Parrott; James Parks; Thomas Prince; James Price; Thomas
Polenson; Henry Parker; George De Passon; Zacharias Roberts; Michael Ryan;
Robert Stevens; H. M. Francis; Sally Smith; Joseph Steingeffer; John Swann;
John Simmonds; Algernon Stafford; Samuel Stevens Jr; Dr. Samuel Thompson; Lloyd
Tilghman; Maria Thomas; John Wallis; James Vincent/Joseph Bartlett, Talb Co,
cautions persons from drawing through his farm and leaving the gates unshut

527. RST Oct 19 1802/James Nabb exec to sell dwelling of late William
Hutchings, Kings Creek Hundred/William B. Smith, living near Easton, offers
reward for negro, Jack, commonly called Morling's Jack

528. RST Oct 26 1802/Benjamin Willmott, Easton, watchmaker, expects to be
absent a few weeks; James Troth will continue the business/Jacob Gibson, Talb
Co, gives detailed explanation for his refusal to grant a license to retail
liquors to James Cowan; mentions Peter Denny and estate of Woolman Gibson;
refers to his own son/Andrew Duncan, Easton, has new gig for sale at Hopkins'
carriage maker's shop in Easton/Letters remaining at P.O. Centreville: James
Blake; James Butcher; Peregrine Blake; Dr. Thomas Burgess; Charles P. Blake; Mrs.
Alphonsa Blake; John Burgess Jr; Mrs. Anna M. Chew; William Carmichael; Samuel
Cooper: P. Callen; Christopher Cox; Edward O. Clark; Henry Elbert; Charles
Elliott; Thomas Earle; John Emory; John Flokner; Peregrine Garnett; Mr. Gambral;
James Hammond; Messrs Harper & Son; Freeman Hawley; John Higgins; Henry Hewitt;
John Holding; Osborn S. Harwood; James Holliday; William Hindman; Miss Kitty
E. Hutchings; Debbe Hollingsworth; Benjamin Harris; James Howard; Richard
Hall; William Kenney; Mrs. Mary Lous; Thomas Lee; Phil. Lloyd; Charles
Letherberry; Joseph Latimore; Stephen Lowrey; Thomas Mason; Messrs. Morris
and Mitchell; John Moore; Mssrs. Jackson and McCutcheon; John Moore, Miss
Hannah McConikin; Paul Michan; Richard Newman; Joseph Oliver; Mrs. Fanny
Palmer; George Primrose; James Porter; David Parsnip; Absalom Penny; Lemuel
Purnell; Will Price; Zachariah Roberts; Margaret Rosetter; Benjamin Rogers;
John Ruth; Rev Elisha Rigg; Jesse Reid; Ralph Rice; Thomas Reynolds; James
Smith; Millinton Sparks; Zebulon Skinner; Charles Sewell; Samuel Sutton; John
Stant; Mrs. Mary Sewell; Emory Sudler; Mrs. Skiner; William E. Sewell; Thomas
Turner; William Thompson; Isaac Warum; James William; Mrs. Ann Wright; Edward
Wright/Letters remaining at P.O. Georgetown Cross Roads: A. Albe; Unit Angier;
William Blocksom; Perry Boyer; William Bordley; Augustin Boyer; Francis Cain;
Capt John Campbell; Samuel Crisfield; Eliza Comegys; Lucy Comegys; Philip
Chrisfield; William Cooper; Samuel Davis; Fanny Demby; John Fitzpatrick; Mary
Field; Abraham Falconer; Dr. Benjamin Hall; Isaac Holt; Jesse Hughes; James
Howard; Cornelius Hurtt; Augustus Leftless; John McDonald; George Murdaugh;
James Pryar; Thomas Price; Joshua Pennington; Elizabeth Pancoast; Isaac
Redgrave; Thomas Seegar; Richard Simmons; John Simmons; Jonas Simmons;
Lambert M. Sewell; William Taylor; Nathaniel Tolson; Etty Wise; Burton West;
John Wallis; Susan Wilson; John Williams/Sale by Amelia Hobbs admin of Henry
Hobbs of QA Co at the farm of the late Richard Grason, lately occupied by the
deceased Henry Hobbs - horses, hogs, sheep, cattle and farming utensils/George
Godwin and Hannah Boutton admin of George Boutton

529. RST Nov 9 1802/Watchmen wanted by Capt Samuel Swan of Easton/Peter Caulk
announces availability of alum salt, James River Tobacco, cider, oranges and
limes at the County Wharf on application to the captains on board

530. RST Nov 16 1802/Sarah Parrott selling property at dwelling plantation of
Benjamin Parrott, dec/John Dawson lost a diamond for cutting glass on the road
from Easton to Oak/James Ritchie, trustee, selling real estate of William
McBryde, late of Somerset Co, lying in Wor Co and Somerset Co/H. Harrison

offers genuine Cane Spirit just received per the schooner Argus, Capt Anderson, from Antigua

531. RST Nov 23 1802/Married Thurs evening last Richard Thomas of QA Co to Miss Margaret Webb of this co/Sale of part of Peach Blossom estate by Graham Haskins, & Co/Notice to creditors of Peter Medford by Moses Passapae, trustee/ Anthony Banning intends to remove out of this county in the course of the winter, offers for sale lots in Oxford/W. Patton explains why he sought relief through the insolvency law

532. RST Nov 30 1802/John Ruth of Hillsborough seeks a blacksmith/William L. Bewley, Oxford Neck, is selling horses, hogs, furniture/John Houston, Somerset Co - "I am in prison for debts which I am unable to pay.." intend to petition the general assembly

533. RST Dec 7 1802/Sale by Joseph Tilford and John Edmondson at Peach Blossom of a large quantity of provender

534. RST Dec 14 1802/Henry E. Bayly and wife and John Landreth, exec of William Nutter dec of Somerset Co/John Nelson admin of Thomas Skinner, Somerset Co/Abjiah Pelham states that his wife, Mary Pelham, has eloped from his bed and board

535. RST Dec 21 1802/Died Fri 10th inst in QA Co, Clayton Wright, a young man esteemed by all/Died Sun morning last in Wye, Mrs. Bordley, consort of Dr. James Bordley, after a very short illness/For rent by Thomas Perrin Smith, the store and compting room presently occupied by Samuel Nicols, with a dry celler under the same/Notice to debtors of William Patton by James Patton, trustee, QA Co

536. RST Dec 28 1802/Sale by Richard T. Earle, trustee, a tract near Church Hill called Springfield, sold by James Brown to Henry Storey, late of QA / We have examined Hoxies threshing machine now seen at Samuel Yarnall's in Easton: Edward Coursey, Owen Kennard, James Cowan, Samuel Yarnall, John Harwood, Robert Lloyd Nicolls, Henry Nicols Jr, Peter Denny, Robert Moore/Sale of Indian corn by Charles Hobbs, Head of Wye, Talb Co/F. & James Nealle exec of Joseph Nealle, late of Talb Co and admin of Jesse Hopkins dec

537. RST Jan 4 1803/Death of William Dimond of QA Co/Betty Dickinson, Delaware Co, Pa, admin of John Dickinson 4th, late of Talb Co/P. Edmondson surviving partner of Edmondson and Prichard/Isaac Poits and Adah Poits admin of William Poits of Caroline Co

538. RST Jan 11 1803/Thomas L. Haddaway, Talb Co, intends to leave Eastern Shore of Md and is selling farm formerly res of Dr. Maynadier, a water lot in St. Michaels, a 100-ton schooner, and 1/2 ownership in the schooner Argus/Abel Griffith of Caroline Co offers reward for apprentice lad named Daniel Miller about 17 yrs old, about 5 feet 4 in, somewhat freckled/William Croney admin of Joseph Blake late of Talb Co/Partnership of Samuel Elbert and Levin T. Speddin, carriage and chair makers, dissolved, to be taken over by Robert T. Speddin and Levin T. Speddin, Easton/James Berry, Gold and Silversmith, announces the opening of his business in the house lately occupied by Ludwick Wainer, Washington St

539. RST Jan 18 1803/Sloop for sale at Miles River Ferry by Nathan Townsend, Hook Town/Died at Easton Fri night last, Josiah Winslow aged 25 and ___ Hayward aged about 19. They placed a large pan of lighted charcoals in their room. The family found them both dead - later judged by an inquest to be caused by suffocation/Sarah Brasscup exec of Sarah Dawson late of Talb Co/Cellia Patridge, Dorch Co, offers reward for negro named Sam, about 24 yrs old and negro named Charles, about 25 yrs old, and a negro girl named Hannah, 10 yrs old

540. RST Jan 25 1803/Married Sun evening last, Capt Freeborn Banning to Miss

Harriet Thomas, both of this county/Charges made by John Sotheren, Wilmington against Charles S. Sewell of QA Co/Tracts at Sudler's Cross Roads, QA Co, late the property of Thomas Sudler for sale by Richard T. Earle, trustee/Samuel Swan resumes tayloring business in Easton/George Rosse admin of Mrs. Eleanor Stevens of Worc Co

541 RST Feb 8 1803/William Rose admin of James Rose, late of Talb Co/William Y. Bourke, Denton, offers reward for negro named Adam, about 23 yrs old

542. RST Feb 15 1803/Sale by James Houston, trustee, of tract Stratford Manor, owned by William Biggs late of Kent Co

543. RST Mar 1 1803/John Stevens Jr lost a watch in Easton/Robert Francis & Co new proprietors of Herring Fishery lately carried on by Thomas Freeman on Tuckahoe Creek near Lewis town/Thomas Nicols, Federalsburg, hiring 3 or 4 journeyman ship carpenters

544. RST Mar 8 1803/Alexander Laing has fresh garden seed for sale/Elizabeth Hynson admin of Jacob Kebler late of Talb Co and also admin of James Hynson late of Talb Co/Nicholas Vallient assuming boot and shoe-making business from John Blake/John Ridue offers reward for negro woman, Peg, about 40 yrs old; she has a sister living in Easton who is free; return to John Ridue, QA Co

545. RST Mar 22 1803/Sale of lots in Snow-Hill owned by Francis Randall dec, by Philip Quinton, trustee/Joseph Ewing admin of John Ewing late of Caroline Co/ William Croney, Talb Co, offers reward for negro girl named Mill, about 17 yrs old, once owned by the late John Barrow; went off with a negro man named Bill formerly owned by Henrietta Bewley; he is about 25 yrs old

546. RST Mar 29 1803/John Gregory admin of Anthony Gregory late of Talb Co/ John Maguire of Dorch Co offers reward for negro man named Govet, 22yrs old, about 5 feet and 1/2 in tall/Sale by James Cheston of a farm on Main Ditch of Long Marsh, Caroline Co adj estate of William Hemsley

547. RST Apr 5 1803/Jane Armstrong admin of John Armstrong renting house recently occupied by the deceased/John Gregory exec of Elisha Hendrix late of Talb Co

548. RST Apr 12 1803/Sale by Gideon Pearce at George Town Cross Roads, Kent Co, of tract on Elk river 2 miles below French-town/John Stewart offers reward for two stolen mares taken from the farm of Mrs. Coursey/Henry R. Hall offers reward for negro woman named Cate who took her male child of 12 months on May last; she is about 19 yrs old, purchased from Matthias Bordley, Wye Island. Her mother still lives on Wye Island; her father lives near Church Hill. Deliver woman and child to John Cain in Centreville for reward/William Atkinson buying cured tan bark/Married Thurs last by Rev Barclay, John Turner to Miss Nancy Coward, both of talb Co

549. RST Apr 19 1803/Henry Bullen of Talb Co offers reward for negro man named Harry, about 21 yrs old; has an uncle living at Wye/Silas Fleming, Caroline Co, publishes certificates attesting to the success of his horse, Inspector, in producing foals in the face of adverse statements of James Stafford and William Billings. The horse was the former property of Vincent Moore. "We believe Inspector to be a good foal getter: Samuel Harington, Caroline Co; from Kent Co: Vincent Moore, Joshua Minner, Ruben Warren, John Gregg, Matthias Clifton/ Letters remaining at P.O. Centreville: Isaac Albert; James Butcher; William Bishop; Charles Bivary; John Clark; John Cox; John Colgan; Mrs. Campbell; William Dunbar; Henry Darden; James Daugherty; Capt Robert Dawson; James Elliott; Alexander Fleming; John Green; Mrs. Hollyday; Anna Hebb; Benjamin Hatchison; Kitty Hutchings; Henry R. Hall; Richard Hull; Emanuel Jenkinson; Samuel Y. Keene; Caroline Lansdale; Margaret Mather; Margaret Meeds; James Meredith; John McFinley; William H. Nicholson; Richard Newman; Charles Price;

-84-

Thomas Pollard; Edward Ringgold; Rev Elisha Rigg; William E. Seth; Robert
Seedars; Cornelia Sothern; Emory W. Sudler; Lucretia Tabbs; William Thompson;
Solomon Young/Letters remaining at P.O. Easton: Medford Andrews; Aaron Anthony;
Charles Bromwell; Samuel Baldwin; David Barrow; Elizabeth Baily; John Baker;
Edward D. Coursey; Susan Cromwell; Sarah Collister; B. Chance; William
Constable; Joseph Collins; Harriet Darnsby; James Dawson; Mary Dawson; Pere.
Driver; Sylvanus Dickinson; Joseph Douglass; Peter Edmondson; James Earle; John
Fleming; William Flint; T. Goldsborough; Ann McGuire; Dorsey A. G.stis; G. R.
Hayward; Allen Holms; Jesse Hincks; Samuel Harrington; John Higgins; William
Haynes; Henrietta Ingram; John Jenkinson; Thomas Jones; William Jenkinson;
Jesse Kelby; Thomas Kemp; Abraham Lewis; Solomon Lowe; Nicholas Loveday; James
Lloyd; Alexander Laing; William Mullican; Anna Martin; Peter Redhead; Benjamin
Ray; William Richardson; William Russum; Samuel Spencer; Mr. Sherwood; Richard
Sherwood; Benjamin Skinner; John Simmons; James Steele; Thomas Stevens; Francis
Sellers; Joshua Taggart; Richard Tilghman; Joseph Toy; Matth. Tilghman;
Cornelius West

550. RST Apr 26 1803/Letters remaining at P.O. Georgetown Cross Roads: Thomas
Bryon; Elizabeth Bateman; Capt Moses Briscoe; William Barrons; John Crow;
Bacheldor Chance; John Chrisfield; Elizabeth Comegys; James Connar; Lucy
Comegys; Stephny Congo; Samuel Davis; Charles Haynes; Rev. Dr. Benjamin Hall;
Capt Gideon Hall; James Hyland; James Howard; Kennedy & Gilmore; Susanna
Medford; William McDaniel; Abraham Millan; Mary Mann; Elizabeth McCluer;
Joseph Mann; William Newman; John Newall; Thomas Price; Joshua Penington; John
Page; Robert Polk; Samuel Penington; Isaac Redgrave; Rev Joshua Reefe; Mr.
___Simmons; John Simmons; Thomas Savir; Daniel Sulivan; Margaret Sims; James
Tennant; William Thomas; Susan Wilson; James Welch; Sarah Williams; James
Woodland/Information wanted by Sailes Cannar, Chancellor's Point Ferry, Talb
Co, on William Cannar, who in a deranged state of mind, left his father's
house last fall and has not since been heard of/Thomas Oram admin of Thomas
Taylor and Timothy Taylor, both of Caroline Co

551. RST May 3 1803/Sale by Eleanor Edmondson exec of Samuel Edmondson, late
of Talb Co, house occupied by Richard Stanfield, Washington St, house where
Thomas Bradshaw lives on West St and house wherein Philemon Willis now lives/
Married Thurs evening last by Rev Joseph Jackson, Andrew Skinner to Miss
Elizabeth Harrison, both of this county

552. RST May 17 1803/James Ridgaway exec of John Ridgaway late of Caroline Co/
Joseph Denny of Centreville offers reward for stolen horse/Samuel Nicols,
Easton, offers reward for negro woman named Henny, about 26 yrs old; it is
generally supposed that she was enticed off by her husband who callls himself
George Hopps, property of the Hon. James Tilghman, of QA Co/David Kerr, Easton,
candidate for Gen. Assembly/Joshua Brittingham, Snow-hill, Worc Co, offers
reward for negro man named Daniel, about 33 yrs old

553. RST May 24 1803/Mary Cooper admin of James Cooper to sell his personal
property

554. RST Jun 7 1803/Farm on West river for rent by Thomas S. Denny, Talb Co/
Married Thurs evening last, James Denny to Miss Nancy Durding dau of Stephen
Durding, all of this county/John Fisher, Talb Co, admin of Andrew Foster
Leverton and also admin of John Banning Merton, both of QA Co/John Gibson, no
longer able to attend to his property at a distance, will sell his mill at the
head of Wye river, commonly called Gibson's Mill

555. RST Jun 14 1803/Married Sun last, John Blake to Miss Lydia Spencer, both
of this county/Sale of property of the late John Thomas of Talb Co, lying in
Worc Co by Jacob Gibson, trustee/Preston Sharpless, Easton, offers excellent
Porter for sale/Robert H. Goldsborough, Myrtle Grove, candidate for state
legislature

556. RST Jun 21 1803/Samuel Helsby and Thomas Newton, near New Market, Dorch Co, offer·reward for apprentice boys bound to farm: James Lord, about 15 yrs old and Keeley Abbot, about 14 yrs old, who may have changed his name to Keely McCollister/Chancery case of John Williams against John S. Alexander, John Murray and William Corbin, heirs of John Sheldon, Worc Co/Sale of land belonging to heirs of William Clark, Kent Co/Elizabeth Duyer admin of William Duyer, late of Kent Co/Garnett, Rasin & Co, Chestertown, announce the running of the schooner, Brothers, lately owned by John Allen of Sassafras River/ William Jones, Kent Co, insolvent

557. RST Jun 28 1803/Charles Gibson appointed Inspector of the Port of Easton/ Died Sat last at James Goldsborough of this county, Andrew Skinner Ennalls of Balt City, aged 64

558. RST Jul 5 1803/Philip Fiddeman, QA Co, admin of John Chaires, late of QA Co, to sell his riding carriage and furniture at his late dwelling near Centreville/Letters remaining in P.O. Easton: Margaret Allen; Thomas Abbott; James M. Brown; Elizabeth Ball; Susan Bordley; Josiah Bailey; Thomas Banning; John Benney; William Barton; Thomas Bell; R. Chamberlaine; William Conner, junr; Matth. Crozier; James Caulk; Commsrs of Tax, Clerk of the County; William Constable; Matth. Durborow; Severn Dawson; Peter Denny; Impey Dawson; James Delihay; Benjamin F. A. C. Dashiell; Andrew Duncan; James Earle, junr; Richard T. Earle; Robert Elliott; John Fleming; J. Goldsborough; C. Goldsborough; Cath. Goldsborough; T. Goldsborough; Maria Goldsborough; Thomas Gordon; Kitty Green; John Griffin; Hugh Garnett; Josiah Hall; Robert G. Harper; Robert Hay; M. Hathaway; Mrs. L. Henry; William Harper & sons; John Jones; Matthew Keene; Samuel Y. Keene; William Lowrey; Luther Martin; William W. McClyn; Dr. W. Mathers; Mary Morgan; M. Miginny; John McClane; John Murphy; Frederick Merkley; Robert Lloyd Nicolls; Thomas Prince; Joseph Purden; William Potter; Robert Riddell; Thomas Russum; James Rue; David Sisk; Robert Spedden; Archibald Surrell; Thomas Smyth; Samuel Swan; Richard Spencer; Francis Shaffer; Samuel Sherwood; Edward C. Thomas; A. M. Tilghman; Joshua Taggart; Lucretia Teakle; Thomas Wood; Hannah Walt; Mary Webb; George Westcoat/Joshua Hopkins admin of Dennis Hopkins, late of Talb Co/William B. Clark and Margaret Clark admin of William Glasgow, Kent Co/Richard Collins admin of Nathan Jackson, late of QA Co/Kinvin Wroth exec of James Wroth late of Kent Co Md/Edward Roberts, living at Miles River Ferry, guardian to Bennet Bracco, offers reward for negro man Gabriel, about 30 yrs old, property of Bennett Bracco, a minor; Gabriel ran away from one of my farm in Tuckahoe/Thomas Hardcastle junr, Talb Co, offers reward for negro man, 21 yrs old, named Daniel, about 5 feet 8 in

559. RST Jul 12 1803/Committed to Worc Co goal, negro fellow, named Joshua, about 25 yrs old who says he formerly belonged to John Beloat, Eastern Shore of Va, who sold him to Mr. Moore of Norfolk from whom he made his escape/Thomas Harper, Easton, taylor/Francis Morling, Caroline Co, offers reward for negro man, Pompey, 24 yrs old/Letters remaining in P.O. Centreville: Peregrine Blake; Isaac Baggs; James Bateman; John S. Blunt; Mary Barton; William Conacan; Francis P. Casey; Samuel N. Copper; Joshua G. Clark; Henry Durden; Richard Duckett; Philip Fiddeman; John Green; William Hopper; Richard Hall; Henry R. Hall; William Morrison; Susan Perkins; Robert Reid; Richard Ridgaway; Benjamin Richardson; Samuel Smith; John Smith; Edward Strong; Francis Schaffar; Littleton D. Teakle; Joseph Thompson; Mrs. Rosa Thomas; Isaac Tilghman

560. RST Jul 19 1803/William Crawford, Caroline Co, to petition for relief from debts/Henrietta M. Blake, QA Co, offers reward for negro, Isaac, about 22 yrs old; his brother is at General Benson's Talb Co/Levin Pollitt, sheriff Worc Co, states he has committed a negro fellow, who calls himself Joshua, about 25 yrs old/Chancery sale of 3000 a. in Caroline Co devised by William Littleton Murray, late of Dorch Co, to children of Alexander Stuart/Land of

Doctor James Wilson, late of Talb Co, near the head of Wye River, to be sold;
John Nabb res on the premises

561. RST Aug 16 1803/James Ballentine, Easton, house plasterer

562. RST Aug 23 1803/Benjamin Skinner, Easton, offers reward for apprentice
boy, Edward Bradshaw, about 15 yrs old, taken off by William Flint, saddler,
Cambridge/A petition for a public road between lands of Alexander Stewart and
land now or lately owned by Richard Gresham near Quaker Lane, to intersect the
road leading from Chestertown to Still Pond/Margaret Ringgold
     exec of John Ringgold, late of QA Co, requests creditors to make
claims at the public house of Richard Peacock, Church-Hill/Open letter from
John Young, Denton, to James Nabb, Talb Co and Robert Orell, Caroline Co
regarding forgery in the petition of Mrs. Jane Green, applying for relief
under the insolvency act/Nicholas W. Easton of Easton to present fireworks
display - 50 cents admission/Robert Spedden, Easton, to run a packet between
Easton and Balt/Peter Edmondson has house for rent in Caroline Co where George
Sewell lives, about 5 miles from Dover Ferry/Henry Hardcastle admin of Perry
Parrot, late of Talb Co/William Dunn renting house presently occupied by
William Hindman/Berry's Mill for sale situated at head of Kings Creek; apply
to William Scott/Sale of land on Grasin Creek, Langford's Neck adj lands of
Thomas Gresham in Kent Co/Sale of Lower Mill on Red Lyon Branch, QA Co, two
water wheel, well calculcated for a merchant mill; apply on the premises to
Joseph Elliott/Elizabeth Blades admin of John Blades, late of Talb Co

563. RST Aug 30 1803/Washington College Commencement - discourse by Gustavus
W. T. Wright of Chestertown. Degree of A. B. conferred on Beddington Hands,
Robert Wright, Gustavus W. T. Wright, Edward W. Pearce, John T. Veazy of Cecil
Co, and Edwin Lorain. Valedictory oration by Edward W. Pearce/R. Chamberlaine
of Peach Blossom offers reward for negro boy named Jake, property of Mrs.
Trippe of Easton; Jake is about 18 yrs old/Robert Orrell states that he will
defend himself against the accusations of Joseph Richardson and John Young by
forthcoming handbills/Robert Stevens, QA Co, insolvent

564. RST Sep 6 1803/Chancery sale of lots of Thomas Groves, Talb Co, dec/
Edward Martin admin of Nicholas Martin, the younger, late of Talb Co/Married
Sun last, James Troth to Mrs. C. Ball, both of this town/John Jenkinson fore-
warns persons from hauling waggons and carts through his woods, Thomas J.
Bullitt excepted; market carts may pass as usual/John D. Thompson advertises
the running of the Warwick Races in accordance the rules of the Chester-Town
Jockey Club/Berne-creek Jockey Club -- N. C. Newton, sec'y/Slaves wanted
between ages 10 to 25, farmilies perferred; apply to: Richard Newman,
Centreville; Solomon Lowe, Easton; Peter Rea, Cambridge; Mrs. ___, Vienna;
John Bloodsworth, Princess Anne

565. RST Sep 13 1803/John Smoot, Dorch Co, candidate for General Assembly/
Robert Worrell, Balt Co, admin Richard Peacock, late of Kent Co Md/James Troth
has selection of watches, chains, seals, keys/William Lambdin admin of Mrs.
Lucretia Haddaway, late, whose residence was 5 miles below St. Michaels/Apply
to James Stoakes for freight or passage on the fast sailing schooner, Anne &
Polly, Clement Vickars, master, running between Easton and Balt/House for rent
in Denton presently occupied by William Boon as a tavern; apply to Alexander
Maxwell, Denton/Edward White, Hunting Creek, Dorch Co, offers reward for three
men: Daniel, age 22; Isaac, age 18; Demsey, age 24

566. RST Sep 20 1803/New-Market Jockey Club races in Dorch Co, Robert Sullivan
- secretary/Creditors of Richard Johns, dec, Talb Co, are requested to make
claims to James Nabb, Talb Co, in order to obtain a decree for sale of real
estate of aforesaid Johns - Stephen S. Johns, Calvert Co/John Sayer Blake, QA
Co, Wye River, offers reward for negro man, Charles, who sometimes goes by the
name of Caesar, about 43 yrs old

567. RST Sep 27 1803/Thomas Wootters requests that claims by settled against the estate of Lamuel Wootters, late of Caroline Co/Samuel Nicols to petition for relief from debts/Died a few days passed, Mrs. Dickinson, amiable consort of Samuel Dickinson of Talb Co/Edward Earle - medicines, liquors, a few boxes of genuine Havana Segars/House for rent presently occupied by Rev Francis Barckley on Harrison & Goldsborough Sts; apply to Mary Trippe, Easton/Henry Smoot relinquishing candidacy for sheriff Dorch Co/John Fisher admin of Andrew Foster Leverton, Queens Town, dec, and Bennett Lowe, late of Talb Co/James Howard offers reward for negro woman, Fan or Fanny, about 28 yrs old who ran away from Thomas Wootters, Ruthsborough; she left a young child 9 or 10 yrs old; sold to me by Mrs. Smith of Block town/Married Thurs evening 15th inst, Anthony Banning to Miss Martha Spencer, eldest dau of Richard Spencer of Kent Co/Edward Earle, Easton, has just opened a druggist business/James Bordley to rent the farm whereon he now resides (Head of Wye)/Died Fri morning last Mrs. Leah Haskins, consort of Mr. Govert Haskins, merchant of Balt city/Chancery case: James Brown against heirs of Henry Storey dec/Milby Purnell admin of Thomas Rigby, late of Worc Co/J. Goldsborough guardian of Nicholas Goldsborough comments regarding the setting of a fire to the woods of Nicholas Goldsborough/Chancery case - Creditors of Robins Chamberlaine: Peter Sharp; Greensbury Goldsborough; John Blake; Thomas Coward J & P. Ruckle; Joseph Osburn: Hugh McCurdy; Jacob Gibson: Richard H. Moale; George Browne; Elizabeth Ennalls; Elizabeth Cole; William Carmichael; vestry of St. Peters Parish; Ennalls Martin; Samuel Baldwin; Samuel Thomas; Thomas Macgill· William Tibbitts; Samuel Browne, admin of W. S. B: William Haskins; Richard Benson; Samuel Chamberlaine: John Needles; Christopher Johnston; Thomas Snowden; Samuel Vincent: George Hoffman; James Baxter; Charles Caroll of Carrollton. Letters remaining at P. O. Easton: Harriot R. Anderson; Mary Abbot; George Anderson; William Atkinson; John Barnett; John Blake; Elizabeth Bentley; Daniel Crouch; S. C. Cone· Solomon Coburn; Alexander Chambers; James Caulk; Jacob Conway; Mathew Crouzier; Marth Deborah; Philip Dickinson; James Denny; Mary Emory; Sarah Edmondson; James Earle; John Erskins; William Frazier; John Fleming; William Gibbs; Thomas Goldsborough; John Gem; Dr. R. Goldsborough; James Goldsborough; James Harrison: James Holmes: K. E. Hutchings; Edward N. Hamilton; Jane Hutchings; John Hale; Edmund Hayward; William Hemsly Junr; William Jordon: Dr. Rev S. Keane; Benjamin Keene; Vachel Keene; Thomas Kirby; Michael Leukis; Corbin Lee· William M. Maynadier; Harriotte McCallah; Solomon Martin· Robert Martin; Mary McGinny; John Mullican; Tristram Needles; I & Jeremiah Nicols; Benjamin Pelton John Patridge; Nancy Parker; Col David Robinson; Amasa Robinson; David Rogers; Andrew Skinner; William Street; William Stevens; Isaac Steele; William Sears; Thomas Smith; Richard Spencer; Mary Sherwood; Richard Stanfield; Archibald Derrell; Anna Maria Tilghman; James Vetich; Anne Wright; John Wroth; Eliza Wood/Committed to gaol of Balt Co, negro woman, who calls herself Rachel May, about 24 yrs old, says she was raised by Col. Ezekiel Fekes, Dorch Co/Thomas L. Haddaway, St. Michaels, offers reward for Jim or James Barnett, negro man, about 30 yrs old/Letters remaining at P. O. Centreville: Frederick Able; James Brown; Mrs. Mary Betton; William Bryon; Basil Biscoe; John Cain; William Caldwell; Mrs. A. M. Chew; Mary Cooper; Daphney Cooper; Henry Costin; John Dodd; Mrs. Hollyday; John Harper; Michael Hopkins; Amelia Hobbs; Nathan Ireland; Paul Michan; Richard Newman; Zacharias Roberts; Thomas Roberts; Andrew Raborg; Richard Ridgaway; Major Stradley; Eliza Sudler; Solomon Scott; William Stinson; Sarah Wood; Samuel T. Wright; Samuel W. Wright; William T. Wright; Ann Wright; Henry Wright

568. RST Oct 11 1803//Mary Cooper admin of James Cooper late of Talb Co/William Jordon living near Easton reports his bay horse strayed or was stolen/Married Thurs last, Wesley Bordley of QA Co to Miss Deborah Fisher dau of John Fisher of this county/Died on 2d inst in Chestertown after a long illness which she

bore with Christian fortitude, Mrs. Maria Lucas, the amiable consort of John
Lucas, 3d, merchant of that town/Henry Nicols junr requests payment of debts
to Samuel Nicols, Talb Co/Charles Gibson and James Clayland, candidates for
sheriff of Talb Co/Samuel Sharpless operating earthen ware manufactory in
Easton, near head of Washington St/Public sale of personal estate of Perry
Parrott at his late dwelling on Kings Creek, Talb Co, by Henry Hardcastle,
admin/Miss Henderson's Boarding School under the joint instruction of Miss
Henderson and Rev Joseph Douglass, for the instruction of young ladies,
Chestertown/Rev Elisha Riggs' School for females now renting at house presently
occupied by William Hindman, Talb Co, shore of Wye River/George Ash announces
forthcoming Elkton Races/William Lowman admin of John Lowman, late of Kent Co
Md

569.   RST Oct 18 1803/Sale of Gibsons Mill; apply to Dr. William E. Seth adj
same - John Gibson, Annapolis/Lemuel Norris, Talb Co, offers reward for negor
man named Dick who calls himself Richard Thomas, about 24 yrs old, property of
Mrs. Mary Goldsborough/Jonathan Kinnamont candidate for sheriff of Talb Co/
James Seth reports his horse strayed or stolen/Married Thurs evening last, John
Maxwell to the amiable Miss Rebecca Coats dau of Doctor John Coats, all of this
town/Died Wed last in QA Co, William Clayton Bordley, a respectable citizen of
that county/Died on the 22nd inst at the dwelling of John Nabb, Head of Wye,
Samuel Hatborn resident of Lancaster Co/Dekar Thompson, Caroline Co, holding
sale on farm he now occupies, owned by Richard Loockerman and lying on Tuckahoe
Creek, opposite Lewis-Town/House for rent on Dover St presently occupied by
Hall Harrison; apply to Sarah Cockayne or James Cockayne, Easton S

570.   RST Nov 1 1803/Samuel Clayton, Easton, to petition for relief from debts/
R. Chamberlaine, Talb Co, offers reward for negro boy named Nick, property of
William Hayward, Talb Co; he is about 19 yrs old/Chancery case regarding land
in Kent Co, mortgaged by St. Legar Meeks of Kent Co to John & Henry Page, now
occupied by St. Leger Meeks, James Brooke, trustee

571.   RST Nov 8 1803/Lott Warfield to petition for relief from debts/House for
rent presently occupied by Mrs. Corse near corner of Washington & Dover Sts;
apply to Peter Denny/House for rent where Rachel Goldsborough now occupies in
Easton/House for rent formerly occupied by John Stevens, New Market, Dorch Co

572.   RST Nov 15 1803/Married Thurs evening last, Jonathan Leonard to Mrs.
Sarah Kirby, both of this county/Died Tues morning last in the 77th year,
Allen Quynn, long a resident of Annapolis and for 25 yrs a member of the house
of delegates/Sale at the Jenkinson Farm near the Trappe by James Ridgaway,
Talb Co/Mills for sale at the head of Chester River, Kent Co, Md; they will be
shewn by William Farrell, tenant in possession; for terms apply to Joshua and
Thomas Gilpin, Phila/John Stevens offers for rent the dwelling house he
formerly occupied in New Market, Dorch Co/Samuel Clayton to petition for relief
from debts/ Zadock Hawley, bottler of Easton Porter Cellar/Lambert Norris near
Easton, offers reward for negro man named Dick,about 24 yrs old

573.   RST Nov 22 1803/House for let occupied by Rachel Goldsborough, Easton/
William D. Baker buying young negroes; apply to Solomon Lowe, Easton/Thomas
Coward is holding sale of personal property at his plantation, Plain Dealing

574.   RST Nov 29 1803/Lambert Reardon, taylor, Easton/Samuel, Easton, renting
house now occupied by William B. Smith on Washington St; also small house same
st presently occupied by William Haynes/James Nabb, Talb Co, seeks to hire a
blacksmith/Owen Kennard, Easton, offers reward for negro man named Perry, 21
yrs old, formerly the property of Charles Groome, Kent Co, dec

575.   RST Dec 6 1803/House for rent, lately occupied by William Tibbles on
Washington St/Philemon Wallis, sheriff Talb Co, offers reward for yellow man
named Levin Cooper, known as Red Levin, condemned for felony; ran away from the

custody of Capt Samuel Thomas of the Easton Packet; he is between 25 to 30 yrs old/Mary Trippe, Easton, offers reward for negro boy, Nick, about 18 yrs old

576. RST Dec 13 1803/William Bromwell, saddle, cap and harness maker in Easton, has removed his shop to the house lately occupied by Thomas Perrin Smith as Post Office and Star Printing Office/Died Sun last at his seat in Dorch Co after a short illness, William VAns Murray, late minister from the United States at the Hague, and minister plenipotentiary to the Franch Republic. As a statesman Mr. Murray stood high, and filled with integrity the several departments which his country had confided to his trust - particularly in bringing about the settlement of the late unhappy difference that existed between the United States and the French Republic/Meeting of St. Thomas's Lodge at Easton, by order of William Harrison, junr, Easton

577. RST Dec 27 1803/Died in N. Y. Tues 13th inst of an inflamation of the lungs, David Denniston, founder of the American Citizen and late partner of the present editor; he was the son of a wealthy and respectable farmer in Orange Co/ Lambert W. Spencer & Co, has removed from their store to the house lately occupied by Owen Kennard opposite the Courthouse; they have an assortment of dry goods, hardward & groceries/Chancery sale at the late dwelling house of Shadrack Keene, late of Dorch Co, a tract called Keene's Misfortune, near the head of Hunga River, Richard C. Keene, trustee/Jane W. Carradine admin of Christopher W. Carradine, late of QA Co

578. RST Jan 3 1804/Letters remaining at P.O. Easton: Thomas Abbott; Anne Akers; Isaac Atkinson; Gen. Perry Benson; Thomas J. Bullitt; William Bryan; Mathias Bordley; Susan Bordley; Hosea Beckley; Rhoda Bland; Solomon Bryan; H. & Thomas Bullin; Elizabeth Bailey; Samuel Bradie; Mary Berry; Richard Bouling; Augestin Boyer Jr; George Bevans; Henry Buckley; Mary Bruff; James Berry; Daniel Cain Jr; Josiah Cox; Spencer H. Cone; William Cox; Samuel Chamberlain; Ellis Chandler; Clerk of Talb Co; Thomas S. Denny; Miss Margaret Denny; Peter Denny; Joseph Dennis; Henry Downs; Miss Martha Deborough; James Dilehay; Haga Davis; Susan Edmondson; James Earle; Thomas Eccleston; Thomas L. Emory; John Fleming; Robert Francis; Robert Geddis; Charles Gulley; Sally F. Goldsborough; Major J. Green; Thomas J. Gulley; Thomas Gordon; William G. Gary; Sophia Grancer; Henry Gardiner; William Hemsley, Jr; Rigby Hopkins; William Hains; Abner Homes; Thomas Hutchins; John Hopkins; Zadock Hawley; Catherine Innis; John Jenkinson; Henry Kean; Ann Kemp; Thomas Kemp; Stanley B. Lockerman; John Landreth; John Landman; John Lunn; Solomon Lowe; Corbin Lee; William Lowrey; Richard Lloyd; William Muley; Sarah Maggs; Monico Mitchell; James Murphy; T. & J. Nicolls; James Price; Nancy Parker; William Pearson; Richard Parker; Ignatius Pearce; Thomas Prince; Henrietta Price; Edward Roberts; Rev Mr. Rigg; Thomas Stevens; ___Saucer; Joseph Stengeffer; Richard Spencer; Thomas Tyler; Dekar Thompson; Dr. James Tilgont, Jr; Robert Tilghman; Eliza Taylor; Thomas Whittington; Anthony Whiteley; Sophia Weaver/Edward Price will manage Gibson's Mill - John Bennett/David Robinson, Easton, has a large number of mules for sale/Chancery sale by Alexander Stuart of real estate devised by Wil.iam L. Murray/William Bryan admin of Peter Green, late of Cecil Co/Margaret Bromwell, living near Hole in the Wall, offers reward for negro man, Jim about 35 yrs old and a negro boy, Bill, about 18 yrs old and Rachel about 17 yrs old and Esther who is about 9 yrs old

579. RST Jan 10 1804/Married Sun evening last, James Clayland to Miss Sally Martin dau of Robert Martin. On the same evening James Wrightson to Miss Sally Neall. Also William Haynes to Miss Hannah Bodfield/Died 31st ult, Solomon Kenton of Caroline Co/Died Fri last in this town, Peregrine Garnett/Died Sat last, Mrs. Mary Cooper, relict of James Cooper/Died Sun last in this town, Charles Baker of Carolline Co/Sale of lots of Joseph Telford, late of Talb Co, on the road from Easton to Goldsborough Neck, opposite the lots of Nicholas Hammond/Joseph Edmondson exec of James Edmondson, near Marshy Creek, Caroline Co/Lambert Reardon, tailor, has removed to the house lately occupied by

-90-

George Higgins, opposite the Post Office/Nathan Bailey exec of William Hay,
late of Caroline Co/Charles Gardiner, Miles River Neck, offers reward for black
horse/William Caulk, Bay Side, Talb Co, offers reward for mulatto man named
Daniel, about 27 yrs old/Sale at Denton of 480 a. adj Joseph Hurd, held in
common by the heirs of Joseph Dixon; also about 1/6 of Chapel Tract, held in
common by Wallace Dixon and heirs of Joseph Dixon; terms made known by James M.
Broom/Benjamin Chambers, President of Board of Visitors and Governors of
Washington College; Daniel McCurtin, sec'y - authorized to accept proposals for
a lady qualified to take charge of a Young Ladies School/James Iddings shall
open a school in the house lately occupied by Edward Markland/John Singleton
offers reward for negro woman, Sinah, property of Miss Polly Goldsborough; her
husband is property of Lemuel Norris (he ran away last fall). Sinah has an
aunt named Balder who is the property of Mrs. Margaret Walker, near Hunting
Creek/Chancery sale by Solomon Scott, trustee of tracts in QA Co: Relief;
Baynard's Pasture; Roes Chance - formerly possessed by George Baynard of QA Co
and which was by him mortgaged to Henry Pratt. Sale to be held at dwelling of
John Patrick on said land/Issabella James admin of John Jones, dec, Talb Co to
sell his personal property at the farm of John Singleton near Hole in the Wall/
Letters remaining at P. O. Chestertown· Unit Ainger; Thomas Adderson; Jere.
Alexander; Samuel Beck, Sr; Lewis Bush; Mary Bruff; John Bowers; James
Blackiston; Sarah Beauman; Hosea Beckly; Dr. Benjamin Chace Sarah Corse;
William Carmichael; Jesse Davis; Richard Darling; John Ewalt; Thomas Edwards;
Joseph Everitt; Josiah Gurley· Richard M. Gresham; James Grant; Richard Graves;
Sophia Granger· John B. Hacket; Thomas Hynson; James Houston; Richard
Hatchison; Upton S. Heath; George Hanson; Elizabeth Haggar; Humphry R. Hall;
Mr. Kendal: Thomas Kemp; Richard B. Mitchell; John Midders; Alexander Murray;
Samuel Miller; Thomas Nicholson; Josias Ringgold· William Spencer; William
Slubey; H. S. Sudlar: James Stoops· Henry H. Stuart; Isaac Todd; William
Thompson; M. Tilghman, Jr; William Thistherwood; Joseph Turner; James Walters;
Rez. S. Wilmer: Amor Williamson: Dr. Whittington; Sarah Woodland.

Letters remaining at P. O. Centreville: Thomas Betton; James R. Blunt; Catha.
A. Betton; Jacob Cruson; Miss Jane Caldwell; Mrs. Susan Clayland; C. W.
Carradine: Henry Costin; Clerk Q. A. Co: John Duhamell; Bennett Downes; Robert
Dawson: Stephen Foreman; Thomas Fitch; C. W. R. Gardner; Joseph Graham Jr;.
Mrs. Holliday; W. Harper & Son; Richard Harris; Mrs. Sophia Keys; Thomas Lee;
Thomas Moore; Daniel McGinnis; Richard Newman; J. H. Nicholson Jr: John Nabb;
Lamuel Purnell; Margaret Philips; William Price; George Reed; Jacob Ringgold;
Cornelia Southern; Charles Sewell; Zebulan Skinner; John Thompson; Isaac
Todd; Edward Turner: J. D. Thompson; Regester of Wills, Q. A. Co; Lott
Warfield; Samuel Wright Jr.

580. RST Jan 24 1804/Pennington & Brookes, Head of Chester, have commenced
coach, chaise and harness making business in the shop formerly occupied by
Henry Covington/Elizabeth Nicholson, living in Centreville offers reward for
negro man, Barnett, about 27 yrs old; he has a wife living with Mr. Henry
Hollyday/Married Sun last by Rev Francis Barclay, William Marshall of Dorch Co
to Miss Sophia Weaver of this county/John Fisher admin of William Fisher, late
of QA Co, to sell his personal estate at the late dwelling house/George Downs,
QA Co, announces availability of his horse, Harmless Shakespeare

581. RST Feb 7 1804/Letters remaining at P.O. George Town Crossroads: Eling
Comegys; Lucy Comegys; Samuel Crown; David Craig & Co; Jacob Colk; James R.
Corse; Abraham Chesterfield; Emory Edwards; Ann Fletcher; William Followfield;
John Greenwood; Joseph Harlan; John Hart; Jonathan Hodgson; James Howard; Rev
Dr. Benjamin Hall; James Jones; John Kennedy; Charles King; Robert King;
Richard Moffett; Hannah Moore; Thomas Nicholson; Hyland B. Pennington; Joseph
Rasin, Jr; Mr. Symmons; John Symmons; Symon Smith; Oliver Smith; Dr. Thomas
Veazey; Robert Ward; Sarah Woodland; Rev Simon Wilmer; Mary Yeats/Chancery
sale by Philip Reed, trustee, of real estate of William Clark, deceased

582. RST Feb 14 1804/Died 26th ult in the city of Phila in the 77th year,
John Beale Bordley, formerly of this state/Died lately in Dorch Co, John E.
Gist, of that county/Died on the 6th inst after a short illness at the Head of
Wye, Rev Elisha Rigg/Died on Wed the 1st inst, Capt George Bell, surveyor of
Worc Co/William Newton exec of Samuel Halsby late of Dorch Co/Robert Setten,
New Market, Dorch Co, wants a young man that understands the tanning and
currying business/Committed to jail in QA Co a negro man named James Late,
about 45 to 50 yrs old/Thomas Applegate junr, Jamaica Point, Talb Co, announces
the sale of house hold and kitchen furniture/James Bowie to sell land near
Easton, late the property of Rev John Bowie; apply to Thomas H. Bowie res near
Easton/Chancery sale by Simon Smyth of the land of William Slipper, dec/Henry
Landen has opened a private boarding house at Quantico Mill

583. RST Feb 21 1804/Married Sun last, Samuel Patterson of Easton to Miss
Peggy Sherwood of Talb Co/Died 6th inst in Northumberland Co, Pa, Dr. Priestly
in his 71st yr/William Richmond admin of Thomas I. Seth, dec/Sheriff's sale of
two lots in Easton, property of Benjamin Willmott taken in execution at the
suit of the state of Md for the use of John Goldsborough/John Dougherty selling
about 20 head of cattle at his place near Pott's Mill/The mill formerly the
property of Thomas I. Seth, late of QA Co, for rent; apply to Philip Fiddeman,
QA Co, or to William E. Seth, Talb Co/Zachariah Turner, near Queens-Town
selling horse named Farmer who was got by the late John Jones's horse Morrick
Ball/Committed to gaol of Kent Co, a negro woman, Jenny about 30 yrs old; says
she is free; she came last from James Smith of Caroline Co; she has delivered
a child since she was committed - William Moffett, sheriff, Kent Co, Md/Sale
at the late dwelling of John Clayland, dec, near Kings-town, by William
Clayland, exec of John Clayland

584. RST Feb 28 1804/Samuel Harrison admin of Edward Harrison/Owen Kennard
admin of James Tilghman, late of Talb Co/ Married Thurs last, William Rose to
Miss Betsey Martin, dau of Robert Martin, all of this county

585. RST Mar 6 1804/Richard Hynson and Elizabeth Hynson admin of Charles Adams,
late of QA Co, request his debtors and creditors settle accounts at Roe's Cross
Roads/Roger Woolford exec of Thomas Woolford, Dorch Co

586. RST Mar 13 1804/Married the 4th inst by Rev Barclay, Dr. Tristram Thomas
of Easton to Miss Mary Ann Goldsborough of this county/Died in Washington Wed
7th inst after a long illness, Gen. Daniel Heister, member of the House of
Representatives from this state/Henry Ringgold will sell the property he now
occupies, 9 miles from Chester Town/Jacob Cruson and Deborah Croney admin of
William Croney, late of Talb Co

587. RST Mar 20 1804/Married Thurs evening last by Rev McClaskey, Thomas
Banning of ths county to the amiable Miss Emme Spencer, dau of Richard Spencer,
Kent Co/William Potter, William Whitely and Isaac Purnell, Caroline Co, notify
that articles of association for the establishment of a new bank in Balt City
will be available for reading at Benjamin Denny's tavern in Denton for such
persons as wish to become share holders/John Blake admin of Eliza Hinson to
sell a part of her personal property by virtue of the order of the Orphan's
Court of Talb Co - at the dwelling of Eliza Hinson dec

588. RST Mar 27 1804/Saddle horse for sale by William Brown, Talb Co/Sale of
tracts, Stratton and Scotts Hardship,contiguous to each other in Tulley's Neck,
QA Co, near the Nine-bridges; Charles Spencer and William Taylor are tenants -
John G. Smith, QA Co/House for rent by recent occupant, Jesse Robinson, on
Dover St next door to Peter Denny's

589. RST Apr 3 1804/Philemon Willis, sheriff Talb Co, offers reward for three
negros who escapted jail, committed for trail for the felonies of breaking
open the store of Lambert Spencer - Dick Wilson, 22 yrs old, property of
William Thomas; Clement Robert, about 21 yrs old, property of Dr. John Coats;

Perry, about 21 yrs old, property of Miss M. Price and under the direction of
Mr. Larrimore of QA Co/Letters remaining at P.O. Easton: Benjamin Anderson;
Capt John Bush; Solomon Brown; John Blake; John N. Benny; Robert Buchanan;
William Bryan; Jonathan Bye; Jubah Benson; Elizabeth Bruff; William S. Bush;
Thomas Bullin; Thomas James Bullitt; James Coulston; Charles Critchet; John
Cooper; Samuel McCarty; Elizabeth Colston; Thomas Cook; James Clayland; George
Dawson; Thomas Daffin; Mary Denny; Miss Margaret Denny; William Dawson; Peter
Denny; Nicholas Dawson; Peter Edmondson; James Earle Jr; Mary Fleming; Jesper
Floyd; Greenbury Goldsborough; Benjamin Gilbert; Littleton Gale; James
Goldsborough; Charles Gully; John Goldsbury; Robert Goldsborough; Miss Mary
Gordon; John Harper; P. W. Hemsley; William Hamsley; Philip Hopkins; Samuel
Hoffman; Christopher Harrison; William Hemsley Jr; Gilberoy Handy; Edward
Hamilton; Col. Haddaway; Solomon Higgins; John Johnson; Benjamin Jones; David
Kemp; Sally Kemp; John Lucas, senr; Edward Lloyd; Alexander Laing; Solomon
Lowe; Daniel Lambden; Patience Loockerman; Foster Maynard; Dr. Ennalls Martin;
Richard Martindale; Sarah Mullikin; Capt Joseph Mirrick; McCallaston; Tristram
Needles; John Nock; Henry Nicolls, Jr; Noah Porter; John Pokley; E. L. Pelham;
S. S. Posey; William Potter; David E. Price; Lambert Reardon; George Rage;
Esther Robson; David Robinson; Joseph Richardson; Hugh Sherwood; Andrew
Skinner; Samuel Stevens; James Smith; Thomas Stevens; Philemon Sherwood;
Joseph Stingeffer; Archibald Serrell; Nathan Thayer; George Thomas; Levin
Tyler; Ann Thomas; Ann M. Tilghman; James Tilghman; Joseph Telford; Nicholas
Vallant; E. Vallant; Mr. Webley; John Woolford; James Willson, Jr; Stephen
Young/John Crozier of Easton, innocent of breaking open the store of Lambert
W. Spencer/Sale of White Marsh, Sassafras Neck, Gassaway Walkins(Watkins?),
manager, lives on the middle farm

590. RST Apr 10 1804/Married Tues evening last in Kent Co, Dr. Edward Scott
to Miss Ann Maria Comegys dau of Cornelius Comegys, all of that county/
Letters remaining at P.O. Centreville: Ann C. Betton; Thomas Betton; James
Bateman; Burgess, Dermes & Co; W. Christopher Caradine; Anna Maria Chew;
Samuel N. Copper; John E. Denny; Henry Downes; John Duhamell; Philip
Fiddeman; Miss Margaret Fiddeman; William Gould; William Harper; Mr. D. C.
Hodges; Richard Harriss; Henry Holmes; William Kearney; Joshua Kennard;
Benjamin Keene; William Legg; Miss Ann Morriss; Samuel Nicols; William
Nelson; Richard Newman; David Nichols; John Patrick; John Quemby; Benjamin
Smith; James Swiggett; John Smith; Mary Seth; Emory Sudler; Scot Esq; Harriet
Sudler; Sary Seth; Horatio Scrivener; William Taylor; Samuel S. Voorhees;
Samuel Watts; Nath. H. White; Charlotte H. White; Samuel Wilson; Major Charles
Wilson; Thomas Wright; Beckey Williams; George Wilson & Son; Eliza Walker/
Phebe Hull, Chestertown, admin of David Hull, late of Chestertown/Thomas
Freeman has taken the farm & fishery of John Ruth near Lewis-town in Talb Co/
James Walker admin of Robert Francis, late of Talb Co/Letters remaining at
P.O. Chestertown: Pegge Atcheson; Unit Angier; James Anderson; Joshua
Browning; John Bowen; Mrs. Elizabeth Caring; James Collins; Jr; John Cox;
Mrs. Nancy Cruckshanks; L. Clarkson; Elijah Denny; Philip Everitt; Joseph
Everitt; Mrs. Margaret Fletcher; Capt W. Graves; Thomas Gale; Richard Graves;
Joseph Garnett; James Higgins; Daniel & David Hull; Charles Heath; Morgan
Hurtt; William Hemsley; Mrs. Isabella Jones; Henry King; Miss Sarah S. Lamb;
William Lindsey - QA Co; Daniel Lamb; Elizabeth McCluer; Mrs. Mary Miller;
John Moore; Charles Maxwell; Rev George Moore; Thomas Moslin, Jr; William
Newman; John Page; John Poley; Tench Ringgold; Joseph Rumney; William Ruth;
Jacob Stevens; Henry Stuart; William Spencer; Thomas Smith, Jr; Thomas Smith
(carpenter); Tempe Tilghman; The hon. James Tilghman; Joseph Turner; John
Tilden; The Rev James Wilmer; Miss Fillis Woodland; Simon Wilmer; Edward
Wright/Charles Gibson, E a s t o n, offers reward for negro man, Abraham/
James Nabb has clover hay for sale

591. RST Apr 17 1804/Democratic Republicans of the several hundreds of

Caroline Co selected members to form a committee at Mr. Boon's tavern: Done Hundred - Robert Hardcastle, junr; Edward Carter; John Boon; Thomas Mason; Choptank Hundred - James Pearce; James Brody; White Turpen; Philemon Harrington; Tuckahoe Hundred - John Ruth; John Tillotson, John Hardcastle; Solomon Cooper; Bridgetown Hundred - Col. William Whiteley; James Summers; Robert Orrell; Solomon Richardson; Great Choptank Hundred - Solomon Brown; Richard Andrew; Francis Elliott; Beachemp Stanton; North West Fork Hundred - Frederick Holbrook; George Collins; Shadrach Lyden; Massy Chaffinch. The following were recommended to represent the county at the General Assembly: Thomas Hardcastle; Peter Rich; John Tillotson; Frederick Holbrook/Aaron Merchant exec of William Merchant, late of QA Co

592. RST Apr 24 1804/John Coats states that William Collins misrepresented a horse he sold to him/John Nabb Head of Wye, reports a stolen mare/William Haslutt, Greensborough, intends to remove from the Eastern Shore next month; he is selling out dry goods, hardware, earthenware and groceris, and a canvass top chaise

593. RST May 1 1804/Proprietors of waggons in Easton announce an increase in their rates to five dollars per diem: Robert Bruff; Solomon Lowe; John Stevens, Jr; John Goldsborough; Nicholas Valiant; James Earle, Jr/George Lake admin of Gabriel Slacum, late of Dorch Co/Chancery sale by Richard C. Keene, trustee, of real estate of Shadrach Keene subject to dower: Keenes Misfortune, and interest in the tracts, Inclosure and Keene's Pastrue - all in Dorch Co/ Nancy Kerby admin of Thomas Newbold, late of Worc Co

594. RST May 8 1804/Died near Chestertown, Mrs. Mary Hynson, wife of Joseph Hynson, on 26 April last/To meet at Mr. Lowe's tavern to supertend arrangements for celebrating the 12th of May: Jacob Gibson; William Meluy; Col. Perry Spencer; Capt Thomas Coward; Samuel Stevens, junr and James Nabb/James Troth, Easton, inform the public that he has new watches, chains, and seals on hand/Nathan Townsend, Easton, reports a stolen mare/Joseph Suliven offers a reward for two negro women who ran away from his sloop while laying in the port of Oxford; one of them was formerly the property of Miss M. Goldsborough/ Philemon Plummer offers reward for a negro man Peter, property of Mrs. Mary Wilson

595. RST May 22 1804/Died yesterday around 11 o'clock, Samuel Dickinson, an old and respectable citizen/William Haslett has established himself in the grocery business, corner of Pratt & South St, Balt/Richard Barroll, Chestertown, Register of Chester Parish, Kent Co, Md reports that the Vestry is engaged in getting subscriptions to support a minister

596. RST May 29 1804/Benjamin Benny, Inspector of Emmerson's Ware House, Talb Co/Purchasing a few young slaves, F. Surget, Charles Bosley, Easton; apply at Mr. Lowe's Tavern/Charles Gulley, Talb Co, insolvent

597. RST Jun 5 1804/Married 23rd ult, Charles Goldsborough of Shoal Creek to Miss Sarah Goldsborough, dau of the late Charles Goldsborough of Horns Point, Dorch Co/Henry Kenton, Caroline Co, gives notice he will not pay on a note of hand which he gave to Thomas Dudley of Talb Co/William Boone and William Crawford, both of Caroline Co, insolvent/Committed to gaol of Kent Co, a negro man named Standley, about 30 yrs old; he says he ran away from Joseph Beard, Annapolis, and belongs to the heirs of William Hambleton, late of QA Co, which John Hambleton of Harf Co is guardian to - William Moffitt, sheriff

598. RST Jun 12 1804/Died Mon morning, 4th inst in Chestertown, Samuel G. Williams, son of Joseph Williams, Chestertown; on Tues following his remains were interred in the Church Yard. He contended a long time with a languishing sickness. He left two affectionate parents/Died a few days past at an advanced age, William Stevens of this county/Died, Mrs. Margaret Hughs, consort

of Col. John Hughes of this county/Mary Ann Benton admin of Samuel Atkinson,
late of QA Co/Joseph Latimer admin of Henry Esgate, late of QA Co/Sale of
house, store, and granary in Greensborugh, part of the estate of John
Steinmetz, dec, late of Phila; apply to Capt William Jackson, Greensborough
or John H. Brinton, Phila/Robert H. Goldsborough, near Easton, offers reward
for negro, Ephraim, about 19 yrs old; his wife named Suck, age about 30 yrs,
ran away Jul last with her child they were lately seen in Dorch Co where his
wife has relations/William Priest, Caroline Co, insolvent

599. RST Aug 7 1804/Married Sun evening last by Joseph Jackson, James
Nicholson of QA Co to the amiable Miss Margaret D. Emmerson of this town/
Died Thurs evening last after a tedious illness, Mrs. Henrietta Maria
Hayward, the amiable consort of Col. William Hayward of this county/Died the
26th ult at Elkton, Davidson David, one of the council of this state/Sale of
210 a. within 2 miles of Centreville - James O'Bryon or Benjamin O'Bryon/
Rent of plantation belonging to Daniel Nicolls, Dorch Co, at the Cross Roads/
Letters remaining at P. O. Georgetown Cross Roads· Mary Ambrose; James Bevans;
Daniel Bryan; Robert Browning· Kessiah Bowers; William Barrans; William
Boardly; William Barns; Nancy Postwick; Moses Briscoe· Benjamin Bryan;
Elizabeth Comegys; Cornelius Comegys; Luscay Comegys; George Corrie; Jesse
Davis; Fanny Demby; Elliott & Tail; Abraham Faulkner; Samuel Golden; Eliza
Grindage; Ann Graves; Joseph & John Hart; Cutbert Hall; James Howard; Harriot
& Tucker; Rev. Dr. Benjamin Hall; Samuel Ireland; Samuel Kerr, Robert King;
John Kenedy; Edmond Lynch; Ann Lambden; John Lathern; Elizabeth Little; B. W.
McReeder; John McDonald· Dr. Maguire; Richard Moffett; Thomas Nicholson;
Hyland B. Penington; Charlotte Ringgold; Joseph Rasin, Jr· Thomas Savin;
Betsey Singles; James Salisbury; John Symons; Mary Woodland; Rebecca Wilson;
Rachel Woodland; Robert Ward John Williams; David Wiley; George Yeats. -
William Pope, Junr., Post Master/Henry Boullin, Miles River Neck, wants to
employ a blacksmith/House for rent where E. Coursey now lives; apply to Henry
Nicols, junr/Sale or rent of 1/3 of the tract called Woolbey Manor, commonly
known as Chancellor's Point, along with two good ferry boats - Sailes Cannar,
William Cannar/John Bowers & Rachel Parrott admin of Aaron Parrott, Talb Co

600. RST Aug 14 1804/Rent of house of William Pope, senr, in George Town,
Kent Co, long celebrated as a tavern abused by William Pope for many
years; also a lot in Georgetown adj Mrs. Wilson's property - Apply to John
Ireland, George-Town Cross Roads or William Pope, Chestertown/William Barton,
Easton, offers for sale two canvas top chairs/Lambert Norris, Talb Co, offers
reward for negro man, Aaron, 21 yrs old/Died Tues morning last in her 73rd
year, the venerable and benevolent Mrs. Ann Hollyday of Talb Co/Samuel
Chamberlaine, Nicholas Hammond, Henry Hollyday exec of Anna Maria Hollyday/
William S. Bush exec of Elizabeth Darden late of Talb Co

601. RST Aug 21 1804/William Clayland, Hillsborough, exec of John Clayland,
late of Talb Co/Rent of house now occupied by Capt Vickars, north side of
road from Easton to Easton Point; apply to Richard Denny

602. RST Aug 28 1804/Married Sun evening by Rev Simon Wilmer, Joseph H.
Nicholson, junr, of Centreville, to Miss Charlotte Gibson of the same place/
Married on the -1th inst at Duck Creek Cross Roads, Delaware, Thomas McDowe
to Mary Denny dau of William Denny of Kent Co/Married on the 14th inst, Enock
Joyce, to Sarah Fields, of the above place/Rent of shop now occupied by James
Faulkner and the shop next to Mr. Lowe's tavern occupied by David Fleming;
also the house occupied by John Millis, one mile from the town on the Phila
road; apply to Thomas Perrin Smith, Easton/Joseph Rasin admin of Susanna
Medford, late of Kent Co Md/William Green admin of Silas Fleming, Caroline Co/
Sale at the house of Joseph Rasin, senr, Still Pond, Kent Co Md, a number of
negroes, stock, furniture/David Robinson, near Oxford, seeking a teacher for
a private family/Perry Benson, Miles River, offers reward for young negro

man, Isaac, about 20 yrs old; has relations in this county and some living in
Delaware near Marshyhope Bridge/Testimony of James Kemp and Charles Vaughn to
the beneficial effect of the waters of Barren-Creek Springs/Married Wed 22nd
ult by Rev Wyatt, David Sharpe of Elk Ridge to Miss Henrietta of Annapolis

603. RST Sep 4 1804/Chancery sale of Grist mill on branch of St. Michaels
river by Hugh Sherwood of Huntington, trustee/Chestertown races to be run by
the filleys of messrs: Thomas M. Forman, Richard I. Jones, William H.
Nicholson and Edward Lloyd - Philip Chaplin, sec'y, Chestertown/Joseph Daffin
to petition for relief from debts/Alexander McClayland, Benjamin Stokes, admin
of Robert Small, late of Talb Co/Sale of property of Morrico Ellors, dec, near
Church Hill, William Stenson, trustee/Thomas Williams, Dorch Co, to decline
the mercantile business and will hold a public sale at his store house in New
Market, Dorch Co/William Dunn, Head of Wye, Talb Co, offers reward for three
negro men: Richard about 40 yrs old; Solomon about 35 yrs old; Benjamin about
25 yrs old/David D. Barrow exec of Thomas Barrow, late of Talb Co; Rent of
house occupied by Edward Markland

604. RST Sep 11 1804/Samuel T. Wright candidate for elector of Kent and QA
counties/Sale of pt of tract, The Advantage, Talb Co on the Choptank river,
by William Patton/Sale at Hibernia, within 1 mile Centreville, mares one of
which is in foal by Major Forman's Ranger, two by Richard Jones's horse,
Suwarrow - John Dames, QA Co/Samuel Thomas, Easton Point, reports the availability of schooner, Louisiana which sails between Easton and Balt/John Coats
of Easton reports horse strayed or stolen/John Willis, Collector of the
District and Port of Oxford/James Claypoole, Chestertown offers reward for two
apprentice boys: William Cooper and James Tigart

605. RST Sep 18 1804/Married some days since, Lemuel Purnell of Centreville
to Miss Charlotte Pratt dau of Henry Pratt of QA Co/Married Thurs evening
last, Lambert W. Spencer of Easton to Miss Anna Spencer, dau of Col. Perry
Spencer of this county/Died last week, William Aikers of this county./ Died
Philemon Hambleton, after a short illness/Died Sat morning last, Mrs. Susannah
Coats, consort of Dr. John Coats of this town/Sale of 60,000 a. in Delaware
Co, Pa, by Edward Tilghman, Phila/John Turner, Talb Co, candidate as delegate
to Gen. Assembly/James Lenox offers for sale in Chester-town house where he
now lives on main st/James Byus, Dorch Co, to petition for relief from debts/
John Miller of Somerset Co, commonly called John Hogskin, to petition for
relief from debts/Nathan C. Newton to petition for relief from debts/Moses
Passapae, Nichols Cross Roads, Dorch Co, offers reward for negro woman named
Jude, about 40 yrs old, likely to be found in the vicinity of Collins' Cross
Roads, Caroline Co/Farms for rent; apply to Sarah Bowman, Kings Creek/William
Y. Bourk, living in QA Co, offers reward for negro man, Moses, about 45 yrs
old, property of Mrs. Blake; Moses has relations in the Jerseys/Henry Downes,
QA Co, to petition for relief from debts/John Roberts, Miles River, admin of
James Hazletine, late of Talb Co/Lambert Reardon seeks sober, steady journeymen tailors/John R. Bromwell, Talb Co, to petition for relief from debts/Sale
at the farm of John Hughes, Miles River of horses, cows, oxen, farming
utensils/The Invinsible Lady now exhibiting at Benjamin Hatchison's tavern
sign of General Washington, in Centreville/Planner Elliott and Sarah Elliott,
his wife, admin of Severn Fitcell, late of Dorch Co/Benjamin Wilmott, Easton,
and William Stevens, Talb Co, and James Turner, Jr, Talb Co, all to petition
for relief from debts/Robert Goldsborough candidate for delegate to Gen.
Assembly/William Welch, Talb Co, offers reward for apprentice lad, Urial
Duling, about 18 yrs old

606. RST Oct 2 1804/John Kemp exec of George I. Dawson, Talb Co to hold sale
at plantation of the dec/Rent of tenement at the head of Shoal Creek in Dorch
Co now occupied by John Vickars, owned by Mrs. Ennalls; also renting farm in
Poplar Neck, Caroline Co, whereon Richard Willoughby formerly lived as

overseer; apply to C. Goldsborough, Dorch Co/Letters remaining at P.O. Easton:
Mrs. Ann Applegarth; William Ashford; Thomas Abbott; Susannah Bordley; John
J. Bell; William Blake; William Bromwell; Henry Berriman; James Benson; Jacob
Bromwell; William Brown; Solomon Bryan; Catharine Blair; Francis Barckley;
Loftus Bowdle; Mathias Bordley; Jabez Caldwell; Patrick Callan; John Clash;
Jeremiah T. Chase; Edward Coursey; Eliz. Caile; Thomas Coward; Mrs. Caile;
John Doherty; Adam Deshler; James Delahay; Stephen Derden; John Dansberry;
Ann Dickinson; Lidia Edmondson; Peter Edmondson; James Earle Jr; Charles
Goldsborough; Z. H. Gregory; Thomas Gibson; Mary Gordon; Rachael A. Curty;
Henry Grose; Caroline Goldsborough; William Garey; John Goldsborough; Josiah
Gurley; Catharine Goldsborough; Samuel Garey; Margaret Gardner; William
Hindman; John Hopkins; Thomas Howard; Thomas Hardcastle Jr; Joseph Harrison;
Thomas Hale; William Kearn; Thaddus Jackson; Dr. Samuel Y. Keene; James
Iddings; Justices of Orphans Court; David Kerr Jr; William Lowrey; Solomon Lowe;
John Landman; Mrs. Lloyd; M. Lambert; Solomon Merrick; Thomas Manely; Haley
Moffitt; George Moore; James Mullican; William Moffitt; Luther Martin; James
Murray Jr; Henrietta Nicolls; Jeremaih Nicolls; Dr. P. E. Noel; Benjamin Nona;
J. H. Nicholson; Laden Ogden; Peter Richardson; Patty Rhoads; E. P. Robinson;
John Roberts; Isaac Spencer; Mrs. William Smyth; Dr. John Stevens; Thomas
Stevens; Robert Speddin; Mr. Shoemaker; William B. Smyth; Richard S. Thomas;
Joshua Taggart; James Troth; John Thomas; Samuel Thomas; Nicholas Valliant;
James Veatch; Henry Willis; Eliza White; Ann Wickersham; James Willson;
William Weaver; James Ward/Samuel Sherwood and Charles Cox, sureties for
Samuel Clayton, late constable of Tred-Haven Hundred, request legal claims be
presented to them/Sale at William Arrington's near Easton/Thomas Applegarth
has opend a dry goods and groceries store on Washington St/Citizens invited
to meet at home of Mr. Scirvin, Chestertown to discuss erection of toll-bridge
across Chester river/Reward offered for strayed horse, William Price at I. B.
or R. Taylor/James Cruckshank, Kent Co, Md to petition for relief from debts/
Bennet H. Clarval, Princess Ann, being imprisoned for the space of 10 months
past, means to petition for relief from debts/Tubman Pollitt, Princess Ann,
to petition for relief from debts

607. RST Oct 9 1804/Married Sun evening last, James Tilghman to Miss Martha
Waller, both of this town/Sarah Fish, Talb Co, to sell on the farm where she
lives, horses, cattle, sheep, farm utensils/Sale at farm of George R. Hayward
in Bailey's Neck, where Thomas Bogs now res, horses, cows, oxen/Mary Bond
holding a sale at dwelling house in Easton, household items, also the time of
a negro woman for seven years/William Kerney, QA Co, to petition for relief
from debts/William Bell Whitley, Caroline Co, to petition for a stay in the
payment on escheatable lands lying in Caroline Co for which he has obtained
an escheat warrant/Jonathan Bready, QA Co, to petition for relief from debts/
Letters remaining at P.O. Centreville: John Brown; James Backman; William
Barney; Senah Busick; Mark Benton; Robert B. Billups; William H. Boardley;
Sam. N. Copper; William Carmichael; Mrs. Sarah Coursey; Edward Coursey; Henry
Downes; James Davidson; John Dames; William Gleaves; Miss Elizabeth C.
Goldsborough; Thomas Garnett; Thomas Hewitt; Turbutt Harris; Richard Harris;
Mrs. Polly Hardiss; Edward Harriss; Mrs. Rebecca Hammond; Benjamin Hale;
Rebecca Kendel; Samuel Kume; James B. Knotts; Miss Kent; Stephen Lowrey; John
Leathurberry; Mrs. Charlotte Nicholson; William Nicholson; William Palmer;
John Patrick; William Rich; Thomas Roberts; Mrs. Jane Rigg; Mrs. Elizabeth
Robinson; Robert Ceders; John Smith; James Smith; Nicholas Smith; Dr. T. R.
P. Spence; Dr. J. I. Troup; John D. Thompson; Sam. T. Wright; Thomas L. L.
Wall/Letters remaining at P.O. Chestertown: James Arthur; Hamilton Bell; John
S. Blunt; Dr. Thomas Bruff; Mrs. Ann Cruckshanks; Mrs. Ann Cuff; Miss Sarah
Calvert; William Collins; George Corrie; Philip Chaplin; John Campbell; John
Connell; Richard Chew; Philip Davis; William Embleton; John Eades; Miss Kitty
Fendell; Isaac Freeman; John Fort; Joseph Garnett; Mr. Guichard; James Harris;

James Higgins; Robert Hall; Nathaniel Hynson; James Harper; James Henderson;
Henry Kennard; John Kennard, senr; John T. Kennard; Rebecca Lucas; Lodge No.
2; Lodge No. 4; Mr. Jane Lard(sic); John Letherbury; Mrs. M. Moore; George
Moore; George G. Medford; Doctor Matthews; Richard B. Mitchell; Miss Ann
McCleon; William Mathews; Mrs.Mary Miller; Joseph Pennington; Daniel Perkins;
Joseph Rasin; Robert Reed; William Russell; Moses Ruth; James Richards; Simon
Smith; Thomas Smith; William Sutton; Daniel Taylor; the honl. James Tilghman;
Samuel Thomas; Mrs. Williamson; Edward Woodall; Mrs. Susannah Walthum; John
Walker; Lyda Warfield/House for rent at present occupied by James Iddings;
apply to Robert Moore or James Neall, Easton

608. RST Oct 16 1804/Died Sat last, John Turner of this county/Margaret
Hambleton exec of Philemon Hambleton/Willaim Wilson and Ann Wilson exec of
John Wilson, Talb Co, near Kingstown/John Vickars and John Simmonds, Talb Co,
to petition for relief from debts/Sale by Daniel Chezum on farm where he now
lives called Barker's Landing, horses, cattle, cows and sheep/Houses for rent
by W. Dunn, Wye River, now occupied by Mrs. Rigg situated on Wye River/Chancery
sale at Long's Tavern in Pricness Anne, the estate of James Ewing, late of
Somerset Co, dec, land in Somerset Co: Howard's Purchase, Turkey Ridge,
Dorman's Folly, Dorman's Addition, Addition and a parcel on Monikin Creek
conveyed by John Walkins late of Somerset Co - sold by Hans Creevey/Jacob
Gibson selling woodland called Turkey Neck Addition adj lands lately occupied
by John Register, dec

609. RST Oct 23 1804/Married Tues last by Rev William Gibson, Dr. Alexander
Stewart of Kent Co to Mrs. Elizabeth Thomas of Wye, this county/Samuel S.
Dickinson exec of Samuel Dickinson/Henry Hollyday, Ratcliffe, selling cattle
and sheep at his farm adj Court-House Bridge/William Clayton, Centreville,
sec'y Centreville Academy/Mecucan Walker, Somerset Co, to petition for relief
from debts/Nicholas Valliant, Easton, offers reward for apprentice boy, Samuel
Ferguson, about 14 yrs old

610. RST Oct 30 1804/Letters remaining at P.O. Georgetown Cross Roads: Mary
Ambrose; William Bordly; Kessiah Bowers; William Barns; Cornelius Comegys;
Luseay Comegys; Elizabeth Comegys; Comegys & Vansant; George Corrie; James
Conner; Joseph Douglas; Abraham Falconer; Sarah Falconer; Ann Graves;
Elizabeth Grundage; Dr. Benjamin Hall; John Hurtt, sadler; Joseph & John Hart;
James Howard; William Haslett; John Kenedy; Robert King; Ann Lambdin; Dr.
John Maxwell; Joseph Mann; Casperus Megines; Richard Moffett; Thomas Nicholson;
Hyland B. Pennington; Elizabeth Rice; James Rayne; William Semans; Sally
Massey; John Symons; Betsey Singles; Mary Savin; Rev Simon Wilmer; Robert
Walter; Rachel Woodland; Mary Woodland; Dr. Robert Ward; James Welch; John
Williams; David Wiley/Lydia Turner exec of John Turner - Nathan Townsend, her
atty/Joseph Durding, Centreville, on account of his bad health to sell off his
stock of goods/Mr. McFarlane opening Dancing School at the house of Mr. Prince
in Easton/Jacob Falconar, Kent Co, Md, to petition for relief from debts

611. RST Nov 6 1804/Married Thurs evening last by Rev Joseph Jackson, David
Kerr, Jr, merchant, to Miss Maria Perry, both of this town/Sale of lot adj
David Nice and Dr. Johnson's lots, near Easton by Thomas McKeale, Easton/
Isabella James admin of John James, late of Talb Co/Richard Thomas & Co has
new guns from London on hand, Queens Town/Hugh McAllister, near Queens' Town
offers reward for negro man, Charles Johnson, about 40 yrs old and a negro
woman, Hannah, about 20 yrs old

612. RST Nov 13 1804/Littleton Dennis Teackle, Princess Anne, selling
mercantile establishment in Princess Anne/John Kennard, Easton, has assortment
of goods for sale/Samuel Abbott atty for Ann Akers, exec of William Akers,
selling horses, cattle, sheep and farming utensils/Alexander Stuart and
Elizabeth Stuart, Talb Co, selling farm near Head of Wye River, late the

property of John Thomas,dec, and where he always resided - Apply to Dr. William E. Seth or Alexander and Elizabeth Stuart/Edward Earle, druggist, has removed to house of Mr. Baldwin/Sale at George town Cross Roads, house now occupied by Henry Wallis, for creditors of John Writson Browning, late of Kent Co, by Robert Browning, trustee

613. RST Jul 24 1804/Joseph Nicholson and George Attwood have purchased two schooners from Capt Dawson called the Centreville and the Farmer; to run as packets and grain boats between Centreville and Balt/John Bowers and Rachel Parrott admin of Aaron Parrott, Talb Co/William Clayton sec'y of Centreville Academy/William and Thomas Atkinson admin of James Cooper/Conference committee of Kent Co of Democratic Citizens - Upper dist: Nathan Smith, James Welch, Caspanius McGinnis; Middle dist: John Gale, John Kennard, Philip F. Rasin; Lower: Capt John Moore, William Crane, Samuel Beck

614. RST Jul 31 1804/Farm for sale occupied by Francis Price near Hole in the Wall/Letters remaining at Chestertown: Levi Alexander; Moses and Aaron Ashley; Mrs. Frances Andrews; Mrs. Sarah Ambers; Elijah Beck; James Bradshaw; Mr. Borall; Hosea Beckley; Joseph Blackiston, junr; George Corell; James Cruckshanks; John Collins; John Campbell; Hezekiah Cooper; Nathaniel Davis; James Eagle; Thomas Edwards; Joseph Everitt; Mrs. Margaret Fletcher; Sweetman Ferman; James Frisby junr; Mrs. Nancy Gibson; Thomas Gale; Miss Mary Hamel; John Heron; Mathew Hawkins; Thomas Hynson; Judy Holland; Upton S. Heath; Mrs. Isabella Jones; Samuel Keenr junr; Richard Keene; John Leatherbury; Richard B. Mitchel; Alexander Maxwell; James Melton; William Newman; Miss Maria Nicholson; Jeremiah Nicols; Joseph Pennington; Daniel Pirkins; John Paley; James Ross; Henry Ringgold; Mrs. Mary Rasin; Joseph Simmonds; James Stoops; Thomas Smith; Henry H. Stuart; William Thomas; Philip Taylor; Richard Tilghman, Mrs. Anna Trulock; Marmaduke Tilden; Rev Simon Wilmer; David Whiteing/John Kemp exec of George F. Dawson, late of Talb Co/Letters remaining at Centreville: James Bateman; Mathias Boardley; Peregrine Blake; Richard Collins; Mrs. Charlotte S. Clayland; Mr. Cuison; Reynolds & Clarke; John Davis; Miss Nancy Edwards; Richard J. Earle; Charles Emory; Mrs. Elizabeth Fiddeman; Mrs. Polly Harris; Mrs. Holliday; Benjamin Hall; Benjamin Hatcheson; Richard Harris; Mrs. Anna Honey; Miss A. M. Kent; Samuel Kerr; James Kerr; James Kindle; Samuel Keene; David Lucas; Daniel McGinnis; Haley Moffett; Hugh McAllister; Charles Neale; Benjamin Obryon; James Pryor; John Patrick; Jacob Pearce; John Southrose; Thomas Sharp; Jesse M. Sherwood; John Scriviner; Peter Sett, jun; Thomas Smith; William Taylor; Mrs. Anne Tilden; Sam. S. Voochus (Voorhees); Mrs. Ann Warfield; Henry Weeden/Creditors of Samuel Nicols insolvent debtor of Talb Co are requested to lodge accounts with Bennett Wheeler, Hall Harrison or Henry Nicols, Talb Co/Patrick Kennard exec of Philip Everitt, late of Kent Co Md

615. RST Jul 10 1804/John Comegys, Kent Co, admin of Abraham Millan and Daniel Greenwood dec

616. RST Jul 17 1804/Married Thurs last by Rev Stockett, John B. Campbell, age 20 to Mrs. Jane Armstrong, both of QA Co/Correction - Married Fri evening 6 inst by Rev Barckley, Josiah Polk junr of Somerset Co to the agreeable Miss Rebecca Troup of this town/Robert Dixon admin of Joseph Dixon/Houses to rent by Thomas Kersey, living on the premises, between courthouse and water, Easton

617. RST Jun 19 1804/Married 17th ult by Rev Walker, William Bowers to Miss Sarah L. Lamb, both of Kent Co/Married Sat 2d inst by Rev Ralston, Samuel Stevens junr of this county to the agreeable Miss Eliza May dau of Col. Robert May, of Chester Co, Pa/Married Mon 4th inst by Rev S. Keene junr, James Hammond of QA Co aged 64 to the agreeable and much admired Miss McClement of Delaware, age 20/Married Sun last Thomas Robinson to Miss Elizabeth Crey, both of this town

618. RST Jul 3 1804/Died in this town on Sun last after a long illness Mrs.
M. Hayward/Letters at P.O. Easton: Thomas Abbott; Richrd Adams; John Blake;
Mrs. Mabel Barns; Rev Francis Barclay; Brian & Roney; Edward Burke; Henry
Bullin; Dr. James Bordley; Miss Matilda Chase; Joseph J. Cartrite; Thomas
Clarke; M. Chamberlaine; Joshua Driver; William Dunn; Solomon Dickinson; Peter
Johnson Down; Philemon Dickinson; James Delehay; Pere Driver; James Edmondson;
James Earle junr; Robert Edgell; Charles Emory; John Etherington; Joseph
Farling; H. M. Frances; John Goldsborough; Thomas Godwin; William H.
Goldsborough; Charles Goldsborough; Greensbury Goldsborough; John Hains;
Joseph Hutchins; Samuel Harrison; John Higgins; Robert Harrison; William
Haddaway junr; William H. Haddaway; Thomas Harper; P. W. Helmsley; E. N.
Hambleton; Rev J. Jackson; Mrs. Silver Johnson; Rachel Kemp; Mrs. Rich Keene;
Sally Kemp; Col. Richard Keene; Dr. Samuel Y. Keene; Rev James Kemp; William
Lowrey; John Lamb; Mrs. F. T. Loockerman; Stanley B. Loockerman; Thomas
Monally; Miss Mary Markland; Richard B. Mitchell; Richard Martindale; James
Nabb; E. L. A. Pelham; Lemuel Purnell; William Patton; Mrs. E. Pamphilion;
Mrs. Primrose; James Price; John Quinby; Edward Roberts; Sally Ratcliff;
Robert Sheddin; Lydia Sherwood; Joseph Stingeffer; William Sands; Richard
Sheath; Hugh Sherwood; Phil. Sherwood; Samuel Swan; James Stanlee; Mrs. A. M.
Smyth; John Shannon; William Stant; Jenifer Taylor; William Tibbles; Dekar
Thompson; Mrs. Eliza Thomas; Charles Twiford; Joshua Taggart; Thomas Vickers;
George Walker; Thomas Wing; Henry Wright; Daniel Whelan; Hugh Work; Samuel
Willson; Stephen Young

619. RST Nov 20 1804/Farm for rent near head of Wye, late the property of
John Thomasdec and where he always res; apply to Dr. William E. Seth or to
Alexander Stuart and Elizabeth Stuart, Talb Co/Sale of lots opposit the Market
Space and Court House; also lot adj David Nice's and Dr. Johnson's lots –
Thomas McKeale/Mr. Lowrey delivered a bill at the House of Delegates, entitled
an act for the benefit of Benjamin Willson of Caroline Co, a minor .../Mr.
Goldsborough delivered a bill at the House of Delegates entitled an act for
the benefit of John R. Bromwell, Talb Co/John Troth forwarns person from
carting or hauling wood across his lands lying in Kings Creek as he has
received considerable injury from persons drawing from Nicholas Valliant's
lands/Sale of yoke of oxen by James Hicks, living in Caroline Co, 3 miles
from Hillsborough/Notice regarding delinquent taxes on lands heretofore
occupied by Stephen Foreman, called Marshlands, lying on Long Marsh, QA Co:
John Browne junr, Collector 16th Dist, Md/John Kemp exec of Margaret Lambdin
and Joseph Cooper dec, both of Talb Co/Rent of store room and cellar in front
of house occupied by Mrs. Mary Dawson, Easton/Rent of house presently occupied
by Miss Fletcher as a school-house; apply to Mary Trippe, Easton

620. RST Dec 4 1804/Petition by Joseph G. Daffin, Dorch Co, for relief from
debts/Tristram Thomas, Easton and George Gillasspy, Phila, admin of William
Geddes, late of Phila, from theOrphans Court of Kent Co, Md/Houses for let in
Easton belonging to Mark Bent: two-storey brick house occupied by Jacob
Loockerman, tavern in the possession of James Faulkner, house occupied by
James Cowan; apply to Owen Kennard, Easton/James Nabb exec of William
Hutchings dec late of Talb Co/Thomas Atkinson and John Tibbles in the tanning
and currying business at Tan Yard at the Head of Wye, late the property of Dr.
Wilson/James Lambdin has taken house at present occupied by Nicholas Valliant;
proposes to open a boarding house/Stanley Vickars offers reward for horse
strayed from Easton Point; owner is Robert Ewing, Kingstown

621. RST Dec 11 1804/Married Sunday 2d inst, Samuel Jackson to Mrs. Jones
wid of John Jones dec, both of this county/Letter to paper from William Handy,
Worc Co, regarding abuse of insolvency act/Farm for rent in Oxford Neck,
property of Mrs. Rachel Thomas; apply to John Singleton, Horatio Edmondson or
to William Thomas/House for rent at present occupied by Lambert Spencer, the
fron being occupied by Joseph Haskins as a store/Sale by William Stenson,

trustee, QA Co, of the remaining part of the real estate of Meriel Ellers, late
of QA Co, lands near Church Hill/Sale of farm where Benjamin Hall, subscriber,
now res, adj Christopher Cox near Centreville/Sale of 240 a. on Long Marsh,
QA Co; Philemon Spencer lives on the premises; apply to Henry Downes,
Hillsborough/John Bennett has established a flour and meal store in Easton;
plans to keep a waggon running at least twice a week from his mill in Wye/
Samuel Brown admin of William S. Bond/Caleb Boyer offers offers for sale
property where he now res in Greensborough

622. RST Dec 18 1804/John Harwood will accommodate 8 boys with board, Easton/
Obediah Garey admin of Richard Ray dec,to sell household and kitchen furniture
at the farm near Chappel, lately occupied by Richard Ray

623. RST Dec 25 1804/Petitions from Bennett Clarvoe, Mininkin Walter, and
John Miller (alias John Hodskin) of Somerset Co for relief from debts/Peitions
from William Kerney and William P. M. Ridgways of QA Co and Joice Insley, Dorch
Co, for relief from debts/Married Thurs last Daniel Cain, age 71, to Mrs.
Elizabeth Watts age 63, both of this co/Sale of work horses by Thomas L.
Haddaway at his farm near White Marsh Church/Chancery sale of lots in Caroline
Co wherof William Gibson died seized: 2 lots in Denton one of which Alexander
Maxwell occupies, 3rd lot at a place known as Walnut Trees, William Crawford,
trustee, Greensborough/Chancery sale by Henry Downes of the real estate of
Brook Thornton dec/John Stevens junr, William S. Bishop, Lambert W. Spencer
have formed a committee of arrangement for St. Thomas Lodge, Easton/John Dodd
and wife admin of Elkanah Meeds, late of QA Co

624. RST Jan 1 1805/Petition from James Turner, Talb Co, for relief from
debts/A new store house for rent on main st fronting the public square and
joining the Eagle Tavern in Chester Town, now occupied by Richard Ringgold;
apply to Isaac Cannell, Chestertown/Woolman Hughey, Talb Co, lost pocket book
in Easton; deliver to Patrick McNeil in Easton or Woolman Hughey for reward/
Sale of lot at Head of Chester; apply to William Ferrell, Head of Chester

625. RST Jan 8 1805/Died Fri 23 Nov last at Mount Vernon plantation, South
Carolina, William Minor senior, formerly of Centreville (heretofore Chester
Mill) in QA Co, for the last 18 years resident of South Carolina aged 66 yrs;
he left a wife and eight children, six of whom under the age of 12/Died Sat
evening last Mrs. Mary Pinkine of this co after a long and painful affliction/
Married Mon 24 ult by Rev Simon Wilmer, Richard Newman of Centreville to Mrs.
Mary Mann of Kent Co/Married Sun 23 ult Daniel Smith to Miss Sally Hopkins,
both of this Co/Married 27 ult, John Hopkins to Miss Ann Pasterfield, both of
this co/Married 30 ult Hugh Rice to Miss Anna Valliant, both of this town/
James Wilson admin of Rebecca King/Sale at the dwelling of the subscriber,
James Greenfield in Hook-Town: two looms and loom geers; attendance given by
Nathan Townsend/Chancery sale by Hugh Sherwood, trustee, of real estate of
James Cooper, dec of mill seat of 114 1/4 a./Henry Johnson admin of John Troth
dec to sell horses and black cattle, sheep, and farming utensils/Mable Lowrey,
Thomas Lowrey, admin of Robert Lowrey, late of Talb Co/James Greenfield gives
notice whereas my wife Margaret Greenfield has left his bed and board .../
Letters remaining at P.O. Chester Town: James Arthur; Henry Briscoe; Samuel
J. Banister; Miss P. Bailey; Joseph Bowsterd; Thomas Berry; James Butcher;
William Brown; Daniel Bryon; John Brice; John Carvill; Abner Coker(?); Anna
Caulk; Henry Cavender; Mrs. Curry, near Church Hill; Mrs. Ann Calvert; John
Duhammel; Abitha Davis; Mrs. Ann Duhamell; Wilson Edwards; Joseph Foreakers;
William Frisby; John Ford; Miss Henrietta M. Foreman; Thomas Foreman; James
Great; Daniel Groome; James Garnett; Mr. Guichard; William Graves; Richard M.
Grisham; John Hall; Lazarus Horley; Richard Harrison; James Henderson; Susana
Hines; Isabella Jones; Mary Jump; John Ireland; William Knight; Lucas &
Garner; John Lucas; Rebecca Lucas; James Lenox & son; Theophilus Russell;
Rebecca Lane; Aquilla Meeks junr; Dr. Mathews; S. Leger Meeks; Mary Mann;
James McCabe; Dr. Charles Price; William Price Senr; John Page; Mary Yeates;

Zacharius Roberts; Ann Ringgold; Isaac Redgraves; Miss Ann Robinson; Margaret Rasin; William Severe; Samuel Johnston; James Stoops; Alex. Surrell; William Stenson; Alex. Stuart; Solomon Scott; Elizabeth Spencer; Starling Thomas; John Thompson; Davis Taylor; Dr. Samuel Thompson; John Tilden; Nancy Thompson; Retent Walters; James Walters; Thomas Wallace; John Walker; George Williamson; Peter Ornald; Robert Wilson

626. RST Jan 8 1805/Letters remaining at P.O. Centreville: John Brown; James Brown; William Barney; John Brown of Joel; John Cote; Mrs. James McCabe; Robert Dawson; Joseph Durding; John Dodd junr; Rev Henry L. Davis; Messrs Frazier & Purnell; Miss Delia Foreman; Daniel Freeman; Charles Frazier; Joseph Graham; Joseph Graham; Jacob Gibson; Frederick G..nce; Henry Honey; Rebecca Hammond; James Kent junr; John Keets senr; Joshua Kennard; James Lenox; John Leatherberry; Miss Mary Minor; Daniel McGinnis; Jessey Massy; Lucy Morgan; John Meeds junr; Samuel Mullican; Thomas Neavite; David Nicols; Samuel Nicolls; Mrs. Julia Paca; Richard Ridgaway; Thomas Rogers; Richard Stockett; Emory Sadler; Jane Rigg; Davis Taylor; Solomon Scott; Mrs. Eliza Tilghman; Thomas Yewell; Mrs. Elizabeth Walker/James Troth, clock & watch making, has removed to the house lately occupied by William Bromwell, next door to Solomon Lowe's tavern/Reward offered for apprentice boys, William Sparks and Richard Sparks, who ran away from the widow of John Turner, late of Talb Co

627. RST Jan 8 1805/Letters remaining at P.O. Easton: William Atkinson; Margaret Allen; John Bennett; Garrison Blades; Capt John Bush; William Bromwell; Solomon Betton; Hugh Bowers; Mary Browning; Solomon Barrett; William Bowers; John Berry; Dr. James Bordley; William Cox; James Colston; John Crouch; John Colgan; James Clayland; Aaron Connelly; Capt Robert Dodson; Joseph Dawson; Mary Dawson; George Dawson; James Earle; Charles Emory; Peter Edmondson; Samuel Elbert; Isaac Faulkner; Duncan McFarlaine; Hannah Freeman; William Farriss; Messrs. Green & Fairbanks; John Goldsborough; James Garnett; Zebediah Gregory; Jacob Gibson; John Gardner; Elizabeth Hay; Turbutt Harriss; Robert Hay; Joseph Huzza; Samuel Harrison; Silvy Hindman; Thomas Hanna; John Jefferies; Henrietta Ingram; Henry Johnston; Thomas Kemp; David Kerr junr; Edward Lloyd; John Lucas 3d; Corbin Lee; A. Lamden; Lloyds Stewart;William Melur; Susannah Mathews; Mikah Martin; Robert Martin; Solomon Martin;Henry Nicols; Cassandra Nicols; Bernard Nadell; James Owens; Noah Porter; John P. Paca; James Price; Thomas Parrott; Dr. Elisha Pelum; Capt Abner Parrott; Perry Prouse; Elisha L. Pelham; James Pursley; John Quimby; John M. Robinson; William Scott; James Seth; Hugh Sherwood; James Stoakes; William Abbot; Edward Turner; Margaret; Trippe; William Troth; Joseph T. Thomas; Anna M. Tilghman; Benjamin Tomlinson; L. L. Thomas; E. Tilghman; Margaret Valliant; Ann Valliant; William Varnum; Thomas Vickars; James Veitch; John Webley; Philemon Willis; Thomas Wickersham; Anthony Whitely; James Wilson; Rev Simon Wilmer; Hugh Workes; Dr. Charles H. Winder; Edward White/Chancery decree - Charles Frazier vs Samuel Parson who removed out of state - regarding sale of a lot in Centreville/Chancery decree to record deed from William Irons to Frederick Armington, complainant, for the tract called London Bridge Renewed in Kent Co

628. RST Jan 15 1805/Peition from Ezekiel Wise, Worc Co, James Cowan, Thomas Ozments and John Vickers, Talb Co, for relief from debts/Died Tues evening last, James Holmes of this town/John Boon exec of Henry Casson late of Caroline Co/James Wilson admin of John Troth, to sell his property and also to sell 5 or 6 young negroes, property of the late Rebecca King, of this co

629. RST Jan 22 1805/Robert Spedden, Easton, candidate for sheriff

630. RST Jan 29 1805/Died Thurs last Mrs. Wood wife of Thomas Wood of this town/Rent of well known stand for a country store, at the Head of Wye, where Doctor Wilson and his brother before him, kept store so long/Rent of blacksmith shop within 1/4 mile of Ruth's borough; apply to Robert Walters near Church Hill or subscriber, John Hacket, living in Centreville

631. RST Feb 5 1805/Mrs. Rigg wid of Rev Elisha Rigg is living in Easton; she has accommodations for 6 children as boarders/John Fisher offers reward for negro man, Caleb, about 25 yrs, formerly belonged to Capt Stanley Robinson; he was living with Thomas Countess, QA Co

632. RST Feb 12 1805/Married Sun evening 2d inst by Rev S. Wilmer, Dr. John Maxwell to Miss Elizabeth Redgrave, both of Kent Co/Died Mon 4th inst Mrs. Leah Bayly, consort of Josiah Bayly, Cambridge/Sale at Hillsborough at the store house lately occupied by William Clayland dec, his goods and chattels by Sam. S. Robinson exec of William Clayland/Sale by Charles S. Sewell, the farm where he now res in QA Co on Post raod to Phila, within 1 mile of Centreville/William G. Garey admin of Elijah Clark late of Talb Co

633. RST Feb 19 1805/James Iddings, removed from Easton to the settlement of Pine Creek, Lycoming Co, Pa, has given authority to William Dawson, constable, to recover accounts due/John R. Giles seeks apprentice in dry goods and grocery store/Bennett Pinkine admin of Michael and Mary Pinkine/James Cobscott informs the public that he has taken the house in Denton lately occupied by William Boon as a Public House

634. RST Feb 26 1805/House to be let lately occupied by Mrs. Rigg on Wye River; apply to William Dunn, near Head of Wye, Talb Co/Deborah Fountain admin of John Fountain, late of Caroline Co dec/John D. Emory, guardian, offers reward for negro, Phylis property of Arthur Emory, minor; she ran away from the neighborhood of Centreville

635. RST Mar 5 1805/Sale of the property of Dr. James Bordley, late of Talb Co by Hugh Sherwood of Huntington, admin/Charles Emory admin of John Sheppard/ Thoams Mason admin of Major Thomas Mason, late of Caroline Co/Ruth North, Talb Co, offers reward for negro woman, Rachel, about 30 yrs, and 3 children: Jim about 10 yrs old; Tom about 6 yrs old; Morris about 4 yrs old

636. RST Mar 12 1805/Letter from Cornelius Comegys junr, Kent Co, Md, regarding the visit of Alexander Stuart junr/Married Thurs evening last by rev Simon Wilmer, Philemon Downes of Caroline Co to Miss Harriet McCallum of this town/Died Fri at Head of Wye, Mrs. Anna Seth, consort of Dr. William E. Seth/ Joseph Bartlett, sec pro tem of the society of the relief of free people of colour, announces a meeting at the court house/Sale at Benjamin Denny's in Denton of following lots: 1. pt of tract Church Grove, formerly Squire's Chance 2. pt of same tract adj land of Messrs. Michael Russum and Anthony 6. lot joining lands of Messrs. James Andrew, Henry Corkin, and David Cisk and at present in the tenure of B. Whitley 3. pt of tract called Littleton's Friendship adj lands of Messrs. Dekar Thompson and Thomas Connelly 4. a lot. which bounds on road leading from Hunting Creek to Greensborough adj lands of Messrs Willes R. Andrew and the late Covey and Easton dec 7. a farm near Collins Cross Roads at present occupied by George Collins, about 400 a. – Alexander Stuart, Kent Co, Md/Charles Henrix requests claims against the estate of Edward Henrix, late of Talb Co, dec

637. RST Mar 1805 Supplement/Chancery sale of farm of John R. Bromwell/James Trippe junr admin of Henry Trippe, late of Dorch Co

638. RST Mar 19 1805/Samuel Y. Keene, Talb Co, offers land for sale in Ky/ Thomas Lesage, QA Co, announces the his horse, Canadian, will stand at the farm of Richard Tilghman 5th/Clement Vickars running packet from Easton to Balt/William Riley, Elizabeth Wright, admin of Hezekiah Wright, late of Worc Co

639. RST Mar 26 1805/Married Thurs lad at Friends Meeting, John Jenkinson to Sarah Parrott, both of this county/Married 5th inst, John Massey, QA Co, to Miss M. Green, QA Co/Sale of land, formerly the property of Benedict Brice in Kent Co Del/Brick house for sale in Cannon St, Chester Town; apply to

Samuel Douglas, Chester Town or Joseph Douglas, Head of Chester/John Harwood
cl rk to the commissioners of the tax for Talb Co/J. Loockerman, clerk of
Levy Court, Talb Co/Peter T. Causey admin of Francis Covey late of Kent Co Del/
Lots for sale in Georgetown, Kent Co, belonging to R. Elliott/John Singleton
of Talb Co to apply to mark and bound tracts: Otwell, Otwell's Addition, East
Otwell, Timothy's Lot, Pt of Feats Lot and pt of Baymans Addition/Chancery
sale of pt of estate of John Winn Harrison dec, most of which is in the tenure
of Andrew Callender/Sam: Elbert, Easton, offers reward for apprentice boy to
the carriage making business named Thomas Torney, about 17 yrs old; it is
supposed that he is in New Castle, Del, with his father

640. RST Apr 2 1805/Marrield 17 ult in Kent Co Del, Samuel Mifflin, merchant
of Camden, to the amiable Ann Hunn, of the same place/Married Sun 2 Feb at
New Orleans, Captain James Sterrett, of the U. S. Artillery, to the amiable
Mrs. Charlotte Copperthwaite of that city/Died Fri 22 Mar last William R.
Wilson of Kent Co of a wound he rec'd in his left arm in a duel/Letters
remaining at the P.O. Easton: William Aikers; Isaac Atkinson; William Ashford;
William Atkinson; Eli Alexander; Memory Adams; Christopher Bruff; Freeborn
Banning; Solomon Betton; Samuel Brown; Garretson Blades; William J. Bush;
William Bowers; Jacob Bromwell; Henry Buckley; James Colston; Levin Campbell;
Thomas Costello; Mrs. Ann Coartz; Marcus Dennison; Charles Dickinson; John M.
Dennison; Philemon Downes; Edward Earle; Lodman Elbert; James Earle; Richard
Edgar; Miss Mary Ennals; Peter Edmondson; Samuel Faudray; James Goldsborough;
Charles Goldsborough; John Goldsborough; William Garey; Miss Mary Gordon;
Henry Goldsborough; Robert Gay; Mrs. Francis Gibson; John Graham; Miss
Elizabeth Hollyday; Mrs. Hollyday; Jeremiah Hopkins; Thomas Hardcastle; Miss
Patience Handy; Henry Haskins; Mrs. Mary F. Handy; Eacock Howes; Thomas
Hayward; Turbut Harris; Amos Hale; Robert Hardcastle; Eseck Howel; M. Howard;
Dr. Johnson; Rachel Jeffries; Peter Johnson; Henrietta Ingraham; Samuel
Jackson; Celia Kinnamon; Rev Sam. Keene junr; John Lucas; Mrs. Lloyd; Thomas
Loveday; Prudence Lambden; Solomon Lowe; Messrs Herster & Miller; Thomas
Monnelly; Hugh Martin; Thomas Mitchel; Bernard Madal; Thomas Maggs; Dr.
Ennalls Martin; John McNeal; Thomas Pearson; Rev E. L. Pelham; John P. Paca;
James Ralston; Samuel Register; Wilson Rochester; John Singleton; Hugh
Sherwood; Thomas Smith; William Seamer; Mrs. Eliza. Skinner; Rebecca Sherwood;
John Smilie; Robert Speddin; Thomas Smith; Edward Turner; Scipio Thomas; John
Troth; S. J. Thomas; William G. Tilghman; Samuel Troth; John Willis; James
Ward; John Williamson; Margaret Walker; Henry Waggaman; Monsieur Le Wasseur;
Leah L. Wilson; William Wallis; Stephen Young/John Page, Kent Co, Md, offers
his dwelling plantation for sale, lying in Swan Creek, Kent Co/James Dixon
about to remove to Pa offers for sale his farm on Miles River and a lot in
Easton adj new brick building of Samuel Hopkins/James Aard, boot and shoe
maker, next door to Mr. Taggart's store and in the house lately occupied by
James Wilson

641. RST Apr 9 1805/Lambert Reardon, Easton, seeks journeyman taylors

642. RST Apr 16 1805/Letters remaining at P.O. Chestertown: James Arthur;
William W. Blake; James Bateman; James Butcher; Mary Burton; Samuel Banister;
Pau. Bayu.; Sarah Clark(?); Philip Chaplin; John Campbell; David Covender;
Luscay Commegys; John M. Denison; George Denniny; Robert Dunn junr; Dorius
Dunn, junr; John Duhammell; Robert Dunn; Rowland Ellis; Benjamin Everitt;
James Fray; Robert Fillington; Charles Fox; Hannah Glanvell; Mrs. Ann Gibson;
Lucas & Garnett; Richard Graves; Ann Grace; Benjamin and James Greenwood;
John W. Gleaves; Mr. Guichard; Woolman Gibson; Mrs. Araminta Hynson; Thomas
Harris; William Hull; Henny Heltzman; James Hollingsworth; Arthur Hull;
William Hollingsworth; Luke Howard; Perigrine Jobson; Isabella Jones; Jesse
Ireland; Dr. Samuel Kerr; The Rev Samuel Kean junr; John Lucas; James Lynch;
James Lang; Jacob Lutz; Rebecca Lowman; Rebecca Lucas; John Latham;

Mrs. Maria Moore; Thomas Numbers; Elisha Osburn; John Peaker; Margaret Pearce; Oliver Smith senr; Solomon Sparks; Major Stradley; Smith Snead; The secretary of the Lodge at Chester-Town; Dr. William Tilden; Samuel Thomas; John Turner; William Thomas; Henry Tears; Miss Harriot Trulock; Robert Waters; The Rev Charles Wallis; John Watters(?); Robert Wilson; Joshua Vanstant; Simon Wicks; Mary Yeates

643. RST Apr 16 1805/Letters remaining at P.O. Centreville: George Attwood; James Brown   Ann C. Betton; Miss Mary Brady; John S. Blunt; Benjamin Crisp; Mrs. James McCane; Mrs. Daphey Cooper; Robert Dawson; J. McClaskey; Joseph Durding; James Durgain; John McDenisson; Farreson Dixon; John Davis; Ann Duhamell; Benjamin Evorite; Mrs. Eliza M. Emory; Miss Arianna Frazier; John Fiddemond; Samuel Frazier; Frederick Glam; Benjamin Hall; Richard Harring; Richard J. Jones; Miss Maria Kent; William Kerney; Stephen Lowrey; Amas Lee; Lawson Lee; Thomas Neavite; Daniel T. Massey; Miss Lucy Morgan; Nicholas Meeds; Jesse Massey; Miss Mary Minor; Daniel McGinnis; James OBrien; Capt Phillips; Dr. W. Ringgold; Mrs. Sarah Ringgold; John Quimby; Dr. W. E. Seth; John Southern; Emory Sudler; Thoams Seegar; Mrs. Mary Saunders; Mr. Smith; Solomon Scott; William G. Tilghman; Clerk QA Co; Charles Wallace; George Williamson; Joseph Wright; Betty Williams; John Young/Married Thurs 11th inst by Rev Dr. Kemp, William W. Eccleston, to the amiable Miss Sophia Richardson, both of Dorch Co/Dissolution of partnership under the firm of Richard Thomas & Co at Queenstown - George and C. Lindenberger, Richard Thomas/Eliza. Thomas renting store and granary formerly occupied by Thomas Williams, New Market, Dorch Co/William Biles, Talb Co, exec of William Biles/Portrait painting by John Bruff at Mrs. Dawson's Easton/Notice to debtors of Green and Fairbanks or Philip Greene/English teacher wanted - Henry Smoot, Richard Walters, Joseph Whiteley, Dorch Co/Edward Harris, Bloomingdale, announces that Young Leonidas will cover mares this season at the subscribers stable in QA Co/Thomas Cecill, Head of Wye, QA Co, offers reward for negro man, Perry about 24 yrs old/John Ridgaway offers dividends to creditors of John Ridgaway, late of Caroline Co dec/Robert Speddin offers reward for a negro man, Will Hopper, formerly the property of John Singleton, about 35 yrs old/Ann Jackson, John Jones, admin of John Jones, Talb Co

644. RST Apr 23 1805/Married Sun last in Caroline Co, Mrs. Sellers to Henry Nicolls, both of that co/Died in Caroline Co on 31 Mar last, James Somers, late sheriff and Collector of that county/Died Sat last at his res near this town in the 72d year, Dr. Moses Allen for many years an eminent physician in this county/Robert Milligan offers a tractfor sale in Cecil Co/John Stevens junr, Worc Co, admin of George Richardson, late of Worc Coand admin of :. Benjamin Purnell, late of Worc Co/Betsy Jones exec of Thomas Jones, late of Somerset Co/Adam Edgar offers for sale a house on Washington St, Easton/John Maxwell res near Simms Tavern, Kent Co, Md, offers reward for two negro man: Joseph, age about 40 and Daniel age about 32, whose wife is the property of Henry Ringgold/John Dodd junr announces that the Canadian horse, Samson, will let to mars this season in QA Co/Moses Butler, living near Turner's mill, Talb Co, offers reward for strayed horse/Dorson Summers, Head of Wye, living on the farm commonly called St. Joseph, Talb Co, offers reward for a negro fellow, John, age about 21; his father is a free negrowho lives in Balt/Carson Bowdle, living in Island Creek Neck, Talb Co, offers reward for negro man, Jim, hired from David Kerr of Easton/Sale of tract on Kent Island by John Walters; apply to Jacob Tolson who lives on the premises

645. RST Apr 30 1805/Died at Duck Creek Cross Roads, Del, 22 Apr, Rebecca Barclett, of this Co, of a short but painful illness; she left a family of children/Chancery sale by Lambert Hyland and Henry F. Carroll/Josiah Bayly to rent mills near Salisbury/John L. Hall atty, Hillsborough, request payment of debts to the estate of Benjamin Elliott, dec/Elenor Valliant, living near Oxford, offers reward for strayed horse

646. RST May 7 1805/Died Sat last at a very advanced age, William Dawson, for
many years Judge of the Orphans Court of this county/Died Sun last in this
town, Jacob Saunders, clerk in the General Court office of this shore/Died
at Balt on Sun week, Mrs. Louisa Harvey Tilden wife of Dr. Tilden of Kent Co,
Md and 3rd dau of Samuel Harvey Howard of Annapolis/Sale at Tuckahoe Bridge
of horses, catte, sheep, horse cart, wheat fan, household furniture, 150
gallons of apple brandy, house, store house and granary, lately occupied by
Francis Sellers dec and William Clayland dec - Henry Nicols, Henry Downes/
William Atkinson informs the public that he has once more got the mill
commonly called Pott's Mill/Thomas Smith is renting store house opposite the
tavern in Georgetown Cross Raods, Kent Co; apply to Ephraim Vansant junr of
said place/William Hughlett admin of Thomas Hughlett, late of Caroline Co dec

647. RST May 14 1805/Mary Moore on behalf of trustees, seeks female teacher
in the Easton Charity School/Perry Lloyd, Talb Co, offers reward for negro man,
Daniel, late the property of John Dickinson, age about 25 yrs/Samuel Thomas has
schooner for sale/Sale of farm belonging to Major James Bruff within 4 miles
of Centreville, also military right to 200 acres in Allegany Co - Joseph H.
Nicholson, Centreville/Sale of lands in Hunting Creek Neck, Caroline Co adj
lands of Charles Goldsborough, late the property of James Edmondson, dec -
Joseph Edmundson, Isaac Atkinson, Isaac Poits/William Jones, near Princess
Anne, Somerset Co, offers reward for negro man, Daniel, age 20/John Ross,
Annapolis, advertises that his slave, Bob or Robert, about 50 yrs, sailed
away in a batteau; he bought him from off the farm of Solomon Frazier, late
representative from Dorch Co where he had run away from the service of his
then master, a certain Levin Mills of said county, since dec

648. RST May 21 1805/Died lately at the seat of Col. Samuel Hughes, Harf Co,
Col. John Hughes of this neighborhood/John and Thomas Meredith have commenced
the mercantile business in Easton opposite the Court House/John Kennard junr
has received an assortment of merchandize/Robert Dawson, William Thomas, admin
of William Dawson/Dissolution of the partnership of Owen Kennard and Samuel
Groome under the firm of Owen Kennard & Nephew/William Patton, Easton, seeks
curier/Richard Larrimore, Talb Co, reports a batteau drifted ashore Feb last
near his houses on the Bay Shore within 2 miles of Haddaways Ferry/Sale of
farm on the main road between Centreville and Beaver Dam Causway; apply to
Lemuel Parnell/William Jackson, Greensborough, admin of Thomas Garratt dec,
late of Caroline Co/Samuel Fairbank, Talb Co, reports a lost pocket book/Sale
of real estate of Edward School, situated on the head waters of Wicomico Creek
about 5 miles north of Princess Ann, Commissioners: John Done, George Handy,
John C. Handy/Athael Stewart reports a lost pocket book

649. RST May 28 1805/Married 21 inst Harf Co, Benjamin Green age 50 to the
amiable Miss Mary Reynolds, age 18, both of that county/ Died yesterday
morning Patrick Crane of Caroline Co/Richard Hatcheson, Swan Creek, Kent Co,
to answer charges made by James Page/Cloudsberry Kerby admin of William
Webster dec to sell his homeland and other items at the late res of William
Webster in Easton and the crops on his farm near Dover Ferry/John Blake to
hold sale at the property called Old Mill/Rent of farm in Talb Co occupied by
George Bromwell and Thomas Bullin; a farm in Caroline Co in the tenure of John
Cooper, Elizabeth Haryon, James Fleharty, William Rumbold, Thomas Hopkins,
Richard illoughby, Nathaniel Perry, Thomas Bowdle and the fields at present
cultiva.ed by several old negroes, belonging to the estate of William Perry;
also for sale houses occupied by John Fleming behind the court house/Chancery
sale by James Earle of lands mortgaged by John R. Bromwell to Elizabeth Lloyd
and Henrietta M. Lloyd/

650. RST Jun 4 1805/Died in Caroline Co, Mrs. Purnell the amiable consort of
Isaac Purnell, loving wife and affectionate parent/Died Tues last in
Chertertown, Richard Tilghman 4th of Kent Co/William Patton, Easton, admin of
Dean Reid, late of Talb Co, dec/Thomas Helsby offers reward for bay horse,
strayed or stolen in Talb Co/Doctor Robert Moore has just received "Doctor
Mace's antibillius Tincture and Pills/Robert Dodson Candidate for sheriff,
Talb Co/William Done, clerk of Somerset Co, gives notice that Nathan C. Newton,
Manucan Walker, Tubman Pollitt and Bennett H. Clarvo are insolvent debtors of
Somerset Co

651. RST Jun 11 1805/J. Maguire Jr, Laurel Hill, Dorch Co, candidate for Gen.
Assembly; also renting his dwelling platation situated on post road from
Vienna to Cambridge; apply to agent, Capt John Maguire/Sale of farm whereon
Capt Weyman res; also the farm on which Archiblad McNeal lives and the farm
occupied by Moses Sherwood adj each other and situated on Broad Creek and St.
Michaels River/Thomas Worrell, clerk of Kent Co Court, gives notice of judge-
ment that James Cruikshank, Kent Co, is insolvent/Exchange of correspondence
regarding delegates: James Page, Richard Hatcheson, Richard Ricaud, Darius
Dunn junr/William Perkins admin of Capt Josiah Johnson, late of Kent Co Md dec

652. RST Jun 18 1805/Married Thurs evening last, Thomas Wood to Miss Nancy
Brown, both of this town/Matthew Tilghman, Chestertown, exec of Richard
Tilghman 4th, late of Chestertown, offers for sale the tract, The Grove
situated in Dorch Co near Hunting Creek adj the lands of Capt Jacob Wright
and Nathan McDaniel and now under rent to Elisha Wright; also selling the
dwelling houses and lots in Chestertown formerly the property of William
Slubey and now under rent to William Bowers, Mary Ringgold and others on the
main street and nearly opposite the market house/Chancery sale of property of
Mary Russell, late of Frederick Co, dec, lying eastward side of the road which
divides Worc and Somerset counties and adj Salisbury - Matthew Keene, trustee/
Chancery sale of estate of Thomas Taylor, dec, in Ross's Neck, Dorch Co - John
Williams, trustee/John Keene, Caroline Co, admin of James Summers, dec,
Caroline Co/James Harrison, constable of Bay Hundred, refutes charge by such
persons accusing him of misappropriating public money/John Page, Kent Co, Md,
is selling his plantation, lying on Swan Creek; also tract called Page's Point

653. RST Jun 25 1805/At Washington College, A. B. degree conferred on:
Ezekiel Forman Chambers; Alexander Hands; and Samuel Sturgis. The degree of
A. M. was conferred on Bedingfield Hands; Edwin Lorain of Matthews Co, Va;
Edward Worrell Pearce; Gustavus W. T. Wright; Robert Wright Jr; John Thomson
Veasey; Dr. Ferguson, Principal of the Seminary; prayer given by Rev Kewley/
Married Thurs 13 inst at Clover - Fields, QA Co, Thomas Emory to Miss Ann
Maria Hemsley dau of William Hemsley, all of that Co/John L. Bozman renting
the plantation he owns on which John Murphey now lives/Sale of brick dwelling
house by Elizabeth Troup in Easton, occupied by Mr. Sarah Troup/A dispute
involving Jervis Spencer, William Spencer, Dr. James Sykes, Dr. Joseph D.
Gordon, Robert Wright Jr, Alexander Stuart Jr (Dover Del), William Douglass
(Dover Del), and William P. Russel/Farm for rent where Ignatius Rhodes now
lives, about 1/2 mil from Easton/James Lambdin intending to leave the state
of Maryland, is selling a lot in Easton on Washington St nearly opposite Mr.
Hopkins' carriage maker's shop/Chancery sale of the estate of William Sparks
dec, pt of tract in QA Co called Pleasant Spring; the case involves Solomon
Sparks vs Robert Walker and Sarah Sparks, an heir of William Sparkes, res out
of state

654. RST Jul 2 1805/900 a. for sale in Kent Co Del, 6 miles of Choptank
Bridge, 12 miles of Frederica Landing, enquire on the premises of the subscriber, W. Hughlett, who wishes to remove to a commercial city/Married on
Thurs 19 ult, Robert Carson of Church Hill, QA Co, to Miss Rebecca Burgess of
same county/John Gardner of this county drowned a few days past, in endeavor-

ing to swim his horse across a branch of Miles river/John Robinson Bromwell insolvent debtor of Talb Co/Elizabeth Charles, Henry Charles, admin of Jacob Charles, late of Dorch Co, dec/Risdon Smith admin of David Bramble, late of Dorch Co/Letters remaining at P.O. Easton: Capt John Bush; Lewis Bionchi; Henry Buckley; Josiah Bayly; Thomas Brascup; F. Bordley; Richard Bewley; Gen. P. Benson; Hannah Bartlett;Thomas J. Bullitt; A. M. Chew; Henry Chamberlain; Capt Thomas Coward; John Chamberlain; Harry Carter; Jeremiah Corden; James Colston; Lewin Cox; Daniel E. Cain; Sally Dean; Solomon Dickinson; Joshua Driver; William Dawson; Mary Dawson; John Earle; James Earle; Joseph Erwin; John Erwin; Capt Joseph Farland; William & Walter Fountain; John Goldsborough; James Garnet; Burton Gunt(?); Charles Goldsborough; Robert Goldsborough; Zachariah Gregoer; George R. Hayward; Mary Jump; Rev Joseph Jackson; William Lowrey; Jacob Loockerman; Edward Lloyd; William Lyles; John Mclean; William Meluy; Ennalls Martin; John McMahan; James Magee; Thomas Maggs; Lucy Morgan; James Murray; Levin Millis; Tristram Needles; William Patton; Dr. Elisha Pelham; Calvin Pierce; Henry Price; Sarah Pearson; Capt A. Parrott; Thomas Prince; William Pierson; Jane Rigg; David Rogers; Edward Roberts; Robert R. Richardson; Bowdin Robins; Mrs. Ridout; Horatio Ridout; George Smith; Mordecai Skinner; Major Hugh Sherwood; William Stevens; William Sands; Joseph Strengeffer; John Stanfield; William Severe; John Smoot; William Scott; Perry Smith; James Sherwood; Levin Speddin; Nancy Steward; William G. Tilghman; James Troth; Commissioners of the Tax of Talb Co; James Vitcht; Philemon Willis; Hannah Webey; James Ward; Springnell Webb; Dr. John W. Young/William Wilson, Ann Wilson, exec of John Wilson, Talb Co/Chancery sale at the house of Mrs. Ellis, a farm in Caecil Co belonging to the heirs of Thomas Ralph, situated on the tidewaters of Bohemia not more than 1/2 miles from Mrs. Ellis Taver and adj the mill of General Basset - William Spencer, trustee

655. RST Jul 2 1805/Brick Tavern in Queens Town for rent where Mr. Moffett now occupied; apply to Alexander Maxwell junr in Denton or Alexander Maxwell at Hall's Cross Roads/Chancery sale at the store house of John Williams at the head of Church Creek, Dorch Co, property of Richard Bright, dec: Brights Addition to the Grove, Forefight, Taylors Range - Thomas Colsten, trustee/ Jacob Falconar insolvent debtor, Kent Co, Md/James Cowan insolvent debtor, Talb Co/Eleanor Tilghman offers reward for negro, Isaac, age about 27, who ran away from the plantation of John Browne in the neighborhood of Centreville, property of Eleanor Tilghman living near Queenstown/James Cruickshank insolvent debtor, Kent Co, Md/Thomas Cecil, Head of Wye, QA Co, offers reward for negro Perry, age about 24/James Stoakes Easton Point, wishing to leave the state of Md offers for sale a house at Easton Point, a good stand for a ship wright/John Bayly offers to rent his part of mills at Salisbury

656. RST Jul 9 1805/Leters remaining at P. O. Centreville: Philemon C. Blake; John Brascup; Miss Sarah Banoa; William Bryan; Turbutt Batton; Mrs. Catharine Betton;Thomas Betton; John S. Blunt; Robert Brown; Mrs. Margaret Brooks; Benjamin Crisp; James Cunningham; Messrs Ignatius;Clarkson & Co; Joseph Durding; John Dames; Mrs. Dames; Mrs. Ann Denny; John Davis; Robert Dotson; William Davis; John E. Denny; James Elliott; Thomas Elliott; John Earle; Benjamin Everitt; Col. Fiddeman; William Gist; Daniel Hollingsworth; William Hackett; Richard Harris; Mrs. Amelia Hobbs; R. E. Harrison; Ben. Hatcheson; Miss E. Lansdale; Miss Sarah Lowrey; Jacob Larrimore; David Lucas; Miss Eliza Lovell; Miss Margaret Meeds; Miss Sarah Morris; Miss Morgan; Mrs. James Nicholson; William Nicholson; Mrs. Jenny Penney; Miss Elizabeth Pearce; John Paca; James R. Pratt; Mrs. Jane Rigg; Mrs. Sarah Ringgold; Milly Sampson; John Southern; Solomon Scott; Barwick Saunders; Isaac Stuart; Commisioners of the Tax; Miss Ann L. Thomas; Joseph Thompson; Robert Tate junr; John I. Troup; Edward Wright; Joseph Wright; Samuel Wright; Mrs. Ann S. Warfield

657. RST Jul 9 1805/Letters remaining at P.O. Chestertown: Rev

-108-

John Armstrong; James Arthur; William Bayer; James F. Brascup; Miss Kitty
Betts; Benjamin Borger; Dr. Morgan Brown; Henry Covender; Richard Colman;
Rebecca Corse; Miss Ann Cannon; George Curry; Miss Mary Cornelius; Capt John
Campbell; James Dawson; John Dawson; James Delihay; Mrs. Elizabeth Davis;
Thomas Eggleston; Rowland Ellis; Joseph Everitt; Robert Fillingame; Mrs.
Charlotte Graves; William Gilbert; Miss Nancy Goodwin; Ann Grace; Mrs. Rachel
Glanville; Lucas & Garrett; Henry Holtzman; William Hull; Jonathan Herring;
Thomas Harris; Luke Howard; William Jackson; Emanuel Jinkinson; James
Ingraham; Daniel Ireland; William Kearney; Nehemiah Kollock; Daniel Lamb of
Joshua; John Leatherbury; John Lucas; Joshua Lamb Jr; John Lodge; Mrs.
Rebecca Lowman; Mrs. Mary Miller; Mrs. Rebecca Maxwell; James Mins; Richard
Newman; Edward Oldham; Joseph Osborn; William Pearce; Risdon Plummer; James
Pryor; James Parker; Richard Ricand; Olion Smith; Joseph Simmonds; Miss
Sudler; William Spearman; James Stoops; Mrs Thompson; John Turner; Mrs. Ann
Tulock; Dr. George Williamson; John Williamson; Alword White; William Wood;
Isaac Wilson; Simon Wickery/Thomas Ozmont insolvent debtor, Talb Co/John
Simmonds insolvent debtor of Talb Co/Farm for rent on which Thomas Raker now
lives on head of Fowling Creek, Caroline Co, by John Stevens junr, Easton/
John Fleming and James George have opened a tayloring shop on Washington St
Easton, next door to Mr. Faulkner's Tavern

658. RST Jul 16 1805/On Wednesday morning last an accident befell the seven
month child of James Dixon of this town in which he was suffocated to death
"by another bed being accidently laid upon the one on which the said infant
was lying."/Died Tues night in this town, Miss Rachael Jefferis of Wilmington
Del, buried Wed last in Friends Burying Ground/Partnership of Charles Frazier
and Thomas C. Earle dissolved, Charles Frazier, Centreville having purchased
the whole of schooner, Nancy & Jane. All orders for the Nancy & Jane must be
left at John R. Giles' store, where the Letter Bag will be deposited./Farm for
rent near Pott's Mill, occupied by Jonathan Hopkins; apply to Samuel Groome,
Easton/John Vickers insolvent debtor, Talb Co/Margaret Ringgold, near Church
Hill, QA Co, offers reward for mare/Benjamin Willmott, William Stevens, James
Roper, all of Easton, insolvent debtors/Alexander Stewart, Kent Co, Md, offers
reward for bay mare

659. RST Jul 23 1805/Married 4 inst, William Kennedy of Duck Creek Cross
Roads, Del, to Miss Ellen Darrack, near that place/Married Thurs evening last
in this county, Levin T. Speddin of Easton, to Miss Margaret Mether of the
city of Balt/Married Thurs last in Centreville by Rev Reed, James Burgess age
58, to the amiable Miss Nevitt, age 18, both of that county/Died Thurs last
at an advanced age, in this town, Mrs. Mary Sharp/Died yesterday at 4 o'clock
in the 54th year of his age, Charles Blair, respectable citizen of this place
after a tedious and lingering illness; he left a daughter - to be buried this
evening at White Marsh Church/Samuel Thomas, Easton Point, candidate for
sheriff, Talb Co/William S. Bishop, Easton, recently pruchased stock and trade
of Dr. Earle now at the house lately occupied by David Kerr Jr, corner of
Washington and Dover sts/Thomas Fountain, Caroline Co, gives notice that his
wife Elizabeth has eloped from his bed and board with their daughter, Matilda/
Mary Hickman admin of William Hickman, late of Somerset Co/Sale of farm
formerly the property of Bazil Sewell dec, on the Bay Shore opposity Poplar
Island and adj lands of Capt Farland; apply to James Barnes, living in the Bay
side or William E. Sewell living in Balt/Samuel Hughes exec of Col. John
Hughes, Talb Co/Sale of two horses by John Mackey, in New Market, Dorch Co/
Mordicai Skinner, Talb Co, offers reward for horse borrowed by a man who
called himself William Brown/Edward Coursey, Wye River, QA Co, offers reward
for negro man called Jim Wye or Jim Smith, age about 32

660. RST Jul 30 1805/Married Tues 23d inst by Rev Joshua Wells, Francis
Rochester, QA Co, to Miss Maria Turner of Stillpond, Kent Co/Sale by exec,
Ennalls Martin and Peter Edmondson the personal estate of Charles Blair at his

dwelling house in Easton/Greenberry Collins seeks employment as overseer; he
has no other family but a wife/Edward Earle, Easton, requests business
payments be made by debtors/Adam Brown, Bolingbrooke, Talb Co, offers reward
for apprentice, Andrew Russel, age about 17

661. RST Aug 6 1805/Benjamin Wailes, Somerset Co, intends to petition under
under the insolvency act/Died Thurs evening last in Easton, Mrs Elizabeth
Sewell of this county of lockjaw, which proceeded from her finger being broke
by her carriage upsetting in turning a corner of the street - to relieve which
amputation was tried, united to the skill of most of the physicians of the
town, but without effect; Mrs. Sewell has left several children and a number
of relatives and friends to lament her sudden death/Sale of farm late the
property of Thomas Rigby dec, situated on Irish Creek - by Elizabeth Rigby
and Sarah Rigby, Deep Neck, Talb Co/Sale of farm of Thomas Buchanan in upper
part of QA Co of about 1000 a. by Jonathan Jester's mill and a place called
Grogtown; apply to Thomas Buchanan in Annapolis or Joseph Thompson who lives
near the premises/Sale of farm in QA Co, about 2 miles from the Nine Bridges,
now rented to John Patrick; apply to William Richmond near Centreville or to
William Tod, the subscriber, in Jersey/William Patton, Easton, has assortment
of leather for sale/Mrs. Neale, intending to leave Centreville in 3 or 4 weeks
offers an assortment of London millinery/Elizabeth Fountain answers notice of
her husband Thomas Fountain, "About three years since, he visited my father's,
quite a stranger and from his declarations of present love, future indulgence,
and the character of his brothers (two pious Methodist preachers) I thought
at least he was a rational being. But two weeks had not succeeded our
marriage, before I found myself tied to an intolerable drunkard...a brother
(William Fountain) has taken advantage of him and prevailed on him to convey
every iota of his estate to him..."/Brick house for sale in which George W.
Thomas and Mary S. Thomas res situated on Chester river, in Chester-town;
also a plantation for sale by George W. Thomas/Edward Harris, QA Co, seeks an
overseer/Peregrine Tilghman, Talb Co, offers reward for mulatto man, Perry
Bently, age about 30; James Edmondson, living near Dover Ferry, offers reward
or a n gro man, Jerry, property of Mrs. King of Easton, age about 22

662. RST Aug 13 1805/Price Martindale candidate for sheriff Talb Co/Margaret
Allen exec Doctor Moses Allen late of Talb Co/Samuel S. Robinson exec of
William Clayland, late of Caroline Co/William Murphy seeks six head of cattle
which staryed away from him, living at Miles river ferry/William Cottman,
Levin Farrington, Lazarus Cottman, exec of William Cottman, late Somerset Co,
to sell his farm situated at head of Wicomico Creek/Mary Goldsborough admin
of Doctor Howes Goldsborough of Cambridge; to sell house in Cambridge where
Doctor Sullivane now occupied as a shop/Anna Maria Tilghman, Plimhimmon warns
trespassers from passing through her woodlands/Benjamin Burrows insolvent
debtor

663. RST Aug 20 1805/New Packet, Resolution, Clement Vickers, master/John
Kennard junr exec of William Hicks, late of Kent Co, Md/Married at Balt Tues
evening in St. Peter's Church, by Rev George Dashiells, the Rev John Armstrong
to the amiable Miss Ann Yellott dau of John Yellot/Married Tues evening last,
William Roberts, to Miss ___Dodson dau of Captain Robert Dodson, all of this
county/Chancery sale of the property of Jeremiah Colston dec: Saint Anthony's,
Chance, Roxall Prakarde agreeable to a deed of bargain from James LeCompte to
Jeremiah Colston dated 1797; also land contained in a deed from Henry Colston
to Jeremiah Colston, known as Cove Hole - Charles Emory, trustee/John Kersey
admin of Impey Dawson, Talb Co, dec/Land in Kent Co Md charged with county
taxes due for the year 1804: 1st dist - Sarah Ferreil; John Martin heirs;
John Rowles heirs; Hynson Smith heirs; Mary Williamson heirs 2nd dist - Samuel
Beck junr; Thomas Deford; Hartshorn, Large, and Co; Samuel Hadley heirs; James
Reed; Hester Reed; Robert Roberts heirs; Edward Scanlan heirs; John H. Stone;
Milcha Thomas; Samuel Thomas; Fisher..(widow); Edward Vidler; Sarah Wiesenthal;

John Bolton heirs 3rd dist - William Ashman; Robert Buchanan; Doctor William
Gleaves; Samuel Gould; Thomas Jones heirs; Archibald McCall; Charles Raley
heirs; John Unick heirs; Joshua Vansant heirs; John Woodland heirs 4th dist
- Malachi Ambrose heirs; William Bantham; Risdon Bishop; William Brown; John
Brown (free negro); Joshua Covington; Joseph Calder; Isaac Calvert heirs;
Hannah Dodson; Rev Robert Elliot; John Field; Mary Falconar; William Gay
heirs; William Greenwood; Francis Heath; Robert Hodson; Richard Hurtt; Henry
Knock; Edward Light, negro; John Massy heirs; Luke Miers heirs; Hannah Miers;
William Miers heirs; James Moody, negro; Stephen Massy heirs; Sylvester
Nowland; Philip Piner, negro; Elizabeth Roberts; Robert Ratcliff; Charles
Rollinson; Daniel Rochester; John Rusey; James Strawbridge, Phila; David
Simpson heirs; Samuel ___, free negro; George Vansant heirs; Alexander
Williams heirs/Chancery sale of the real estate of Levin Gunby, late of
Somerset Co - Tubman Lowes, trustee/Chancery sale of the real estate of Joshua
Collingham dec, tract called Bacon Quarter in Wor Co/Nancy Handy admin of
Major James Handy, late of Worc Co dec/Samuel Turbutt admin of Sarah Carey
dec, late of Talb Co/Nicholson & Attwood, Centreville seeks young lad to
stand in a grocery store/Richard Willoughby seeks employment in farming
business/Baynard Wilson, Head of Wye, Talb Co, offers reward for negro, Dick

664. RST Aug 27 1805/Married 28 ult, William M. Hardcastle of Thomas, Caroline
Co, to Miss Anna Colston dau of Henry Colston of this county/Died Thurs
evening last, James Ruth, QA Co, aged 61/Robert Henry Goldsborough candidate
for sheriff Talb Co/I declare William Barroll, Esq., of Chestertown to be a
scoundrel - T. M. Forman/Phil St. John Downes admin of Alexander McCallam dec/
Thomas Hardcastle to petition to open a canal down Old Town Branch/James
Lenox, Church-hill, requests payment to the late firm of Lenox and McFeely,
Impey Dawson has new schooner called Dawson, Capt Edward Auld/Sale of farm by
James Dixon, situated on the Miles River, at present occupied by Samuel Troth/
Outten Toadvine, Purnell Toadvine, exec of William Toadvine, Worc Co/Property
for rent occupied by Abraham Broome, nest door to P.O. on Washington St,
Easton/Thomas James Patterson, sheriff of Dorch Co, offers reward for Henry
N. Parrett, a tailor, about 5 feet 6 inch high, marked with small pox, 26 to
30 years old, jailed for debt, escaped on the 7th inst

665. RST Sep 3 1805/House for rent on Washington St, occupied by William
Thomas - James Wilson junr, Easton/Cloudsberry Kirby admin of William Webster,
late of Easton/Sale of coachee by William E. Seth, Head of Wye/Hugh Sherwood
of Huntington admin of Doctor James Bordley, late of Talb Co/Hatfield Wright
exec of James Wright late of Caroline Co/Mathew Tilghman, Chester Town,
requests payment of debts to partnership of Richard Tilghman & Son/Henry
Costin admin William Diggans, late of Talb Co/Farm for rent in Caroline Co
near Thomas Hardcastle by William Barroll, Chester-town/Chancery sale of real
estate of Collison Hadaway dec, part of tract Miles End - William W. Hadaway,
trustee/Ezekiel Gillis, Somerset Co, to peition for relief from debts/

666. RST Sep 10 1805/Married Thurs last Jonathan Spencer to Miss Nelly
Robinson, both of this county/Died 3 inst at his farm in QA Co, Charles
Frazier, late speaker of the House of Delegates/Patrick Kennard exec of Philip
Kennard exec of Philip Everitt, Kent Co, Md/Michael Lamb, Melescent Lamb, exec
of Mary Medford, late of Kent Co, Md/Rachel Thomas selling at her farm in
Oxford Neck, horses, cattle and sheep/Sale of lot on road from Easton to
Kings-town adj farm where subscriber, Samuel Register, now lives/Chancery sale
of real estate of John Thomas dec in Talb Co by John Gibson, trustee/James
Seth, Talb Co, forewarns persons from passing through his land enroute to
Dixon's Neck/William R. Stuart, Centreville, assuming the packeting and grain
carrying business formerly conducted by the late Dr. Charles Frazier/James
Fookes of Thomas, living near Salisbury, offers reward for negro woman, Venus

667. RST Sep 17 1805/Died Fri morning after a very short illness, in this
town, Mrs. Deborah Dickinson/John Kemp exec of George I. Dawson/Silas C. Bush,

Princess Anne, Somerset Co, to peition for relief from debts/Mills for sale
by William Thomas, situated on Prickly Pear creek, Kent Co Md/James Byus,
Dorch Co, to petition for relief from debts/Sale of late dwelling of William
Akers dec by Samuel Abbott for Ann Akers/Sale of plantation on Broad Creek,
Talb Co, also plantation in Dorch Co, heretofore the dwelling place of Robert
Rolle; apply to John Rolle/Sale of young negro woman with 2 children by John
Goldsborough junr, Myrtle Grove/Robert Tuite, QA Co, has stray steer/Solomon
Scott, sheriff QA Co, reports runaway negro from QA Co jail called Phill, 13
to 15 yrs old; lived for four yrs past with David Rodgers near Royal Oak,
Talb Co/Richard Waters of William to petition for relief from debts

668. RST Sep 24 1805/Chancery sale at Mr. Cannell's Tavern, Chester Town,
pt of real estate of late George Hanson, called Holsten and Crow's Addition
commonly known as St. James - Thomas Worrell, Chestertown/Rent of farm in
Hunting Creek Neck, Caroline Co, where James Edmondson late res/Sale agreeabe
to the will of John Stewart dec, Dorch Co, at the dwelling house formerly
William Dail's, 4 miles below Cambridge, by William Colston, administrator/
Farm for sale, Talb Co, whereon John Burgess now lives; apply to George
Parratt who lives near the premises/Margaret Williams admin of Nathan Williams
late of Dorch Co; indebted person are requested to make payment to Robert
Williams, legal atty for Margaret - K. Williams, living in New Market/Samuel
Dixon candidate for sheriff QA Co/John Thompson, Chestertown, has opened an
Academy in Chestertown/Garrettson Blades near Dover Ferry, Caroline Co, offers
reward for dark brown mare

669. RST Oct 1 1805/John Turner, Talb Co, declines to be candidate to Gen.
Assembly because of broken leg/Sale of house where James Trippe junr, now
lives; the front on Race St is occupied by Mr. A. Fleming, merchant/James Cook
Kent Co, to petition for relief for relief from debts/John Lambdin insolvent
debtor/Thomas S. Cook, QA Co, offers reward for negro woman, Flora, age about
40, who ran away from James Cook of Kent Co Md/Wilson Regester has commenced
a currying business in Easton in shop adj David Nice's/James Walker admin of
Robert Francis, late of Talb Co/Robert Minnish to petition for relief from
debts/Letters remeining at P.O. Easton: Margaret Allen; William Atkinson;
Thomas Atkinson; Thomas Abbott; John Armeson; Solomon Betton; Henry Banning;
John Blake; Major Benny; Edward Barwick; John Bullin; James Barns; Richard
Bewley; William Barrell; William Benton; Solomon Bryan; James Bowie; Francis
Barckley; Eugene O'Connor; William Carmichael; Robins Chamberlain; Lydia
Corse; John Cain; Elizabeth Cail(?); John Crowder; Thomas Cook; Patrick Crane;
Richard Collison; Joseph Cox; John Coark; Jacob Conway; Daniel Caesa; Edward
Coursey; Joseph Dawson; Rebecca Daffin; Henry L. Davis; Rachael Eccleston;
John Edmonson; Walter F. Fountain; Samuel Findley; Maria Goldsborough; James
Goldsborough; George Gale; Daniel Grafton; Margaret Gardiner; William Haney;
Elizabeth Hamsley; Henrietta Hayward; Alexander Hite(?); Robert Hardcastle;
Edward N. Hamilton; Maria Harris; Sophia Harrison; Joseph Huzza; Sarah
Jenkinson; Joseph Jackson; Rev Samuel Keen sen; Rev Samuel Keene junr; Gen.
James Lloyd; Edward Lloyd; Mrs. Lloyd; Kenny & Lorain; John Lucas 3d; Solomon
Low; Jacob Loockerman; Sarah Mullican; Frances Mansfield; James Nabb; Edward
Needles; Kitty Nicolls; Hector McNeill; Hannah Osborne; James Purseley; Lydia
Pearson; Nancy Pacifield; Thomas Pearson; Elisha L. Pelham; Abner Parrott;
John Quimby; John Ruth; Thomas A. Reardon; Polly E. Ridgeway; Peter Redhead;
William S. Richardson; Mr. Roberts; Thomas Stevens; Alexander Stuart junr;
William Sands; Daniel Stephens; Samuel Stevens; Robert Spedden; Joseph
Stangeffer; Rebecca Sherwood; Samuel Troth; WilliamTibbles; Colonel Richard
Tilghman; Sipio Thomas; James Veitch; David Walker; Sharker White; Sarah
Wilson; James Walker; Hugh Work

670. RST Oct 8 1805/Thomas Lea, Robert Milligan exec of Cantwell Jones, New
Castle Del, selling his about 3 miles from Cantwell's bridge/Robert S. Gamble,
QA Co, to petition to cut a ditch from Ringgold's Head Dam, QA Co, through

Beaver Dam Branch to Long Marsh ditch/Ann Auld exec of Samuel Auld, late of
Talb Co/J. Faulkner and J. Brascup have entered in the a partnership of the
tailoring business, Easton, next door to the P.O./John Huffington to petition
for relief from debts/Joseph Haskins offers reward for negro Tom, age about
50, well known in the neighborhood of Isaac Purnell/Letters remaining at P.O.
George-Town Cross Roads: Angello Bennet; James Beetle; Caleb Briscoe; George
Corrie; Capt John Campbell; Mary Capelle; Cornelius Comegys; John Cacy; James
Cowharding; Samuel Davis; Thomas Dulany; Fanny Denby; William Downs; Elizabeth
R. Graves; Charles Haynes; James Howard; William Harper & son; Daniel Knock;
William Knight; William Nicholls; George Little; Daniel McCarty; Sarah Noell;
Rebecca Newnam; Ann Parsons; William Price; Eben Palmer; Newman Runnalds;
Nancy Robinson; John L. Smith; William Spearman; John Symons; Sarah Smith;
Robert Scott; Betsy Singles; James Stephenson; John Turner; Samuel Voorhees;
James Welch; James Walters; Dr. Simon Wilmer; Mary Yeates

671. RST Oct 8 1805/Letters remaining at P.O. Chestertown: William Abbot;
Jeremiah Alexander; Jacob Banbury; George Bordley; Jacob Bunee; Mrs. Amelia
Burk; Mrs. Mary Cooper; John Campbell; Samuel Crouch; Edward Coppage; Mrs.
Anna Caulk; Miss Ann Caldwell; William Corse; James Dawson; James Frisby
(Worton); Richard Filingame; Joseph Forman; William & Thomas Glenville; James
Greenwood; Nathaniel Hynson; Daniel Hull; Kinzey Harrison; Master James
Holliday; John C. Hynson junr; Mrs. Isabella Jones; Daniel Lamb; John Lucas
3d; Samuel Lacock; John Leatherbury; Sarah Leek; James Larey; Thomas Morgan;
Thomas Nicholson; Miss Eliza & Phillis; Nunom Reynolds; John M. A. Rankin;
Dr. John S. Reese; Edward Robinson; Nathan Smith; Henry Steiner; Edward
Stevenson; Alward White; Joseph Wilkinson; Samuel Weatherhead; William
Usselton

672. RST Oct 15 1805/George Spry and Araminta Spry his wife, admin of John
Graham/Sale by Joseph Bartlett, Wakefield near Easton, furniture, wind mill
and other articles/Mary Bond gives notice to debtors that notes are now in the
hands of Thomas J. Bullitt of Easton/Sale of cattle by Samuel Smith and John
Fisher/Joshua Graves, QA Co, admin of James H. Graves, late of Kent Co/Sale
of lot on Kings' Creek pt of three tracts: Kingston, John's Neck, and Middle-
spring by Thomas Atkinson, Easton

673. RST Oct 22 1805/Sale at the late dwelling house of Robert Vinton dec on
Miles River Neck/Sale of negro boys and girls by Sarah Dickinson at the
Trappe/David Sisk admin of Isaac Whittington/Edward H. Smith to petition for
relief from debts/Oliver Hammond, Dorch Co, requests immediate payment by
debtors

673. RST Oct 29 1805/Died Wed morning last at his father's in this county,
the Rev William Ridgeway, eldest son of James Ridgeway after a long and
painful illness/Died Fri last, Mrs. Frances Gibson, widow of Woolman Gibson,
late of this county/John Pennington to petition for relief from debts/Sale at
the late dwelling of Rebecca Vinton dec in Miles River Neck/Sale by Joseph
Bartlett/Bennett Jones, Easton, reports a stray gelding/Anthony P. Sumption,
near Centreville, offers reward for apprentic Joseph Owings, age about 17

674. RST Nov 5 1805/Died Tues 22 ult, Samuel Baldwin of thic county, merchant
of this town for many yrs; he left a wife and several children/Died Thurs last
in QA Co, James Clayland junr, one of the associate judges for said County/
Died Sat night last in this town, Mrs. Elizabeth Caile, in her 73d year/
William E. Seth exec of Frances Gibson/Sale of house occupied by Thomas S.
Robson on Landing Road near West St - by John L. Kerr, Easton/Chancery sale
of real estate of William S. Bond by John H. Howard, trustee/John Graham to
petition to straighten the road from Easton to St. Michaels

675. RST Nov 12 1805/Married 22 Oct at Mount Harmon, Richard Barroll of

Chester Town to Miss H. C. Wyncoop dau of the late Dr. Wyncoop of Del/Married
Sunday evening last, James Cockayne to Miss Elizabeth Troth, both of this
town/Died Fri last in Cambridge, Mrs. Anna Redhead wife of Peter Redhead late
of this County/William Frazier exec of Mrs. Dickinson, Easton/Phebe Hull admin
of David Hull, Kent Co Md dec/William R. Stuart exec of Charles Frazier, late
of QA Co/House for rent occupied by William Patton on Harrison St; apply to
Mary Trippe, Easton/John Higgins junr; Thomas Stevens, Talb Co, offer reward
for two negro boys: James Hackett, age about 20, and Levin Brooks, age about 16

676. RST Nov 19 1805/Mary Hayes admin of Dr. William Hayes, late of Caroline
Co/Married 14 inst in Friends Meeting at Coolspring Del, Samuel Johnson of
Germantown to Jennett Rowland of Cedar Grove/Store house and granaries for
rent at Pemberton's Landing on Tuckahoe Creek, property of the heirs of James
Nicols, late of Balt town dec; apply to James Fisher, Talb Co/Sale at
Bloomingdale, QA Co, the seat of Edward Harris, several plough horses by
Elijah Covington, overseerSale on Jamaica Point, Bolingbroke, Talb Co, horses
and cattle by Langford Higgins at his farm/Sale by John White junr of Phila,
offers for sale the farm ofhis father, John White dec, situated in Caroline
Co 1 mile below Whitleysburgh/Hugh and Edward Auld will run packet from Easton
to Balt/Benjamin Blunt admin of Thomas Countis, late of QA Co dec/Solomon Lowe
about to decline from inn keeping

677. RST Nov 26 1805/Married Tues evening last at Washington city, Perregrine
Ringgold of Kent Co to Miss Bobby Smith of that city/Died Sun evening 10th
inst, Mrs. Nancy Arringdale wife of John Arringdale of this county after a
short but painful illness

678. RST Dec 3 1805/Married 14 ult QA Co, Lewis Bush of this county to Miss
Elizabeth G.(?) Osborne of QA Co/Died Thurs last Miss Nancy Baldwin eldest dau
of the late Samuel Baldwin of this county/Died Sun evening last at the seat
of Robert H. Goldsborough of this county, Mrs. Sarah Collester(?), aged 74,
suddenly/Sale at the late dwelling of William Dimond, late of QA Co of about
20 to 30 negro slaves by William Murphey, QA Co/Chancerysale by Margaret Black
in Kent Co Md, property of George Black/Nathan Peacock gives notice that his
wife Milcha has absconded from his bed and board/John Bruff, St. Michaels,
offers reward for apprentice,Thomas Kemp, age about 14

679. RST Dec 10 1805/Married Thurs evening last by Rev McClaskey, John
Meredith, merchant, to Miss Sally Troth, both of this town/Robert Bruff,
Easton, exec of Christopher Bruff, to hold sale at his farm/Charles Emory
admin of Samuel Baldwin/John Boon exec of Henry Casson and admin of William
Casson, late of Caroline Co; also offers for rent house presently occupied
by John L. Hall as a tavern in Hillsborough/Philemon C. Blake junr, QA Co, has
two young negro women for sale/John Stevens junr seeks to hire lad for house
work/Robert Dawson, William D. Thomas, admin of William Dawson dec of Miles
River Neck/Sale at late dwelling of John Daugherty dec near Potts Mill by
Robert S. Harwood admin of J. Dougherty/Tristram Bowdle gives notice to those
with claims against James Bowdle/William Frazier exec of Deborah Dickinson,
late of Talb Co/Obediah Garey admin of Richard Ray dec, late of Talb Co/
Harrison & Kemp ship builders, St. Michaels

680. RST Dec 17 1805/Sale at farm where Christopher Bruff lived on Choptank
river by Robert Bruff exec of C. Bruff/Chancery sale of estate of Levin Gunby
by Tubman Lowes, trustee/Sarah Brascup exec of Mrs. Sarah Dawson/Thomas
Wayman admin of Thomas Wayman late of Talb Co/Sale by Orphans Court of Talb
Co at former res of Francis Gibson of 2 negro men andl negro woman by William
Seth exec/Taxes on property owed in QA Co: Joseph Bruff - Todley Point,
Neglect; James Harris - Persenett's farm; Caleb Rickett's heirs - one lot;
John Hardcastle - Costin's Park Point; James Byrn - Manor Point; Levin
Clarkson - Seegar's Hazard, Pock Hickory Ridge; Capt John Campbell - land

adj mill work(?); Gafford's heirs - Sarah's Portion; William Harris heirs - Contention Point; Lazarus Title's heirs - House and lot in Kingstown; Joshua Miers - Bridgewater, Tilghman's Friendship, and Hazard's Addition/Rent of store house and grannary and dwelling house formerly occupied by William Clayland dec and lately by the subscriber, John Lucas 3d/William Cannon, Jabez Callwell, admin of Sailes Cannon dec, late of Talb Co/House for rent presently occupied by Mrs. Holmes Washington St - Freeborn Benning, Talb Co/John L. Hall atty for Betila Elliott, admin of Benjamin Elliott, late of Caroline Co dec/ Sale of negro women by Philemon C. Blake jun, QA Co/Shop for rent occupied by James Faulkner next to P.O./Chancery sale of real estate of Thomas Boon of Caroline Co dec at Denton - William Potter, trustee/Sale of brick house formerly the property of James Lambdin, Washington St, Easton; apply to James Earle junr or to William Harrison junr/Sale at the late dwelling of Samuel Baldwin on farm owned by heirs of the late Joseph Parsons - Charles Emory, admin/Horatio Edmondson of Talb Co, near Easton, offers reward for negro Levin Banthom, about 5 feet and about 30 yrs old/John Kersey admin of Impey Dawson/ House for rent presently occupied by James Roper; apply to Solomon Lowe at the Star office

681. RST Dec 24 1805/John L. Kerr, William S. Bishop,Steward St. Thomas Lodge, announce dinner at Capt Frazier's tavern in Easton, for all Ancient York Masons/John Stevens junr, Easton, having declined business and transferred all stock to John Kellie/Michael W. Hopkins, Centreville to open an Academy in Centreville/Married Tues evening 10th inst, William Harrison of this county to Miss Martha Dent of Balt/William Morrisson, living in Centreville, offers reward for Nathan Starkey, apprentice

682. RST Dec 31 1805/Rev Francis Barclay to open a school in Easton/Benjamin Hall has opened an apothecary shop in Centreville

INDEX

When a name is mentioned more than once in the same issue parentheses are
used to indicate the number of times the name appears.

Single Names

This first section of the index lists first names of persons, usually
slaves, for whom no last name is given.

Aaron 600
Abby 146
Abe 336
Abraham 298, 590
Adam 26, 522, 541
Ambrose 456
Andrew 180, 270
Amy 42
Ann 129

Balder 579
Barnett 580
Benjamin 358, 603
Bill 545, 578
Bob 119, 139, 141,
200, 647

Caesar 75, 566
Caleb 263, 631
Cassa 167
Cate 159, 438, 482, 548
Charles 138, 142, 146,
159, 299, 539, 566
Clem 352
Cloe 340
Cuff 331
Cumfort 182

Daniel 83, 165, 173,
197, 368, 552, 558,
565, 579, 644, 647(2)
Darkey 185
Dave 62
David 61, 167, 469
Davy 62, 79
Dawson 60
Demsey 565
Denis 274
Dick 90, 129, 137, 153,
154, 291, 293, 466, 487,
569, 572, 663
Dumfries 221

Easter 181, 263

Edmund 4
Eli 132
Elisha 368
Eliza 671
Emanuel 117
Ephraim 598
Esther 289, 578

Fan 129, 567
Fanny 485, 567
Flora 669
Florah 165
Frank 294

Gabriel 558
George 4, 203, 518
Govet 546
Grace 182
Grace (granny) 294
Grant 173

Hagar 235
Hannah 167, 539, 611
Hannibal 4
Harris 635
Harry 4, 99, 103, 104(2),
328, 399, 414, 433, 469,
549
Havannah 167
Henny 142, 552

Ibby 167
Isaac 66, 83, 296, 560,
565, 602, 655
Ishmael 134
Israel 153

Jack 3, 56, 61, 194, 260,
484, 485, 527
Jacob 5, 108, 119, 140,
162, 182, 188, 293
Jake 563
James 139, 452
Jenny 583

Jeremiah 346
Jerry 661
Jesse 295
Jessemine 493
Jethro 134
Jim 469, 523, 578,
635, 644
Jinny 487
Job 53, 368
Joe 33, 167, 173,
205, 368
John 346, 367, 452,
644
Jonathan 412
Joseph 644
Joshua 559, 560
Juba 89, 108, 141
Jude 605

Kate 489

Leven 15
Levin 73, 137, 331,
346, 452

Mabb 71
Maria 294
Mary Ann 164
May 220
Memory 343
Milly 340(2)
Mingo 66
Moses 66, 605, 649

Nace 491
Nancy 357
Nat 35
Ned 110, 141, 200,
222, 226
Nell 107, 129, 210
Nelson 305
Nick 575
Nuba 78

Single Names

INDEX

Marriages and Deaths in the Newspapers of Lancaster County, Pennsylvania, 1821-1830

Marriages and Deaths in the Newspapers of Lancaster County, Pennsylvania, 1831-1840

Marriages and Deaths of Cumberland County, [Pennsylvania], 1821-1830

Maryland Calendar of Wills Volume 9: 1744-1749

Maryland Calendar of Wills Volume 10: 1748-1753

Maryland Calendar of Wills Volume 11: 1753-1760

Maryland Calendar of Wills Volume 12: 1759-1764

Maryland Calendar of Wills Volume 13: 1764-1767

Maryland Calendar of Wills Volume 14: 1767-1772

Maryland Calendar of Wills Volume 15: 1772-1774

Maryland Calendar of Wills Volume 16: 1774-1777

Maryland Eastern Shore Newspaper Abstracts, Volume 1: 1790-1805

Maryland Eastern Shore Newspaper Abstracts, Volume 2: 1806-1812

Maryland Eastern Shore Newspaper Abstracts, Volume 3: 1813-1818

Maryland Eastern Shore Newspaper Abstracts, Volume 4: 1819-1824

Maryland Eastern Shore Newspaper Abstracts, Volume 5: Northern Counties, 1825-1829
F. Edward Wright and Irma Harper

Maryland Eastern Shore Newspaper Abstracts, Volume 6: Southern Counties, 1825-1829

Maryland Eastern Shore Newspaper Abstracts, Volume 7: Northern Counties, 1830-1834
Irma Harper and F. Edward Wright

Maryland Eastern Shore Newspaper Abstracts, Volume 8: Southern Counties, 1830-1834

Maryland Militia in the Revolutionary War
S. Eugene Clements and F. Edward Wright

Newspaper Abstracts of Allegany and Washington Counties, 1811-1815

Newspaper Abstracts of Cecil and Harford Counties, [Maryland], 1822-1830

Newspaper Abstracts of Frederick County, [Maryland], 1816-1819

Newspaper Abstracts of Frederick County, 1811-1815

Sketches of Maryland Eastern Shoremen

Tax List of Chester County, Pennsylvania 1768

Tax List of York County, Pennsylvania 1779

Washington County Church Records of the 18th Century, 1768-1800

Western Maryland Newspaper Abstracts, Volume 1: 1786-1798

Western Maryland Newspaper Abstracts, Volume 2: 1799-1805

Western Maryland Newspaper Abstracts, Volume 3: 1806-1810

Wills of Chester County, Pennsylvania, 1766-1778